The Dispossessed State

The Dispossessed State

Narratives of Ownership in Nineteenth-Century Britain and Ireland

Sara L. Maurer

The Johns Hopkins University Press
Baltimore

© 2012 The Johns Hopkins University Press
All rights reserved. Published 2012
Printed in the United States of America on acid-free paper
9 8 7 6 5 4 3 2 1

The Johns Hopkins University Press
2715 North Charles Street
Baltimore, Maryland 21218-4363
www.press.jhu.edu

Library of Congress Cataloging-in-Publication Data

Maurer, Sara L.
  The dispossessed state : narratives of ownership in nineteenth-
century Britain and Ireland / Sara L. Maurer.
        p.   cm.
  Includes bibliographical references and index.
  ISBN-13: 978-1-4214-0327-4 (hardcover : acid-free paper)
  ISBN-10: 1-4214-0327-7 (hardcover : acid-free paper)
  1. English fiction—19th century—History and criticism.
2. English fiction—Irish authors—History and criticism.
3. Property in literature. 4. Land tenure—Government
policy—Great Britain—History—19th century. 5. Land tenure—
Government policy—Ireland—History—19th century. I. Title.
  PR878.P728D57 2012
  823'.809—dc23   2011021305

A catalog record for this book is available from the British Library.

*Special discounts are available for bulk purchases of this book. For more
information, please contact Special Sales at 410-516-6936 or
specialsales@press.jhu.edu.*

The Johns Hopkins University Press uses environmentally friendly
book materials, including recycled text paper that is composed of at
least 30 percent post-consumer waste, whenever possible.

For Don, inalienably

Contents

Acknowledgments   ix

Introduction   1

1 Disowning to Own: Maria Edgeworth's Irish Fiction
and the Illegitimacy of National Ownership   19

2 The Forbearance of the State: John Stuart Mill and
the Promise of Irish Property   55

3 Native Property: Young Ireland and the Irish Land Acts
in the Victorian Proprietary Landscape   89

4 The Wife of State: Ireland and England's Vicarious
Enjoyment in Anthony Trollope's Palliser Novels   133

5 At Home in the Public Domain: George Moore's *Drama
in Muslin*, George Meredith's *Diana of the Crossways*,
and the Intellectual Property of Union   167

Afterword   206

Notes   211

Works Cited   223

Index   237

Acknowledgments

The ideas in this book were fostered at Indiana University, under the intelligent and generous guidance of Andrew H. Miller, Patrick Brantlinger, Deidre Lynch, and Janet Sorenson. There too, Purnima Bose and Eva Cherniavsky first sparked my interest in colonial and postcolonial issues in literature. And in teaching me to teach writing, Christine Farris and Kathy O. Smith taught me much I needed to know in order to write this book.

At Notre Dame I have been particularly indebted to the assistance and collegiality of Graham Hammill, Susan Harris, Susannah Monta, and John Sitter. Whether they realize it or not, David Wayne Thomas and Katherine Zieman made crucial interventions into this research. While she was chair, Katherine O'Brien O'Keeffe's advocacy created the conditions under which it was possible for me to complete my manuscript. Chris Vanden Bossche's contributions to this project, both administrative and intellectual, are unmatched by any colleague. I am grateful to Chris Fox, Maud Ellmann, Luke Gibbons, and the Keough-Naughton Institute for Irish Studies at the University of Notre Dame, whose faculty and visiting fellows have enriched my understanding of Ireland far beyond the nineteenth century. At the same time, the scholarship of graduate students Brook Cameron, Heather Edwards, Nathan Elliott, Benjamin Fischer, Jessica Hughes, Lara Karpenko, Maggie Nerio, and Teresa Huffman Traver made the nineteenth century a rich and enjoyable place to be.

During the writing of this book Sarah McKibben and Naunihal Singh provided daily support and encouragement. I benefited from the writing advice and box wine of Wendy Arons, Robert Goulding, Margaret Meserve, Emily Osborne, and Sophie White. I am grateful too for the long-distance encouragement of Kathy Psomiades. Jeanne Barker-Nunn, Ivan Kreilkamp, Todd Kuchta, Richard Higgins, Maureen Martin, and Nick Williams all provided me with useful advice during the final stages of the project. Mary Jean Corbett's careful and knowledgeable review of this manuscript on behalf of the Johns Hopkins University Press proved indispensible. Matt McAdam has been the model of an efficient and responsive editor. I am grateful, too, for Glenn Perkins's attention to this manuscript during copyediting. All errors remain my own.

Research for this book was funded in part by the Institute for Scholarship in the Liberal Arts at the University of Notre Dame and the Keough-Naughton Institute for Irish Studies at the University of Notre Dame. Parts of chapter 1 have been reprinted from "Disowning to Own: Maria Edgeworth and the Illegitimacy of National Ownership" in *Criticism: A Quarterly for Literature and the Arts* 44, no 4, © 2002 Wayne State University Press, with the kind permission of Wayne State University Press. An earlier version of chapter 4 appeared as "The Nation's Wife: England's Vicarious Enjoyment in Anthony Trollope's Palliser Novels," in *Troubled Legacies: Narrative and Inheritance*, edited by Allan Hepburn, © 2007 University of Toronto Press, and is reprinted here with the kind permission of the University of Toronto Press.

I would not be the sort of person who wrote academic books were it not for the high quality of my very first interlocutors—my parents, Larry and Sharon Maurer, who modeled for me an ethic of hard work and intellectual curiosity, and my siblings, Micheline Maurer, Laren Botello, Kierstin Maurer, and Travis Maurer, who kept me on my toes and kept me laughing. During the composition of this book I remained human due to the abundant friendship of Dana Baker, Aparna Balaji, Gail Bederman, Cara De la Cruz, Tina DeVries, Doug Dillaman, Amy Eldridge, Devasena Gnanashanmugam, Alexandra Guisinger, Michelle Harm, Julie Hiipakka, Suzanne Link Freeman, Joy Lewis, David Nickerson, and Irene Kim Park.

Don Fessenden provided, and continues to provide, unprecedented support both relevant to and far afield from book writing. I thank him for all the ways he contributed to making this book possible, but I know I owe him for so much more.

Finally, all thanks to the Creator, who broke the chains so I could lift my hands.

The Dispossessed State

Introduction

The nineteenth century witnessed a revolution in thinking about property that was also a revolution in thinking about the state. The commonsense understanding of property at the opening of the century might be read in Thomas Macaulay's 1833 argument for a coercive enforcement of order in Ireland: "[Mr. Macaulay] thought there was no situation in the life of a public man more painful than that in which he found himself, under the necessity of supporting the suspension of the Habeas Corpus Act, and the even temporary abolition of trial by jury. These were sacred portions of our Constitution, older than Parliament itself—their origin was lost in the darkness of ancient times. . . . [But] what were the Habeas Corpus and Trial by Jury intended for? Why, to be the means, not the ends, of protecting life and property."[1]

Macaulay's reluctance to impose coercive measures on Ireland gives way to his conclusion that all laws exist to protect life and property and thus are simply means to that end. For Macaulay, no law is sacred that does not protect property, which, like life itself, exists prior to any state institution. That this position was one of consensus, not partisanship, is evident from the argument of his opponent on the matter of Irish coercion. John Romilly, while condemning the coercion that Macaulay reluctantly advocated, argued from precisely the same basis as Macaulay, contending that proposed searches of Irish households could never lawful: "Was it not clear that the authorized breaking open of houses was nearly as great a breach of order as unauthorized murder?"[2] In both views, the preservation of property was equated with the preservation of life. Property, like life, is assumed to pre-exist the law, not to be constituted by it. Law itself can only be legitimate if it respects that fact.

Yet by the late 1870s a new way of thinking about property and its relation to the institutions of the state had started to take hold, as Matthew Arnold's claim made clear: "If it is the sound English doctrine that all rights are created by law and are based on expediency, and are alterable as the public advantage may require, certainly that orthodox doctrine is mine. Property is created and maintained by law. . . . Legal society creates, for the common good, the right of property and for the common good that right is by legal society limitable" ("Equality" 46).

Arnold's assertion that property exists for the sake of the social order, rather than the social order existing to preserve property, represents a complete reversal of Macaulay's and Romilly's assumptions. For Arnold, all property rights originate with the state and end when the state withholds its recognition and enforcement. Arnold's assertion that his stance is "sound English doctrine" is somewhat ironic—he knew well that his claim was not universally accepted. Still, by this point in the century, Arnold was part of a group of thinkers who revolutionized the way the state was conceived. Instead of a state whose purpose was to preserve and respect property rights that preceded the state, Arnold's state created the order of property over which it presided.

This book explores this shift in thinking in both fiction and nonfiction. Drawing on the political, economic, and legal theory behind these changes, it explores how journalists, political theorists, and fiction writers imagined the fluctuating relationship between a person's orientation toward property and a person's orientation toward the state in the nineteenth century. My purpose in writing it is twofold. First I aim to flesh out what has previously been a rather limited discussion of how Victorians thought about property. Scholars of Victorian literature and culture tend to think of property in terms of its redefinition under the influence of an increasingly pervasive market-driven culture. Jeff Nunokawa tells us of Victorians "alarmed that market values had managed to engross everything under the sun" (4). Andrew Miller observes that for the Victorians, "the penetrating anxiety" was "that their social and moral world was being reduced to a warehouse of goods and commodities, a display window in which people, their actions, and their convictions were exhibited for the economic appetites of others" (6). In these terms, no property was safe for actual keeping. The new world of capitalism was one of endlessly circulating objects, all primed for exchange rather than ownership. All its inhabitants could do was hanker nostalgically for a lost world in which property was inalienable, permanently attached to them in a way that secured and reinforced a stable identity. Often this nostalgia meant longing for a relationship to property that they imagined had once been available to owners of land.[3]

But the dynamics that made up Victorian concepts of proprietorship far exceed the two poles of alienable and inalienable to which this narrative attends. The idea of Victorian property was split along a number of axes. Victorians disputed whether property was a culturally embedded, historically determined relationship or an abstract relationship whose dynamics were immutable and instantly recognizable. They told stories in which property in land signified communal interconnection and stories in which it signified a zone of absolute, exclusive individual control. They argued about whether property had evolved from a primitive state in which ownership and kinship were practically identical to a modern condition in which property was wholly a matter of free contract. They alternated between thinking of ownership as a relationship between one owner and one owned thing and considering it more as a bundle of variable rights and privileges that might be negotiated among several parties. All these competing ideas about property were crosscurrents through which property passed when Victorians imagined it to modulate their relationship to the state. I take them all into account in telling the story of how Victorians gradually abandoned the idea that property existed prior to the state. In doing so, I suggest that the stories we tell ourselves about market thinking in the nineteenth century—the yearning for permanent attachment to property, the fear of alienating oneself along with one's labor, the rage for a sense of self-possession—are not always the most accurate narratives concerning Victorians and their property.

My second aim in describing how Victorians thought about property and the state is to make more visible the entity that presided over the multinational United Kingdom of Great Britain and Ireland. In the story of how Victorians imagined their property to define their relationship with the state, it is apparent that the British state presided not just over a collective body identified as British but over both British and Irish affairs, even though it treated each in a markedly separate manner. Understanding Ireland to be always a part of British state formation in the nineteenth century allows us not only to comprehend how Ireland was visible to the Victorian British Isles, which we mistakenly tend to think of in exclusively British terms, but also to see how Ireland helped shape what the British thought of themselves. When inhabitants of the British Isles thought in terms of property and the state, they often thought in terms that linked Irish and British culture.

The Anglo-Irish and British writers featured in this book who wrote about Ireland under the Act of Union—Maria Edgeworth, Anthony Trollope, John Stuart Mill, George Moore, and George Meredith—were also always writing about the powers and potentials of the British state; therefore, they were always writing about property. Although the idea of property as a natural right increasingly fell out of favor during the nineteenth century, these writers saw in Ireland a dynamic in which the state could treat property as the end for which the state existed, the boundary the state could not cross. Perhaps most paradoxically, all these writers imagine that the state of dispossession, especially dispossession from the land that they strongly associate with the Irish, has unifying potential. Edgeworth and the journalists who wrote as "Young Ireland" celebrated dispossession as the founding moment of a community forged around persisting possessive feelings directed at the lost property; dispossession was more available as a communal experience than ownership of property ever could be; thus, it might be the experience that allowed an entire community to resist state interference. In contrast, Mill, Trollope, Moore, and Meredith saw a unifying power in the state's ability to address dispossession. They imagined that the state could redistribute property and its enjoyment in a way that might draw owners into a closer relationship with the state. By examining these Victorians' preoccupation with dispossession as a starting point for an Irish relationship, this study seeks to add some precision to how we think about colonial possessions and colonizing dispossession.

The British State and Irish Dispossession

While scholarly attention in Victorian studies often fixes on the rising influence of the middle class, it nonetheless remains true that those who owned landed property retained a strong political influence throughout the nineteenth century, even as landed property's economic power gradually waned. But in the global context of the British empire as well as in the semicolonial case of Ireland, land always reigned supreme. In his influential *Cultural and Imperialism*, Edward Said argues that landed property remains the bottom line of the British empire. "At some very basic level, imperialism means thinking about, settling on, controlling land that you do not possess, that is distant, that is lived on and owned by others" (7). But even this absolute statement is imprecise in its characterization. Trying to define imperialism at its most fundamental level, he offers a definition of imperialists as controlling and settling land they "do not possess," that is "owned by others." The dichotomy would seem a simple one, with imperialists exercising control over distant lands against the claims of an indigenous population who own and live on it. But the dichotomy is not so simple—imperialists "settle" on land, indigenous peoples "live" on it. Imperialists "think about" land that is "distant," but how that distance is maintained after they make their settlement is not clear. Said implies that indigenous attachment to land is distinguished by its lack of distance, its lack of a conscious cognitive attachment even, whose absence perhaps indicates how fully naturally the connection is. There is no need to think about owning land for those who simply *are* the owners. What is not clear is how one retains one's identity as the owner of land that is imperially claimed by someone else from somewhere else. Perhaps that is why, when later in his book Said reasserts that "the actual geographical possession of land is what empire is in the final analysis all about," it is a possession that—grammatically at least—happens without any identified owner at all (78).

Said's imprecision in describing the difference between imperial possession and native ownership reflects his work's larger argument that those in possession of land—those whose control of it seems simply part of the natural order of things—may have no moral right to it whatsoever. At the same time, his wording also reflects how difficult it is to identify a principle that explains how one might recognize who *does* have moral rights to the land. Said and other postcolonial critics have exposed the imperial biases of property's definition both in western law and in European philosophy. As a result, they often reject abstract theories of property in favor of an ethic of native attachment. Against a Lockean vision of property created by one's own labor in the earth, a vision they rightly show to be the product of cultural biases, postcolonial scholars tend to join anticolonial nationalists in their assertion of a highly particular, nonpropertized, indigenous attachment to the land that precedes the imposition of an imperial law. Political scientist Uday Singh Mehta, for example, posits that an indigenous sense of "territorial togetherness," collective in nature and premised on a sense of the "textured realities of a locally imagined and physical landscape," serves as "a marker of a people's sense of autonomy" (120, 122, 127). This assertion of an attachment that defies European—and, most pointedly, British—definitions of property avoids appealing to any central body for its legitimation. It exists prior to formal government and abstract theorization. Felt and experienced rather than defined and regulated, this sort of attachment to property appears to lie outside any system that might transfer or reassign ownership. While a community might expand the number of people who feel an attachment to its property, it could never effectively ensure the extinction of such feelings in people who once had them. In Mehta's formulation, regardless of whether such an attachment is recognized by a governing body, the indigenous connection to the land is inalienable.

This book examines the attractions such a vision of property had, not for anticolonial nationalists, but for the colonizing culture against which they struggled. Attending to the backdrop of debates over the nature of property in Irish and British land, this book reads a group of British and Irish writers drawn toward Irish claims of a native attachment to the land—claims articulated in much the same terms Mehta uses. But their attraction was not exclusively—or in some cases at all—about correcting injustices committed by Britain. For the authors who are the subjects of the following chapters, such Irish nationalist assertions of rights to property, made in an environment of rather rigid and often coercive state control, offered a positive model for imagining Britain's own continued respect for individual property rights.

It might seem counterintuitive to argue that nineteenth-century writers imagined Ireland as the site of a property that was secure in the face of government interference. After all, the British Victorian stereotype of Ireland was that popular unrest there made it a territory where neither life nor property was safe. This popular unrest, however, was undertaken in the name of a collective Irish attachment to land, a right that resisted all British attempts to redefine it. In 1867, for instance, the group alternately known as the Fenians, the Irish Revolutionary Brotherhood, and the Irish Republican Brotherhood issued a declaration that I offer as representative of numerous declarations that came before and after, justifying rebellion against the British state: "Our rights and liberties have been trampled upon by an alien aristocracy, who treating us as foes, usurped our lands, and drew away from our country all material riches. The real owners of the soil were removed to make room for cattle, and driven across the ocean to seek the means of living, and the political rights denied to them at home. . . . But we never lost the memory and hope of a national existence. . . . The soil of Ireland, at present in the possession of an oligarchy, belongs to us, the Irish people, and to us it must be restored" (Provisional Government 76–77).

This particular assertion of rights of property was the opening shot in a campaign of violent resistance designed to drive the British state entirely out of Ireland. It was a manifesto uncompromisingly hostile to British rule, one that advocated violence against the British as legitimized by the need to restore the moral order of property. And yet, as I argue, its vision of the native right to property as perfectly preserved in the hearts of the Irish people had a reassuring aspect. After all, for many Britons at this time, property seemed to be disintegrating into a nothingness of infinite alienability and modular bundles of rights. In Ireland however, property was still imagined as a right to an actual spatial zone, one whose prerogatives could not be extinguished by mere state policy.

The Irish resistance to state interference was a crucial reminder to writers in this study of what property might be. One of the foundational myths of English liberty and English representational governance was the Lockean idea that the state was fashioned out of consenting men whose rights to property preceded its establishment. In Locke's formulation, a man *"puts on the bonds of Civil Society . . .* by agreeing with other Men, to joyn and unite into a Community, for their comfortable, safe, and peaceable living one amongst another, in a secure Enjoyment of their Properties" (7:95). Locke imagined property as the protective zone that buffered subjects from the power of the state, as the line that the state could not cross because the whole purpose of the state's existence was to protect property for individual enjoyment. When Irish activists continually justified their resistance to the British state by invoking the rights of property, they attributed to Irish property unusual powers to resist even the most well-developed state, which the British government in Ireland most definitely was. Victorian Ireland, neither fully colony nor co-nation, was a zone the British state governed with a sophisticated and centralized set of institutions. In contrast to Britain, which prided itself on minimal government and local administration well into the late nineteenth century, Ireland was the space where all British citizens could read the British state's potential for power over everyday life.[4] Thus, fantasies that Irish land might be property that protected its owner from state interference were also fantasies of Irish property as able to resist a state that was both the same as—and yet far more invasive than—that which governed Britain. In such a view, Ireland was the site where a fully developed set of state institutions might nonetheless coexist with property that operated as if the state could act only beyond its boundaries.

As the following chapters show, when writers turned their attention to property in an Irish context, they turned to property in a situation where the state exercised more power over defining and redistributing property than it ever did in Britain, yet it seemed to have less power for making such definitions and distributions stick. The state's simultaneously exaggerated and attenuated powers were a result of the anomalous semicolonial situation of Ireland in the nineteenth century. Ireland, as it was incorporated into the United Kingdom, provided the specter of the state's potential power to simply make the rights of property disappear. This was true for more than just the native Irish Catholic population, whose property rights had been erased by two hundred years of penal laws imposed by the conquering British. The Act of Union with Britain also eliminated the representative rights of two-thirds of the landed members of the former Irish parliament and had been intentionally designed to decrease the social and political power that the Irish Protestant landholding class exercised over the Catholic population. With this decrease in power for the Anglo-Irish landholders came a centralized, state-sponsored police force and state-sponsored education system, long before either were centralized in Britain, where similar tasks were left to the supervision of local landowners.[5] Thus Ireland constituted a situation in which a centralized state—the same state that in Great Britain was so well known for its respect for the rights of private property—actively intervened in the life of individual citizens and downplayed the mediating role of a propertied class, which in Britain was imagined as the paternalistic firewall between the state and its citizens.

But Ireland was also most nakedly the site of prolonged resistance, both discursive and physical, against such incursions by the state. During the nineteenth century, the British came to understand Irish national character as possessively attached to the land. Through low-grade guerrilla warfare, mass meetings, parliamentary obstruction, armed uprisings, and even the assassinations of British officials, Irish nationalists justified their resistance by invoking a communal attachment to the land such as Mehta attributes to indigenous populations. But in nineteenth-century Ireland, such attachments were always intertwined with a British interference. Thus, the Irish assertion of property rights centered somewhat paradoxically around a rhetoric of dispossession. Irish nationalists framed the Irish experience as one of having had rights to the land, of having been robbed of them by the British state, and of still experiencing them, nonetheless, as a palpable attachment. The exceptional nature of this attachment, they implied, came about because legal channels of connection had been denied to them. This was a narrative that at least a portion of the British public proved willing to buy. In her wildly popular best-seller *The Wild Irish Girl* (1806), Sydney Owenson treated the unusually durable sense of Irish attachment to land as a simple part of the Irish landscape. In the tale, the absentee landlord's son, on his first trip to Ireland, is introduced to a lodge his father has leased not in terms of its present-day status but as having been at one time "the best part of what remained of the patrimony of the Prince . . . whose great forefathers once owned the half of the barony, from the Red Bog to the Sea Coast" before the family's dispossession under Cromwell (37).

Both British and Irish audiences during this period accepted the idea of an Ireland where the history of an ancient Irish title and the conquest that disrupted it might be read in every field and allotment. What Owenson romanticized, Irish nationalists advanced as fact: Irish land was teeming with a cultural memory of rights that could not be erased by the mere legalities of British rule. Many suggested that it was precisely the imposition of such legalities that kept alive possessive sentiments. Irish parliamentary member Isaac Butt, for instance, argued that the Irish idea that property had been taken from them was "kept up in the minds of the people by the acts of the present oppression" (48 n 1).

The rhetoric of dispossession, whether a product of authentic group memory or of state provocation, was employed by two very different groups in Ireland: the Anglo-Irish Protestant class, protesting that they had been robbed of an independent Irish parliament that was their right as property owners, and the primarily rural Irish Catholic underclass, who protested that their land had long ago been stolen from them by Protestant invaders. In both cases, state interference with property rights led each party to publicly assert property rights that existed prior to the state and that persisted outside of their legal channels. Having been dispossessed, the Irish framed themselves as connected to their property in a way that mere legal rights never could achieve. At the same time, this cathexis, taking hold as it did outside of legal channels, could never be legitimately defined as the exclusive experience of just one dispossessed group.

The notion that the Irish, especially Irish Catholics, felt an intense connection to the land was brought home by almost constant guerilla warfare carried on throughout the nineteenth century. The Irish Catholic secret societies, composed under various names—Defenders, Rockites, Ribbon Men—violently enforced an Irish moral economy of fair rents, fair practices by the landlords, and exemption from tithing to the Protestant Church of Ireland. While this resistance could be organized on a national level, as it was in the Tithe Wars and the Land War, its most striking feature was its widespread persistence orchestrated at the local level, even when no national framework supported it. Additionally, the second half of the century saw the development of the Irish resistance movement on the international stage. Emigrants who fled Ireland during the famine subsequently joined forces in North America as the Fenian Brotherhood, the overseas counterpart to the Irish Republican Brotherhood in Dublin, with both groups explicitly committed to acts of violence in the name of freeing Ireland from Britain's rule. Their international campaigns—a plan to attack a Canadian military fort, an attempt to take Chester Castle in northern England and seize its arsenal, and the deadly bomb intended to free men imprisoned after the Chester plot was uncovered—only intensified a British perception of a fundamental and undisruptable Irish attachment to their homeland, one that did not disappear even when the Irish left Ireland.

As a result of this unrest, most Britons viewed Ireland as a place where life and property were singularly unsafe. But in its resistance to British law, Ireland proved a proprietary landscape exempt from many of the contradictions of British property at the time. Irish property rights still seemed to carry with them one of the most important functions of the Lockean ideal of property, an ideal that no longer seemed available in a commercial Britain: the function of marking off a zone into which the authority of the state could not enter. This privacy was all the more attractive because, in the Irish context, it also sidestepped the socially atomizing effects of British private property. The equation of the Irish property rights in land with a deeply felt Irish national character made land the site of a communal identity, not a barrier to it. But perhaps most attractive to the writers I examine was the perverse logic of inalienability they found in the Irish attachment to property. If Irish land could not be estranged from its owner by hundreds of years of British state interference, then surely it could be considered equally immune to the alienating forces of the marketplace. The entanglement of, on the one hand, Irish claims to land and, on the other hand, their experience of dispossession from it suggested to these authors that the colonized Irish land had become the sort of property that could never be given up. Because Irish attachment to land stood outside of legal definition and economic valuation, no legal or economic channels existed to make its loss a possibility. Irish property was property that could only be kept, not lost.

In my first chapter I show that Maria Edgeworth, in her Irish fiction, leaned heavily on this idea that Irish property could not be lost because its title could never be proven. In her Irish national tales *Castle Rackrent* (1801), *Ennui* (1809), and *Ormond* (1817), Edgeworth assigns the role of ruling Ireland not to the state but to those who own land. Rather than establishing a correspondence between land ownership and native attachment, or even land ownership and hard work and deservingness, Edgeworth applies the stereotype of native Irish attachment to the soil to the Anglo-Irish, suggesting that such attachment unites them to the Irish in a shared sense of dispossession. Nonetheless, as her final Irish novel, *Ormond*, shows, this is a strategy neither the Anglo-Irish nor Edgeworth herself can sustain in the face of increasing British state involvement in Irish lives.

While Edgeworth worked with a vision of property as a right that preexists the state, the journalism of John Stuart Mill championed the idea that the state could create rights in property and in fact *should* exercise such power in Ireland. Chapter 2 examines Mill's writings on Ireland, in which he argues that the state can assuage an Irish sense of dispossession by sponsoring the redistribution of land in small lots that would be farmed by their proprietors. But even Mill, opponent of a conception of property as a natural right, imagines the space of such property to be so completely autonomous from state interference that it is animated by an almost supernatural "power of property." Mill, in his advocacy of a purely expedient and state-defined assignment of property in land, imagines landed property to be a space the state might create but cannot control.

Chapters 1 and 2 examine two opposing visions of property that shaped discourse on Ireland. One vision imagined property to predate the state; the other imagined the state to create property rights in order to set up a zone from which it then excused itself. Chapter 3 demonstrates the attractions that Irish nationalist assertions of indigenous property rights had for those caught between two such opposing visions. The chapter offers a broad overview of several competing narratives about property in the land that shaped Victorian discourse. Property as a zone of individual freedom, the landed estate as the interconnected fabric from which society is built, and, finally, the notion of property as simply a bundle of rights all clashed at midcentury, making ownership in Britain seem just as unsatisfactory as dispossession. Focusing on the Young Ireland journalists also writing at midcentury, I argue that their imagination of the Irish proprietary landscape posed elegant, but exclusively Irish, solutions to the problems that troubled of British property. The chapter ends by examining the Irish Land Acts of 1871 and 1881, acts that legislators billed as restoring indigenous property practices to the Irish. Showing how advocates of the Irish Land Acts married the ideas of legal theorist Henry Sumner Maine to the nationalist rhetoric of an exceptionalist Ireland, the chapter argues that the idea of indigenous property as an experience available only to indigenous people was actually put to imperialist uses. In the Land Acts' interpretation of indigenous property practices, Ireland might be owned in its particularly native way by the Irish, while still leaving ample room for its control by the British.

Chapter 4 argues that Anthony Trollope's Palliser series of novels also imagines the Union of Britain and Ireland to be enabled by a dynamic in which one party has formal ownership while the other claims different, less defined rights to the same property. In Trollope's fiction legal holders of property cannot be the enjoyers of their own property, and he depicts legal owners as needing to be joined to the dispossessed in order to have someone who might enjoy their property in their place. For Trollope, this dynamic serves as a model of how the state works. Integral to this vision is Trollope's way of imagining the wife as responsible for enjoying property she can never own, a position he suggests is analogous to Ireland's relationship to the British state.

Chapter 5 ends the book by considering the state's definition of what cannot be property at all. Fiction by the Anglo-Irish George Moore and the English George Meredith deals with the state's ability to keep objects, corporeal and incorporeal, from being private property. This new focus, I argue, was a response to the proposal of the first Home Rule Bill, which threatened that the British state might be dispossessed of Ireland altogether. Both supporters of Home Rule, Moore and Meredith invoke the state-defined zone of the public domain—that is, the legal space in which the state declares an object no longer individual property in order to guarantee its availability to all citizens—as the dominant trope through which to think about Ireland's possible transition to independence. Public domain is also the device through which Moore and Meredith imagine that Britain's sacrifice of dominion over Ireland will be made no sacrifice at all.

In choosing which texts would contribute to this narrative about state and property, I have relied on the criteria of subject matter over an author's national identity. Quite often the authors I include have an unclear identity in relation to Irishness. Perhaps only the writers associated with the Young Ireland movement can unambiguously claim status as "authentically" Irish. The longtime collaboration of the Anglo-Irish landlord class with British rule has made their inclusion in the Irish canon a point of controversy. The extent to which Maria Edgeworth might have identified with British, Anglo-Irish, and Irish interests has been a hotly contested topic over the past two hundred years, with the fact of her subordinate gender position complicating whether or not one understands her as identified with landlords or their dependents.[6] Moore's status as Anglo-Irish landlord is equally problematic. His enthusiastic, although only intermittent participation in the late-century Celtic revival and the early days of the Abbey Theater would seem to identify him solidly with Irish cultural nationalism, but his long-term residence in London and his love and emulation of continental literature associates him with a more cosmopolitan disavowal of nationality altogether.[7] Meredith, with no Irish ancestry at all, stubbornly aligned himself with a Celtic frame of mind, insisting that a Welsh lineage endowed him with a Celtic racial sympathy for the Irish; he also considered himself half-Irish because his mother, who had never been to Ireland, had the maiden name of MacNamara.[8] It would be difficult to categorize Trollope or Mill as anything other than British, although Mill was asked to stand for parliamentary election for an Irish district after the publication of his journalism on the Irish land question.[9] Mill's possible Irish parliamentary career as the Irish Tenant League's member suggests what I hope to establish in this book: that the British state enabled a system of identification in which being representative of Britishness or Irishness was not always a matter of *being* British or Irish. It is unquestionable that the deep divides of irreconcilable religious identities, markedly different cultural heritages, and the brutal unevenness in the distribution of material wealth barred a widespread identification between populations in Britain and Ireland. Nonetheless, the authors I include in this study all show that such an identification, grounded in a shared state rather than a shared nation, was at least cognizable to some in the nineteenth century.

Scholarly Contexts

In telling the story about Irish property in the British imagination, my intent has been to unearth some of the ways that the multinational structure of the United Kingdom shaped what we know as British literature. This project has been ably carried out on imaginative literature from the Romantic era. Katie Trumpener's monumental *Bardic Nationalism* (1997) established the idea of a nineteenth-century trans-Celtic sphere of letters dominated by Irish national tales, Scottish historical novels, and Celtic folk songs and poetry. In the time since Trumpener's book first appeared, research on Celtic influences in Romantic-era literature and culture has produced some of that field's most important work. Ina Ferris's *The Romantic National Tale and the Question of Ireland* (2002), Evan Gottlieb's *Feeling British: Sympathy and National Identity in Scottish and English Writing, 1707–1832* (2007), and Ian Duncan's *Scott's Shadow* (2007) have all explored the influence of Scottish- and Irish-identified writing on the formation of a large body of British literature. Little of that attention, however, has extended into the Victorian era. To date, Mary Jean Corbett's exhaustive *Allegories of Union in Irish and English Writing, 1790–1870* (2000) and Gordon Bigelow's *Fiction, Famine, and the Rise of Economics in Victorian Britain and Ireland* (2003) remain the only full-length studies to take into account the impact of Ireland on British Victorian literature.[10]

The field of Irish studies, however, offers rich models for thinking about Ireland in the nineteenth-century British imagination. As Joe Cleary points out, "If colonial cultures are more dependent than metropolitan ones, they may sometimes be compelled for the same reason to be more innovative and experimental, less insular and more receptive to developments elsewhere" (57). Such has clearly been the case for several influential studies of the colonized culture of Ireland to whose innovations in placing Irish culture in a theoretical and global context I am indebted. Seamus Deane's *Strange Country* (1997) has provided a masterful account of Enlightenment rationality by focusing on accounts of Irish culture as the Enlightenment's other. David Lloyd's essays have demonstrated that the Irish novel challenges some of our basic assumptions about the relationship between the novel and nationalism.[11] Julia Wright's *Ireland, India, and Nationalism in Nineteenth-Century Literature* (2007) overturns simple notions of an imperial metropole and colonized periphery through a careful excavation of Irish responses to a colonization of India in which the Irish identified both with colonized and colonizer. Works positioned squarely within Irish studies, such as Margot Backus's *The Gothic Family Romance* (1999), Luke Gibbons's *Edmund Burke and Ireland* (2003), and Heather Laird's *Subversive Law in Ireland, 1879–1920* (2005), have illuminated reasons why Irish property might matter to British literature.

The pattern my work uncovers—of a British state interested in treating property as something that was off limits to it, even if such property originated with state legislation and enforcement in the first place—accords with recent work done by Anne Frey, Lauren Goodlad, and Pam Morris. All three persuasively argue that the nineteenth-century British state was marked by habits of governmentality, Michel Foucault's term for a modern strategy of the state in which to govern at all means to identify areas from which the exercise of government must be restrained.[12] Frey, Goodlad, and Morris recruit Foucault's term to challenge earlier Foucault-inspired literary and cultural criticism that tended to play up the pervasiveness and coherence of the powers of the British state. Instead, Goodlad's and Frey's work in particular foregrounds the necessary freedom required for governmental power to work, a freedom it paradoxically must work to create in order to exert any power on its subjects. The nineteenth-century writers featured in this book express such presuppositions when they concern themselves with property rights the state must create in order to respect. When Mill imagines the freedom of the peasant proprietor, made free by a property procured for him by the state; when Anthony Trollope imagines a dynamic in which legal owners decline to exercise their rights so that others may enjoy their property for them; even when Moore and Meredith imagine a zone of resources made inalienable through the state's creation of a public domain, they all might be understood as trying to imagine what Foucault calls "this new art of government," whose paradoxical task is "introducing additional freedom through additional control and intervention" (*Birth of Biopolitics* 64).

In focusing on property as the space of freedom created by the state, my study, however, departs from Goodlad's and Frey's focus on the pastoral methods involved in modern governmentality. Both Goodlad and Frey emphasize the role that a pastoral ethic plays in creating a state that both devises and commits to its own limits. This pastoral ethic is one that encourages leadership through an intimate knowledge of subjects. The modern "pastor" of the British state may or may not hold an official state position, but like the Christian Good Shepherd who knows each one of his flock individually, he (and it is usually a he) is responsible for acquiring personal knowledge of individuals and applying it for the good of the state. At the same time, this modern pastor must allow individuals to know him well enough so that he might provide them with guidance in the context of an individualized relationship.[13]

While the writers I examine sometimes draw for evidence on information collected in a pastoral mode, they do not imagine the state's involvement with property to be pastoral in manner. In their telling, to assign property rights to a citizen of a state is not, for the most part, a way for the state to come to know its subjects; rather, it is a way for the state to become known to those subjects as the power that accords them freedom. The distribution and recognition of property rights become, in an age of governmentality, functions that do not lean heavily on pastoralism's individuating tactics. The writers I examine do not uniformly treat owning property as an individuating condition, one that inevitably confers an atomizing singularity on its beneficiaries. In fact, they often highlight property's functions of unification—unifying an owner with the ancestors and heirs to whom he owes the property, unifying an enjoyer of property with the legal owner, or unifying a legal owner with the state whose laws make him such.

The writing I examine exhibits at best a vexed relationship to the norm of the self-possessed individual as fully enclosed, fully autonomous, owing nothing, as C. B. Macpherson tells us, to society for the skills and capabilities he or she owns like free-market property. In my analysis such characters do appear, but they are something less than normative. Just as often as I find characters asserting their autonomy and anxiously cordoning off their individual personhood from the determining interference of others, I also find characters troubled by the contradictory metaphors of property. These characters are often alarmed by the experience of official ownership, reluctant to defend themselves as if they were individual property, and routinely glad to cede the enjoyment of their property, even in their own selves, to someone else. For these characters, property in one's self, just like property in land, works best when it can be shared, sacrificed, returned, and poured into the pool of the public domain. All such proprietary strategies have their advantages.

Tracking the realist novel's fictional incarnations of these uneasy property-owning individuals through the nineteenth century may also help us understand the sudden nonfictional late-century interest in communal rights to land and shared cultural property. Studies on the politics of liberalism in the late nineteenth century—Joanna Bailkin's *The Culture of Property* (2004), Eugenio Biagini's collection *Citizenship and Community* (1996), and Paul Readman's *Land and Nation in England* (2008)—have begun to unearth a wide divergence between capitalism's preference for perfectly individual, perfectly alienable, property and late-century British liberal politics, which began to take the side of collective property in land, in labor, and in cultural artifacts. To these studies this work adds a consideration of how ideas about property could not be separated from the multinational condition of the British state. It also adds a longer view in which to contextualize the liberal party's late-century so-called conversion from the voice of individual property rights to the champion of collective and national property. Examining Britain's long literary engagement with Ireland since the Union, one can discern a much more vexed liberal relationship to property much earlier in the century. While Victorian home visitors, journalistic investigators, and aspiring members of the clerisy provided a pastoral sense of individuation to the population, property may have been more available than we so far have allowed as a terrain on which one could project one's desire for more communal experiences. Certainly, my examination of representations of Irish property reveal not a longing for the individualizing power of property but a most definite envy for its status as the stage for communal experiences—even the communal sense of dispossession.

Writing in the aftermath of the Indian mutiny, Lewis Pelly argued in the *Westminster Review* that the English were prone to feel more guilt than was warranted over their treatment of India, protesting, "We have taken no man's estate—filched no man's property—invaded no man's conscience." His argument indicates the extent to which a British sense of what constituted a legitimate and illegitimate state action still depended on the idea of respect for property in land—a respect that in his formulation is equal to respect for a man's own conscience. But coming as it does in the middle of a long history of the assignment and reassignment of land rights undertaken by the East India Company, it also rings more than a bit disingenuous. If one first uses the law to define a tax collector as an owner (as Pelly asserts Cornwallis did in late-eighteenth-century India) and then revokes that law in order to recognize a village community as having a collective attachment to the soil, slightly other than proprietary in nature (as land resettlements in British India did in the mid-nineteenth-century), has no property been taken? If a government can simply reengineer the rights and responsibilities that are grouped under the heading of property, then can any limit exist to the government's assigning of and revoking rights? And if a government can assign and revoke rights in property, then what was the ultimate end of a state that in Britain, at least, had always defined itself as existing primarily for the protection of property? How could Pelly have made such a claim in anything other than bad faith? My aim in this book is to suggest that Pelly's claim—and even more importantly, a host of claims about British respect for Irish property rights—clearly served a self-interested function. However, their immediate sense of self-interest might have had less to do with keeping the empire profitable and under control and more to do with trying to stabilize their own sense of how they hoped that property might work at home.

CHAPTER ONE

Disowning to Own

Maria Edgeworth's Irish Fiction and the Illegitimacy
of National Ownership

Maria Edgeworth's reputation has been tied persistently, if contradictorily, to
property. Edgeworth is well known for declining to express a sense of ownership over her own writing. Her refusal stems in part from Edgeworth's close
collaboration with her father. He often assigned her topics and themes upon
which to write and was heavily involved in editing her work. At least once, in
Essays on Professional Education (1809), he published under his own name a work
primarily written by her. The entirety of the credit she gives her father for her
own writing success can be summed up in one anguished note to a friend—
"Where should I be without my father? I should sink into that nothing from
which he has raised me" (Butler, *Maria Edgeworth* 207).[1] Additionally, because
male authors—Walter Scott, Gerald Griffith, the Banim brothers—borrowed
without crediting the comic, thick description of clashing cultural manners she
innovated in her Irish tales, Edgeworth has seemed a figure unusually divested
of her own intellectual property.[2]

In contrast to this image of Edgeworth as robbed of credit for her contributions to English literature, twentieth-century critics envisioned Edgeworth to
be confidently assertive of what was due to her as an Anglo-Irish, land-owning

Protestant in Ireland. The members of her class maintained a monopoly on the land and leadership of the nation, which cast them in a colonizing role in Ireland. Edgeworth, Tom Dunne contends, disdained the Irish peasantry, believing "that the civilization of Irish life involved its Anglicization in every facet," an Anglicization she thought should be carried out through "a benevolent, improving landlordism" ("Maria Edgeworth" 6; "A Gentleman's Estate" 98). Terry Eagleton's account of Edgeworth's Irish fiction similarly concludes that Edgeworth's final sympathy lies with the colonizer, not the colonized, her "language trad[ing] in power while striving to be innocent of it" (176). Sharon Murphy has repeated the same argument, arguing that Edgeworth's fiction is largely motivated by her ambition to "justify and facilitate the continuing presence of the colonizing class that she herself represents" (42).

This chapter will consider these two visions of Edgeworth—the modestly dispossessed author and the jealously possessive colonist—not as contradictory, but as two sides of the same coin. In Edgeworth's fiction an initial act of dispossession lies at the root of many characters' convictions that they are proprietarily connected with a piece of property. Edgeworth plays with this paradox for its laughable effects. Her Irish novels offer comedies in which proof of ownership remains veiled by the passage of time, and the impossibility of recovering it is what guarantees an attachment to property in the future. In Edgeworth, this promise holds as true for those who have lost their ownership as for those who make spurious proprietary claims.

The idea that ownership and dispossession might become indistinguishable over time is one of Edgeworth's answers to the problems of Union. Hastily passed after the Irish rebellion of 1798, the Union was supposed to reconcile Ireland to Britain, but the Irish had never stopped perceiving the British as a conquering presence in their country. Edgeworth's plots anticipate an era when memory of Britain's takeover of Ireland might be lost in the distant past, when British and Irish would not look so very different. In doing so, they look forward to a time when possession and dispossession might come to look like the same thing. Edgeworth unites these two themes in her enshrinement of the estate as a microcosm of the nation itself, a nation not yet in existence but one that would be formed by a blending of British and Irish character.[3] She envisions the landed estate as an autonomous piece of property, able to internally reform without outside intervention. She imagines the nation, too, as evolving toward improvement and reconciliation without outside intervention.

The figure of the autonomous estate as autonomous nation is of course not Edgeworth's invention. At the time she was writing, it was prominently associated with Edmund Burke's conservative attack on the French Revolution in *Reflections of the Revolution in France* (1790). In it, he roundly condemns the French National Assembly's attempt to legislate France into radical reform. Such a reform could never occur in Britain, he asserts, because Britons "assert our liberties as an *entailed inheritance* derived to us from our forefathers, and to be transmitted to our posterity." The legislation of one generation cannot tamper with such liberties because they are as unassailable as property: "We hold, we transmit our government and our privileges, in the same manner in which we enjoy and transmit our property and our lives" (33). In order to imagine the nation that can reform without revolution or without the meddling of a conquering power, Edgeworth relies on this Burkean vision of the nation and its governing structures as an internally evolving estate. Known for her admiration for Burke, Edgeworth wrote novels that imposed a narrative structure on his logic, a logic that Luke Gibbons describes as a focus on "the continuous modification of custom and practice between distant origins and an uncertain present" with the aim of "heal[ing] the wounds of history, and in particular, the originary violence through which conquests, or revolutions, established new political regimes" (171).

Edgeworth's Burkean strategy at first might seem a betrayal of her Enlightenment principles, whose tenets she promulgated in her educational literature, but her translation of Burke's motif of a property as a tradition evolved from immemorial time winds up not only acknowledging some of its anti-Enlightenment faults but actually using those faults to fuel her plots' resolutions. The fault to which she most often returns is one raised by Thomas Paine in the first part of *The Rights of Man* (1791).[4] Against Burke's celebration of British traditional rights inherited like property, Paine asserted a set of "natural and imprescriptible" rights, which he held as the only proper end for which governments might be created. Among these were "liberty, property, security, and resistance of oppression" (54). Burke's claim that all rights were anchored in historical and cultural context and did not exist in any universally generalizable form, Paine contended, was the fallacy of all those "who reason by precedents from antiquity": they stop at an arbitrary point rather than going all the way back to the beginning. If Burke's readers pushed his sense of precedent a little further back in time, Paine argued, "we shall find a direct contrary opinion and practice prevailing; and if antiquity is to be authority, a thousand such authorities may be produced, successively contradicting each other" (*Rights* 25). Rather than refuting Paine's logic, Edgeworth's tales celebrate exactly that feature of the nation as inherited property. They portray the Irish estate as the vessel of a gradually accumulated history that changes both property and property-holder, until the bond between them can no longer be traced back to any clear origin and in that way becomes indissoluble. Without one clear legitimizing source to authorize it, no identifiable mechanism exists to undo it.

However, this is a strategy whose effectiveness for Edgeworth eroded in the second decade of Union, as an increasingly interventionist British state made it difficult to imagine union proceeding on organic terms of traditions changed imperceptibly over time. In this chapter, I offer a brief analysis of her children's tale "Simple Susan" to illuminate a larger trend in two of her Irish novels— *Castle Rackrent* (1801) and *Ennui* (1812)—a trend in which Edgeworth makes dispossession the paradoxical source of legitimacy for property holders. Then I will turn to her last Irish novel, *Ormond* (1817), to explore how the creeping involvement of the British state apparatus in Irish life drained her common-law Irish comedies of some of their force.

The National Tale and Keeping What Is Lost

I begin to explore Edgeworth's strategy of celebrating dispossession by examining the scene of a supposed crime, one in which Edgeworth is denied credit for her own work. During the last days of his life, Walter Scott's thoughts turned confusedly toward Maria Edgeworth. Both Scott, with his historical popularizations and fictionalizations of Scottish history, and Edgeworth, with her tales of Anglo-Irish landlords on their Irish estates, were seen as developing the distinct narrative style of the national tale, a popular Romantic genre of the novel set in the Celtic regions of the British Isles.[5] Yet in discussing the female authors of the day, Scott was unable to remember the name of the writer whom he credited with first inspiring him to write novels of a specifically Celtic national character. Making no reference to his published declaration of a desire to "emulate the admirable Irish portraits drawn by Miss Edgeworth" (Lockhart 493), nor to the well-known story that Edgeworth's *The Absentee* (1812) revived his flagging commitment to the manuscript of *Waverley* (1814), an older Scott instead recollected her early didactic sketches for children in *The Parent's Assistant* (1796), dwelling vaguely and condescendingly on her powers of sentimental expression: "Ay, Miss Edgeworth: she's very clever, and best in the little touches too. I'm sure, in that children's story, where the little girl parts with her lamb, and the little boy brings it back to her again, there's nothing for it but just to put down the book, and cry" (qtd in Lockhart 493).

It would be difficult to make an argument about the conscious motivation behind such comments. Recorded as evidence of Scott's declining mental faculties (he was, after all, a personal friend of Edgeworth's), the anecdote nonetheless is suggestive of the gender dynamics behind Scott's position as canonical novelist. Marilyn Butler reads his comments as a distancing gesture, in which he pays his "last compliments to his women rivals for their beautifully done small work" while defining himself as an author working "on a bigger scale" (Introduction 3). It certainly was not the first of Scott's attempts to distinguish his work from Edgeworth's; Katie Trumpener notes his tendency to downplay in his own criticism those works by Edgeworth that most clearly influence his own (139). Even in senility, Scott reduced Edgeworth's literary accomplishments to feminized "little touches" most relevant to home, hearth, and childhood. Yet if the force of the anecdote is in the estrangement—either by the effects of old age or misogyny—between two of the national tale's most prominent authors, it still highlights a tendency of the national tale beyond its careful recording of national "habits, manners, and feelings" (Scott 493). For what is at the heart of "Simple Susan," the Edgeworth tale to which Scott refers, is also what is central to every national tale: the pleasurably nostalgic mourning of what is lost, along with its simultaneous restoration. I use Scott's chance comment to illuminate Edgeworth's approach to the national tale. Examining "Simple Susan" as a prologue to more extended readings of Edgeworth's Irish novels helps outline Edgeworth's vision of an illegitimate ownership, one that keeps lost things lost even after they are regained. The illegitimate owners who populate Edgeworth's novels experience Anglo-Irish Union as an arrangement they cannot defend, legitimate, or condemn. In writing of an Ireland illegitimately owned, Edgeworth creates a vision of an unauthorized and unauthorizable bond that leaves Britain unable to disentangle itself from Ireland, making it the most secure, because it is the least legitimate, sort of property.

Critics often have focused on the transmission of property in Edgeworth primarily to make arguments about the gender dynamics involved in these scenes. Katie Trumpener describes such scenes as ones in which "an English character travels to a British periphery [and then] under the tutelage of an aristocratic friend, he or she learns to appreciate its cultural plenitude and decides to settle there permanently. Each national tale ends with the traveler's marriage to his or her native guide, in a wedding that allegorically unites Britain's 'national characters.'" (141).

While the marriage plot cannot be separated from the gender inequities it normalizes, it also implies an erotic energy that does not always imply automatic subjugation for the wife. Mary Jean Corbett notes that national tales imagine amicable and intimate relationships between Ireland and England by glossing over power disparities involved both in the gender dynamics of a marriage and in England's colonizing relationship with Ireland. But Ina Ferris's emphasis on the tales' dizzying hybridity—the way they use romance to confound the boundaries between "us" and "them," "here" and "there"—demonstrates that the erotic power of the marriage plot might confuse accepted property relations in the interests of Union ("Narrating"). Marriage might, as Corbett argues, be a fitting allegorical vehicle for welcoming Ireland into Great Britain's fold while keeping the region femininely disenfranchised from its own property. Yet it might also, as Doris Sommer argues happens in Latin American national tales, skew gender dynamics, imagining women to be key players in domestic partnerships of such national importance that "fathers of nations couldn't afford to lord it over mothers" (15).

With their emphasis on domestic affections, national tales provide a psychological model for the cultivation of patriotic attachment similar to that articulated by Burke in his *Reflections on the Revolution in France*. But Burkean political theory and national tales also require the medium of inanimate property as part of that cultivation. The country secure from revolution, Burke explains, is one in which "we have given to our frame of polity the image of a relation in blood . . . adopting our fundamental laws into the bosom of our family affections" (34). Yet in Burke's model and in the national tale, this merging of familial love and love of country winds up less focused on ties of affiliation among nation or kin and more focused on the attachment to physical objects that stand for family. Burke envisions the English constitution "as an entailed inheritance derived to us from our forefathers, and to be transmitted to our posterity; as an estate specially belonging to the people of this kingdom" (33). While Burke explains that "to love the little platoon we belong to in society. . . . is the first link in the series by which we proceed towards a love to our country," his rhetoric orients that love not toward other people but toward the physical objects collectively owned by the "little platoon" of the family (47). For Burke, the "sense of habitual native dignity" that stabilizes England emanates not from a spirit of brotherly love but from a freedom conceived in distinctly materialist terms: it "carries an imposing and majestic aspect. It has a pedigree and illustrating ancestors. It has its bearings and its ensigns armorial. It has its gallery of portraits; its monumental inscriptions; its records, evidences, and titles" (34). The French revolutionaries' ambitious decimal planning disrupts this patriotic orientation toward physical objects. Burke condemns it on the grounds that, "No man ever was attached by a sense of pride, partiality, or real affection, to a description of square measurement" (198).

The Irish national tale, with its marriage plot embedded among belabored expositions of landscape, castles, portrait galleries, and monuments, also narrates erotic and patriotic attraction as emanating from physical objects. In Edgeworth's plots, these objects are the subjects of property disputes that an appeal to the past only complicates. For Edgeworth, if the nation is an inheritance, perpetually owed to its descendants, Ireland's problem lies in being owed to more than one line. Edgeworth draws both on Anglo-Irish complaints that Union robbed their children of ruling power in an Irish parliament and on an Irish Catholic tradition of viewing Anglo-Irish estates as land that had been stolen from their forefathers.[6] The power of hereditary rights, which Burke saw as permanently securing a nation to its landholders, could also be invoked by Irish Catholics as being strong enough to cancel a conqueror's claims to a piece of land.

The paradox of inheritance in Ireland, then, is that its Anglo-Irish holders cannot own it, since they illegitimately seized it from the Irish children to whom it was owed. Yet those Anglo-Irish holders cannot give up Ireland because they already owe the land to *their* children.[7] In *The Wild Irish Girl* (1806), the bestselling novel by Sydney Owenson (later Lady Morgan), the marriage plot provides an elegantly simple solution to this impasse, joining the competing claims of future generations into one family. The marriage of native Irish and Anglo-Irish causes both property and oppression, English rule and Irish disinheritance, to be passed down to the same family line. Desire and deservingness coincide, suturing over the paradox at the center of inheritance.

Edgeworth's Irish fiction, by contrast, confronts this contradiction and refuses to end with Irish and Anglo-Irish neatly united in possession. Robert Tracy notes that all of her Irish novels after *Castle Rackrent* (1800) hint at a crosscultural romance only to dissolve it and replace it with an intracultural union. He reads these "flirtations with the theme of intermarriage" as an awareness and deliberate rejection of Owenson's model of marital reconciliation as national reconciliation, a rejection motivated both by Edgeworth's disdain for what she called Owenson's "disgusting affectation and *impropriety*" and by her allegiance to rationality over romance ("Maria Edgeworth" 5). For Tracy, the possible intercultural unions in each of Edgeworth's Irish tales indicate her awareness that "for the Anglo-Irish to rule, it is not enough to have legal right or British protection." Tracy reads the disruption of those possible romances as Edgeworth's reluctance to legitimate Anglo-Irish ascendancy through the more imaginative channel of Irish tradition. While I agree with Tracy that this pattern in Edgeworth's plots comes close to an admission, in his words, "that legal title and fair dealing are not enough to justify an Anglo-Irish landlord's possession of his estate," I do not read the absence of claims for Anglo-Irish legitimacy in Edgeworth's novels as any scruple about endorsing Irish tradition and identity (22). Instead, I interpret Edgeworth's plots as expressing scruples about legitimacy.

In their wariness of legitimate ownership, Edgeworth's tales imply also a suspicion about any centralized authority that might claim the power to confer such legitimacy. In this she holds much in common with Burke, whose inclination is to see landed property as a phenomenon whose origins are obscured in preconscious times. And in this she works very much against Enlightenment belief in legislation as the way to encode and insure a respect for universal rights. But her Burkean view contains in it traces of the Enlightenment suspicion that any justification of property as naturalized by history is necessarily biased in its selection of a point at which origins become obscured. Blending these two viewpoints, her solution is to imagine origins as so thoroughly lost that no party might easily claim their property.

For Edgeworth, writing about Ireland requires writing about the profound uncertainty at the core of all property. Catherine Gallagher describes Edgeworth's novelistic debut in *Castle Rackrent* as setting up a "pattern . . . in which owning is constantly seen to rest on the action of disowning, and, conversely, the claiming of continuity is exposed as a fictional activity that results in dispossession" (*Nobody's* 296). My sense of Maria Edgeworth as an author of disownership is in large part indebted to Gallagher's argument that a propertyless mindset was crucial to Edgeworth's work, both in rationalizing her position as female writer deeply influenced by her father and in allowing her to articulate the position of the Anglo-Irish. In following Gallagher's path through the themes of disenfranchisement in Edgeworth's Irish novels, I wish however to emphasize the power of Edgeworth's disownership to bind irrevocably the Anglo-

Irish to the Ireland they could never legitimately claim title to, and hence could never give up. For Edgeworth, illegitimacy, rather than being a badge of shame that a Protestant inhabitant of the British Isles would be eager to pass over, offered possibilities as a figure for national unity.

The illegitimate ownership Edgeworth envisions to be the power that binds Irish and Anglo-Irish promises a fullness of possession. Within it are both the full right to enjoyment and the sacrifice that operates as the founding moment of a national unity that Edgeworth clearly wants Irish and Anglo-Irish to enjoy and, perhaps more vaguely, wishes to extend to British and Irish together. Her plots of illegitimate ownership attract critical attention for the way they elude easy identification with the interests of either colonizer or colonized. *Castle Rackrent* is particularly indeterminate, or, in the words of Declan Kiberd, as "ambivalent in form as it is undecidable in attitude" (248).[8] Such readings search for evidence that might amount to Edgeworth's claim for Anglo-Irish legitimacy and find its absence remarkable. That such legitimizing claims are considered the main proof of a colonizing point of view suggests an oversimplified approach. For Edgeworth, the lack of legitimizing claims serves the Anglo-Irish ascendancy more than would explicit claims of authority. Without legitimacy, Edgeworth demonstrates, the Anglo-Irish can become full members of the Irish nation through a common longing for ownership, remaining undivided by the actual ownership, which might create antagonistic interests. And if the Anglo-Irish might, why not the British as well?

Simple Susan's Sacrifice and the Security of Nonownership

Edgeworth began her career writing for children, that audience of the perfectly and blamelessly dispossessed. While she authored many children's tales in which the propertyless status of youth allows children a freer range of action than adults have, "Simple Susan"—the tale Scott recalled as her best writing—provides a full articulation of the advantages of dispossession. In "Simple Susan," as in the national tale, what is lost or about to be lost makes up the central interest of the plot. Like the national tale, the story relates a clash between custom and new commerce-driven habits played out over one particular piece of land: in this case, a small tract the villagers would like to keep common for their children's May Day celebrations but which the opportunistic Attorney Case would like to enclose for his garden. The dispute leads first to Case's abrupt recall of a loan to the heroine's father, Farmer Price, the loss of which requires his conscription into the militia. This emergency prompts the loyal Susan Price to offer her lamb for slaughter to Attorney Case in exchange for a delay of her father's departure. In this offer lies the paradox of "Simple Susan" and the paradox of all of Edgeworth's national tales—what is given up is never actually lost, often because it is never even owned. So that her father may stay an extra week with his family, Susan gives away her lamb, only to have it returned to her by the butcher, who concludes that he cannot accept it as meat because "It is a sin to kill a *pet lamb*" (emphasis in original, 117). Susan herself had entertained such scruples, worrying that a lamb that "feeds out of hand" and "follows me about" could not be a medium of exchange (104). The butcher confirms her suspicion and takes from his own stock to appease Case. Farmer Price gets his week's reprieve, and Susan pays nothing at all.

This moment of loss, which is not loss at all yet produces the same redeeming effect, provides the central motif for the story when a song by Llewellyn, a traveling harper, ends the Price family's woes. When the blind itinerant's "Susan's Lamentations for Her Lamb," inspired by Susan's grief, wins a prize, the harper sends his money to the Price family, freeing Farmer Price from his military obligation. Llewellyn claims, "I am in a great measure indebted to your sweet daughter Susan" for the honor he has won (133). Susan's lamentations (for a lamb she ultimately did not lose) are treated as the thing taken; the bard has carried them away and forged them into a song. These actions require him to use the language of compensation. He hopes to clear the "debt" he has incurred against her emotions, the loss of which she never registered.

Susan's fluency in fair and careful bargains—her refusal to pay an unfair ransom for her guinea hen, her public role in judging a bad shilling for the neighborhood children, and her carefully rewritten bills and receipts for bread-baking—structure the story around a logic of exchange that is nonetheless belied by a plot in which something so clearly comes from nothing. It is not that Susan is exempt from the general economy, a willingly passive receiver of gifts. Her last name, Price, links her filially to the rules of market exchange. And in that filial relation lies the sleight-of-hand that permits her losses that are not losses to yield gains that most definitely are gains. It is as daughter that she acts, so what she gains is clearly never hers. The money that seems most logically "hers," what she earns by baking bread and rolls for the local baronet's household, is never legally hers. Edgeworth makes this explicit in directly quoting the text of Susan's bill: "Sir Arthur Somers, to John Price, debtor" reveals all the money

Susan has made to be owed already to her father and thus never hers to give to him (105).

Susan's position in the story as a nonowner secures for her more property than mere ownership could. She is willing to give up her lamb for her father's sake, but it turns out that the lamb is not hers in a way that permits such a sacrifice. Likewise, even Susan's anguish over her pet's potential loss cannot be estranged from her. Llewellyn takes the incident as plot for his ballad but unambiguously refers to her by her real name, inspiring the local baronet's family to take a personal interest in her. Llewellyn's commitment to paying Susan back for the feelings he has "borrowed" from her is less about a nascent sense of intellectual property than it is about Edgeworth's notion of the profound security of a certain type of property that cannot be considered property at all.

A succinct articulation of this paradox comes in the tale's final confrontation over the land in dispute, when Attorney Case offers to give up his claim to the land. The baronet refuses this gesture, scoffing, "A man cannot give up that to which he has no legal title" (106). His point, that one cannot control the alienation of a thing if one is not the owner, is intended to deflate Case's pose of generosity and to disprove the attorney's claim to the land permanently. Yet the ambiguity of the baronet's statement serves just as well to insist on a nonowner's irrevocable attachment to the object of which she or he is not proprietor. The sentence that denies the nonowner's right to offer the land to another can, by extension, deny the nonowner's ability to abandon the land at all or refuse to enjoy its advantages. Cloaked in the very words that chase Farmer Price's tormentor off the land, and out of the village altogether, is the story's declaration of enforced enjoyment for the nonowner. Susan cannot lose her lamb because she has no legal title to it. Likewise, she cannot display her emotions without compensation because she can have no legal title to them either. Most importantly, the children cannot lose their May Day commons because they are its ultimate owners, as inheritors, and because they can never actually come into the ownership, as children.

The bardic figure of the blind harper signals possibilities for the intersection of national identity with this secure nonownership. The figure of the bard would have been familiar to Edgeworth's audience; a wanderer, his function is to sing songs and tell tales that are not of his own composition but have reference to the history and unity of the nation. He is authorized by property that cannot be owned but that is committed to memory and so can never be taken away.

Edgeworth's Irish fiction imagines this secure nonownership to be the catalyzing force behind the national unity that draws together Irish and Anglo-Irish. Her novels *Castle Rackrent* and *Ennui* (1809) feature plots in which peasants legally reclaim title to Irish land. Yet the novels never allow this fantasy to operate as a national consummation in which the nation is permanently, because materially, reclaimed by the Irish. Rather, each reclamation is incomplete, serving to acknowledge the illegitimacy of the Anglo-Irish ownership that inevitably reasserts itself. Each plot joins the disinheritance of the colonized Irish to an articulation of the illegitimacy of Anglo-Irish rule, blurring the differences between the two types of nonownership and making of them one category. Not only does Edgeworth co-opt a sense of colonized woundedness and apply it to the very people who already hold the land; she also makes holding the land itself a position that can only be permanent if it is entirely bereft of a centrally verifiable legitimacy.

The Randomness of Right: *Castle Rackrent* and the Logic of Union

Edgeworth's exploration of losses that remain losses, even after they are regained, resonates with her contemporaries' construction of Irish identity. At the time she wrote, several strains of Irish nationalism organized around the idea of what no longer belonged to the nation. Members of the Protestant Ascendancy, primarily of landlords who had been granted estates seized from Irish Catholics in the seventeenth century, fashioned themselves the true people of the Irish nation, united around what they saw as the loss of their own legitimate constitution at Union. Their mid-eighteenth-century agitation for a more powerful Dublin parliament had been framed not as a progressive reform but as the restoration of aristocratic prerogatives that had been taken away. The result of this agitation, the convening of a parliament in Dublin in 1782, forged the collective identity of the Anglo-Irish as a people vigilantly mindful of having once been robbed of power.[9] After Union's dissolution of the Dublin parliament, Anglo-Irish identity quickly coalesced again around this same sense of having been deprived of power so that, as Robert Tracy points out, Anglo-Irish writers considered themselves chroniclers of a decaying society (*Unappeasable* 17). At the same time, the rural Irish Catholic population, over whom the Anglo-Irish ruled, also derived a sense of identity from their long history of land and rights lost to the English invaders. To the United Irishmen, these were the "men of no property" whose collective resentment would give teeth to a nationalist uprising (Boyce 128).

The defining power of lost property and rights intensified with the 1798 United Irishmen uprising. The movement's wholesale adoption of a Republican agenda from the French Revolution entangled both Irish nationhood and the Anglo-Irish Union in questions about the stability and mutability of property. The United Irishmen's leaders hoped for a nonsectarian Ireland based on universal rights. They wanted to expand the category of those who mattered as members of the nation by changing the privileges and responsibilities attached to property. Because Union was a direct result of the unrest occasioned by such ideas, its proponents and opponents alike participated in a debate that connected stability of property with national governance. At the same time, both sought to preserve for the nation a power that transcended the matters of mere ownership to which the revolutionaries sought to reduce it.

Advocates of an Irish Union with Britain said government restructuring was the only way to guarantee the security of property. The paradoxical argument for Union was that the only way to protect property, defined primarily as Anglo-Irish estates and their attendant privileges, from both the Catholic Irish and the menace of revolutionary France was to remove its political control further away from Ireland altogether. In arguing for Union, Catholic pro-Unionist Theobald McKenna admits that the national pride prompting him to write in favor of parliamentary consolidation may appear contradictory, but "on political matters . . . you must often subtract when you would expect to add, and divide where you had hoped to multiply." Those against Union, he explains, would "reason forward in a direct line" equating parliamentary control with a national control of property (np). Yet pro-Unionists and their opponents alike were not shy about reasoning along that "direct line" of equation when confronting the question of compensation to borough members who would lose parliamentary seats, a traditional source of income, under the plan of Union. Historian G. G. Bolton argues that this response indicated a political climate in which national autonomy might very well be calculated in monetary figures without any sense of contradiction. Westminster's offer of 15,000 pounds in compensation to every parliamentary member who lost a borough in the merging of the parliaments, and the fact that not one eligible member failed to apply for such compensation, confirms that those in power agreed in viewing parliamentary Union as, in Bolton's words, "virtually the nationalization of a form of private property" (161).

Both sides, however, approached the issue of compensation in a way that belies Bolton's claim that the Union took place under conditions in which "the difference between a borough as property and a borough as the rights of the representation of the people" was not yet a difference at all (162).[10] The debate itself required that property and national affiliation be both identical and differentiated. Even when those engaged in the debate acknowledged the incommensurability of private compensation with the public rearrangement of government, they proved unable to disentangle their own arguments from that very equation. Delivering the second proposal of Union to the House of Commons, Robert Stewart admitted that the question of paying those who lose "influence" in the new configuration was "a subject of the greatest constitutional delicacy" (5). Yet he concluded that the solution involved a legitimate exchange: "If this be a measure of purchase, let us recollect that it will be the purchase of peace" (41).

Anti-Unionist discourse more explicitly cast the pro-Unionist sin as selling the nation and pocketing the cash. The speaker of the Irish House of Commons, John Foster, condemned the compensation plan as "a base and humiliating bribe" (50). Anti-Unionists warned that England would liquidate the Irish nation into cash to pay off English war debts while Westminster's control of taxation, public works, and trade law would always be tailored to enhance English commerce. Anti-Unionists tried to demonstrate both the illegitimacy of taking political control from the Irish and the disastrous economic consequences of Union, which often led them into contradictory claims about the nature of the nation itself. In castigating Unionists' disregard for the sanctity of the Protestant constitution of Ireland, Foster still relied on the very terms of exchange he claimed could not be applied to the question. He argued that "a full and entire" Union could not take place, parliamentary combinations notwithstanding, because there were simply too many conflicting financial interests standing as barriers. Such an argument assumes economic forms to be arbiters of national destiny. His conclusion with the Burkean assertion that "Our freedom is our inheritance and with it we cannot barter" is more prescriptive than descriptive of a legal or metaphysical impossibility. He had already imagined the possibility of that exact transaction, declaring that "if England could give us all her revenue, and·all her trade, I would not barter for them the free Constitution of my country" (49).

Both the pro-Unionist argument that Irish property would be more secure once guarded by a distant parliament and the pro-Dublin argument that such an arrangement could never be constitutional assumed that the party with legitimate rights to the nation was by definition always out of reach. Pro-Unionists argued that national government *should* rest with Westminster because, from a distance, Westminster could better filter out the "passions and caprices" that had endangered Ireland (McKenna 39). Anti-Unionists argued that the location of power was already removed; instead of being in the immediate hands of property owners, it rested in the hands of generations unborn, in whose trust the Dublin parliament held both property and power. Yet neither of these positions successfully imagined Ireland's governance as exceeding mere property. The borough compensations revealed the extent to which the idea that governance was a right and inheritance of future generations translated national control more firmly than ever into a form of property; money paid to excluded members was counted as part of the estate and paid out to its trustees for debts and marriage settlements attached to the estate, not to any particular individual. Within the inalienability of entailed real property was concealed the conversion of parliamentary seats into cash value. In order for either Union or an assertion of Irish national autonomy to work its affiliative magic, the exclusive nature of property—the belongings that might well disrupt belonging—needed to be submerged. Landed property, the emblem of both permanent ownership and familial belonging, provided such a camouflage.

Castle Rackrent, Edgeworth's Irish novel authored before Union, uses the camouflage of its eponymous landed estate to confound the identities of fictional characters, real author, and native Irish. The oft-repeated story of the tale's genesis is that Edgeworth was beguiled by the dialect of her father's steward and set out to write a story as he would tell it. The book's preface advances the notion that the serving man, John Langan, is the tale's true "author." The editor claims only to be transcribing the story of an illiterate servant, a tale whose authenticity is ensured by retelling it "in his own characteristic manner" (6). Edgeworth's advent as author, and the commentary she produces on the Union, are both marked by this public disowning of her own work: the Anglo-Irish daughter of the landlord insists that the work is not hers but the native voice of the Irishman who serves her. The rhetorical gesture is standard for eighteenth-century texts, in which novels are routinely presented as editorial discoveries, true tales of real people appropriated for their edifying possibilities. But in a book preoccupied with inadequate landlords and suffering tenants, Edgeworth's acknowledgment that what appears as hers is actually an Irish product seems an allegory of the relations between the landed class and the Irish peasants.[11]

Daniel Hack offers a more wary reading of what such empathy might accomplish, noting that the assumption of shared experience often masks a displacement and absorption of the very experience receiving compassionate consideration. The preface's smug anticipation of the time "[w]hen Ireland loses her identity by an union with Great Britain" bears out Hack's suspicion that Edgeworth's empathy launches a takeover of native Irish culture. Yet the preface also suggests that no identity can be securely stolen. While disowning Edgeworth's narration as simply Thady's "own characteristic manner," the editor also calls the reader's attention to the evanescence of all manners called one's "own": "There is a time when individuals can bear to be rallied for their past follies and absurdities, after they have acquired new habits and a new consciousness. Nations as well as individuals gradually lose attachment to their identity, and the present generation is amused rather than offended by the ridicule that is thrown upon their ancestors" (7). Both Edgeworth and Thady, Ireland and Great Britain are subject to the inevitability that, even in the most secure of property arrangements, what might be called one's "own" will wind up attached to a markedly different entity in the future, even if it is never explicitly alienated. The power of authorship ceded by Edgeworth emerges as a perpetual act of disowning anyway.

Castle Rackrent imagines a world in which the bond of ownership might be activated by even the most arbitrary of physical connections. Significantly, this theme arises during the tale of a parliamentary election, the most public of rites linking property to national participation. As Sir Condy attempts to win a place in the Dublin parliament, he gathers up tenants willing to present themselves at the polls as freeholders. When asked the qualifying question, "Had they ever been upon the ground where their freeholds lay?," the tenants all answer in good conscience that they have, since Condy has trucked in sod from his farm on which each man has briefly stepped. The tenants in question have adhered to a strict legal form of "having" property and, in doing so, have transformed themselves into the freeholders that they are not, a transformation that has repercussions for the entire nation. Lest the reader miss the national implications of this trick of literal attachment, the editor provides two footnotes, one assuring the reader that "This was actually done at an election in Ireland" and the other relating an anecdote in which the Duke of Sussex reveals his Irish title to Irish seminarians in Rome. The seminarians, dismayed to find that despite his title he has never "trod upon Irish soil," promptly arrange for Irish dirt to be spread upon a marble slab in Rome so he may stand on it and rectify his absence (34). In making the Burkean move of understanding national attachment as the stuff of literal and material property, the seminarians are able to commit a dizzying act of geographic rearrangement.

But such " 'cuteness,' " as the editor calls it, is not an exclusively Irish trait. In English Shropshire, where a woman must not appear outside the house after childbirth until she has been "churched," the editor notes, a woman is able to get around the constraints on her movement by taking a tile from the roof and wearing it over her head whenever she is inclined to go visiting. By this method she may "safely declare to the clergyman, that she 'has never been from under her own roof till she came to be churched' " (66). The anecdote includes all of the features made familiar by Burke's image of the unshakeable nation as an estate—the domestic affections that Burke claims tie subjects to nations, the properly virtuous women who both secure those affections and guarantee a legitimate line of national inheritance, and the physical stronghold of the house itself—in an anecdote that proves all of those objects to be highly mobile. In fact, the strictness with which the women interpret the bond that holds them under the roof yields them more mobility than would a broader interpretation. A literally physical attachment of woman to roof tile liberates her from the house that is supposed to confine her.

The trick that transforms domesticity into mobility makes Thady's subsequent semantic distinction about his association with the Rackrents an especially astute distortion of belonging. When asked by a stranger if he "belongs to" Sir Condy, Thady replies, "Not at all . . . but I have lived under him, and have done so these two hundred years and upwards, me and mine" (34). The anecdote of the Shropshire women's headgear has rendered the word "under" suspect. Sir Condy, whose tenure could not literally have lasted 200 years, is only the roof tile under which Thady is able to wander freely in his own conversation. It is no surprise that, after this declaration, Thady proceeds to spill Condy's financial secrets to the stranger, who will later use the knowledge to bankrupt the landlord.

But in light of the very English Shropshire anecdote, Thady's equivocation cannot be read as a specifically Irish instance of trickery. Rather, it comes from a too literal insistence on attaching person to property, an insistence that ultimately makes a person's identity more mobile than looser constructions would. Such a reading goes against the grain of criticism that, in outlining an Irish novelistic tradition, places *Castle Rackrent* as the founding text of a characteristically Irish incoherence.[12] Most critics focus on the surplus of character motivation within the book and the surplus of meaning in the book's layers of editorial apparatus as generic features made necessary by the chaos of Irish history.[13] Seamus Deane connects Edgeworth's formal choices to a profoundly disordered Irish social context. He reads her as failing to tame "the excessive, uncontrollable nature of a history that is not yet finished" in her "strange, fractured, and unstable narrative" that is "*the* symptomatic discrepancy of the Irish novel" (39–40, emphasis in original). Similarly, Eagleton reads the confusion of *Rackrent* as the inevitable loss of "formal equipoise" involved in an attempt to "mime a history of ceaseless upheaval" (183).[14]

But the claim that social and literary chaos is the unique preserve of the Irish ignores the *Rackrent* credo that all persons and nations are bound to lose their characters.[15] Gallagher observes in Richard and Maria Edgeworth's *Essay on Irish Bulls* (1802) a tendency similar to the effect worked by *Rackrent*'s attribution of proprietary wordplay to both Irish and English sources. In writing on comical Irish misuses of English, the Edgeworths trace out genealogies of verbal blunders, beginning with contemporary attribution to an Irish speaker and working back to the same joke's manifestation in folklore and literature from an array of countries and time periods. Their conclusion is that many examples of Irish word folly cannot be called anyone's "rightful property" (Gallagher 291–92). If the blunders are not properly Irish, Gallagher argues, they are not properly the Edgeworths' either. Only in the act of writing can the Edgeworths assert their difference from the propertyless Irish, by selling what they have established is neither their property nor Irish property.

Yet what works for the Edgeworths in a culture of commodifiable literacy plays out differently in the questionably literate society of *Rackrent*, where the absence of written titles becomes an engine for generating inalienable rights. After the death of Sir Murtagh, Thady notes the new establishment's neglect: "the tenants even were sent away without their whiskey" (11). The editor offers a gloss for the ostensibly transparent word "their": "Thady calls it *their* whiskey; not that the whiskey is actually the property of the tenants, but that it becomes their *right* after it has been often given to them." The editorial voice that in other places is quick to point out a "common prejudice in Ireland" or an Irish tendency to "metaphor and amplification," in this instance corroborates that the traditional expectation is actually their right (58, 62). As with the tricks of movable property, the editor acknowledges that "in this general mode of reasoning respecting *rights* the lower Irish are not singular," furnishing an example of an eastern despot with a reputation for transforming one-time gifts into expected annual tributes (58). This gloss prefigures the description of Lady Murtagh Rackrent's despotic exploitation concerning duty payments from tenants, so that no peasant approached the estate "without a present of something or other" (12). It is difficult to ignore the text's implication: the Anglo-Irish, too, are liable to claim something as their right after it has been often given to them.

Rackrent details with equal attention the potentially tyrannical and potentially liberating aspects to such a Burkean world in which rights might emerge from indistinct points in the past. Such customary duties tyrannize as mere written titles cannot. The *Rackrent* editor links the landlord's wife, tenants, and the footnote's "Sublime Ottoman" in the illegitimate creation of obligations from illegitimate causes. One-time events turn suddenly into traditional commitments that cannot be circumvented. If the Rackrent tenants' rights are violated when they are denied their traditional funeral whiskey, then Lady Murtagh's expectation of traditional "presents" is itself legitimate. But there is something potentially powerful for the powerless in this dynamic. If both landowners and land-letters can incur obligation because of single acts, then each moment contains within itself the possibility of creating new relations and debts between them. If the movable sod upon which a tenant stands becomes his property once, and allows him to wield the political power of the vote, then the conditions for that momentary ownership and suffrage to develop into a native right have already been met.

In contrast to this power of custom, the novel implies that writing offers no safe repository of title. The one truly literate character in the novel, Thady's son Jason, first attracts the attention of the future Lord Condy because of his "book-learning." The friendship continues when Condy makes Jason agent of the estate. Jason's abilities in writing and calculating—written forms of control— permit him to become Condy's primary creditor and then to take over the estate altogether. Yet the advantages of literacy prove a very tenuous hold over the land. The book ends with Jason and Condy's widow going to court over the title of the estate because the written transfer of title cannot be verified as legal. "Others say, Jason won't have the land at any rate," Thady concludes, and in a book where those with the least verifiable title have the most right, Edgeworthian law, at least, seems to favor the widow (54).

It is the widows, after all, who survive the disasters of Rackrent with worldly goods intact, despite the (ostensibly) written marriage settlements that assign those goods to their husbands. Lady Murtagh, after her husband's death, whisks away all "blankets and household linen, down to the very knife cloths" because, as Thady reports it, they were "all her own, lawfully paid for out of her own money" (15). Thady has already mentioned the various sources from which Lady Murtagh draws funds, so his description of the linens as "paid for out of her own money" contradicts his earlier explanation that she "got all her household linen out of the estate from first to last" without any expense. He notes that she obtained "duty yarn from the tenants," had it spun for free for her at the estate's charity schools, and then woven for free by estate weavers (12). This contradiction foregrounds Lady Murtagh's claims of ownership even as it casts doubt over it. The apposition of the two terms, one of ownership, one of acquisition—"all her own, lawfully paid for out of her own money"—suggests the two to be equivalent. If one term turns out to be untrue—"lawfully paid for out of her own money"—then both must be untrue. The narrator can name no means, other than purchase, that would accomplish ownership. Lady Murtagh's earlier attachment to the linens eludes definition, positioned as it is between traditional community tribute and illegitimate extortion. Torn out of the context in which they first came to her, the linens attach to Lady Murtagh in a way it is difficult for the narrator to specify. And yet they still do. Her exit from the story suggests that it is always better to have an unclear connection to the property one claims than to claim property on clearly defined grounds that can then be contested. The same point is implied in the case of the nameless Lady Rackrent, Sir Kit's Jewish heiress bride. Throughout her marriage, in which her husband terrorizes and imprisons her in an effort to obtain her jewels, this Lady Rackrent never loses her diamond cross, as if the absence of an intrinsic correspondence between Jewish owner and Christian symbol secures it to her all the more.

Ennui: The Landlord's Miseducation

While Edgeworth abandons the ironic excess of her first novel in her subsequent works, the morally didactic tone of her second Irish novel permits an even more explicit and thorough exposition of the skewed logic of inheritance. *Ennui*'s melodramatic switched-at-birth plot renders absurd the notion that genealogy intrinsically connects one to property. Yet its staid middle-class ending fails to narrate hard work as the proprietary glue that binds owner to estate. The story follows the Earl of Glenthorn, lord to both English and Irish estates, through his dissolute upbringing, profligate gambling, divorce, and the bankrupting of his English estate. After his return to the Irish estate he can barely remember, his Irish nurse reveals that he is her natural son, switched not long after birth with the heir, whom she raised as her own, and who is the current village blacksmith. Glenthorn immediately cedes his estate to the rightful heir—the blacksmith, Christy. Yet this restoration of title backfires. The former blacksmith's wife pours the fortune into jewelry and expensive hangers-on. The house itself burns down when the blacksmith's son, mistaking his chambers for his native mud hut, places a candle up against the wall. This tragedy causes the true lord and former blacksmith to renounce all claims to the estate. Conveniently, by this time the former Earl of Glenthorn has married the woman to whom the estate is next entailed.

The reversals and undoing of reversals in the story teasingly promise an allegory about who will inherit Ireland, only to make any clear line of inheritance incomprehensible. Christy, the blacksmith and rightful heir, has no sense of the estate as his own and can barely understand the revelation that he is the hereditary lord. While lord of the castle, he longs for useful work such as he did at the forge, but even his furtive attempts to fix a castle lock are foiled. Yet, much like Burke's dutiful guardians of property, he cannot refuse his inheritance because he feels he owes it to his son, Johnny. Perhaps in this predicament, Edgeworth acknowledges the hereditary rights of the native Irish and the barriers that a lack of education has placed between them and those rights. But the man whose lack of education has barred him from effective lordship is, by birth, Anglo-Irish, and not native Irish at all. And if the book contains within it an Edgeworthian faith in the role education might play in a nonviolent Irish emergence into power, then the education she bestows on her hero is a startling one. Glenthorn's reckless abandon as an English aristocrat almost kills him, while his ignorance as an Irish lord inspires a peasant uprising.

Critics argue that Glenthorn's stint in the middle-class world of professional education and honest effort displaces the aristocratic system of hereditary property with a more bourgeois model in which property is earned through labor. Marilyn Butler sums up the plot of *Ennui* as one in which Glenthorn "represents successively two different class styles, which are also two different social philosophies and systems. . . . Glenthorn acts for the Anglo-Irish ruling order, by abdicating his old role of feudal ruler . . . and by re-training as (eventually) a professional administrator" (Preface 33). Yet Butler's and others' arguments rely for evidence on the administrative policies of Richard Edgeworth, which Maria would have observed as her father's constant companion on his estate errands. Elizabeth Kowalski-Wallace traces the novel's observations on property administration to the pair's experience as landlord and sidekick: "As a landlord, Glenthorn learns precisely what Maria Edgeworth and her father learned"

(165).[16] Thomas Flanagan goes so far to assert that Glenthorn's encounters with Ireland are "not fiction at all, but an exposition of [Richard] Lovell Edgeworth's theories of politics, economics, social arrangements, education, and morality" (83).

This confusion of fictional and biographical detail results in a failure to distinguish Richard Edgeworth's labors from the labors of the Edgeworthian hero. In authoring the second volume of her father's *Memoirs* (1820) after his death, Edgeworth revisits many details of estate management that first appear in her Irish novels, especially *Ennui* and *The Absentee*. But in the *Memoirs*, these details form a narrative in which her father, an altruistically motivated landlord, returns to his Irish estate and, through careful study of current political economy, successfully dismantles feudal practices and traditional arrangements in favor of those promoting industry among the tenants.[17] However, no Edgeworth hero ever achieves the same kind of administrative wisdom that she attributes to her own father as landlord. Even though she exposes the spurious nature of any claim to right through inheritance, her fictional plots never quite cohere into stories where labor leads directly to legitimate ownership. Even in *Castle Rackrent*, Jason's rise to the estate as bourgeois agent guarantees no security of property, as seen in the unresolved claims to the estate at the novel's end.

In contrast to *Rackrent*, *Ennui* focuses on the more orthodox plot of education, a narrative closely associated with the spirit of the self-made middle-class man. But while Glenthorn undergoes both an education about Ireland and a reeducation of the heart, he never fully acquires a working knowledge of estate management. While at his Irish estate he becomes acquainted with local habits and problems, but he responds only with fitful charity, irregular attention, and political missteps. Making a random stab at addressing tenant poverty, he builds his faithful Irish nurse an English-style cottage, only to watch it disintegrate when its maintenance proves a mystery to her family. He tours Ireland, but, after visiting spots recommended by travel books, he acknowledges that he "had seen nothing of the country or of its inhabitants" (251). He conceives a great affection for his swaggering jokester of an Irish serving man, Joe Kelley, only to be framed by Kelley as the ringleader of a tenant rebellion.

Throughout Glenthorn's tenure as lord of his Irish estate, it is his agent M'Loed who provides administrative wisdom. In conversations with M'Loed, Glenthorn insists on patently uneconomic policies—such as giving marriage portions for all daughters on the estate and financial incentives to those with children—while the agent sternly advocates policies based explicitly in Adam

Smith's *Wealth of Nations* (1776) and implicitly on Thomas Malthus's theories of population. Thomas Flanagan misrecognizes this relationship as one of tutelage, explaining that only "after Glenthorn has thoroughly mastered the art of administering Irish affairs under M'Loed's guidance" does the lord find out that he has been switched at birth (84). Yet Flanagan's chronology is faulty. Glenthorn, while respecting M'Loed's wisdom, never acquires—or even tries to acquire—it for himself. In fact, it is only after his dispossession, at the estate of Lord Y——, a friend he has won through his renunciation of the estate, that Glenthorn comes to an understanding of the landlord's proper role in property management. Viewing "the neat cottages, the well-cultivated farms" of his friend's land, he is struck with "how little I had accomplished, and how ill I had done even that little, whilst the means of doing good to numbers had been in my power" (296).

This moment of revelation, coming as it does at a moment when Glenthorn has lost his estate, his name, and any purpose in life, suggests that what makes Glenthorn a fitting landlord by book's end is not his time working with M'Loed. Rather, dispossession, driven by his own recognition of the illegitimacy of his title, allows him in the end to reclaim it. Without the extremely public acknowledgment of his illegitimate position, Glenthorn would never have won either Lord Y——'s friendship or, through that friendship, the esteem of Glenthorn's future wife (and next heir to the estate), Cecelia De la Mere. While the trajectory of Glenthorn's fate leads him to undergo a period of hard work before his return to his estate, labor and study alone cannot win him his property. After all, the earnest work ethic of Christy, repeatedly described as industrious and able, fails to secure him the estate. Christy's claim as the natural heir is trumped by a superior claim based on illegitimacy. Glenthorn's overdetermined lack of title to the estate—his lack of inherited title due to his biological identity, his lack of economic title due to his failure to improve the estate, and his lack of moral title through his long history of dissolution—wins him the estate back from Christy, whose biological identity gives him only a legal title.

The ineffectiveness of hard work in this scenario is surprising, given Edgeworth's enthusiasm for the tenets of classical political economy and her commitment to evangelizing about them in almost of all her works. But her vision of attachments to property that are virtually self-generating, persistent even through shifting regimes of legitimacy and extreme revisions of identity in the owner and transformations in what is owned, is in some ways the logical condition of property under a laissez-faire economics. Political economy in Edgeworth's day dictated that no state apparatus should interfere in the workings of the market. Her vision of property that transcends interference, attaching where it is most expressly forbidden by recognizable authority is actually an extreme manifestation of laissez-faire policies. Truly free-market property is that which might seek protection from the state but whose freedom is only coherent if its definition, its constitution as property, is entirely outside of the state's hands. In this way free-market property looks a lot like a Burkean estate, both entirely constituted by an internal logic, both naturally resistant to legislative interference.

"Unlawful Possession Could Not Satisfy Me": The Feeling of Owning

The name of Edgeworth's novel refers to Glenthorn's apathetic experience of the ownership of his immense estates. *Ennui* offers itself as a paradoxical title concerning the psychological texture of owning. "Among the higher classes, whether in the wealthy or the fashionable world, who is unacquainted with *ennui?*" Glenthorn asks, connecting property ownership with apathy, boredom, and an "insatiable longing for something new." As he narrates it, actual ownership is a distorting phenomenon. He notes that as lord of his English estate, "my mind was distended by the sense of the magnitude of my possessions" (162). His narrative is full of fidgeting, yawning, and dull inclination toward sleep, all of which receive more textual attention than do explanations of his financial or social situation.

For Glenthorn, ownership disturbs consciousness, reducing the owner to restless somnambulance. Any emergence into actual awareness disperses ownerly control. He describes his youth as a series of receding promises that ownership could be fully experienced. Unfettered by disciplining parents or guardians, he boasts that he was "completely master of myself" while still a boy. This mastery, though, holds no enjoyment. He is briefly beguiled by the novelty involved in the "pleasure of property" when he comes into his estate but quickly sinks back into jadedness. "Every casual visitor, all the strangers, even the common people" who visit his grounds draw more enjoyment from the park than he does. In his retrospective overview he moralizes that "want of occupation, and antipathy to exertion, rendered me one of the most miserable men upon the earth," but it is the loss of control, not the active exertion of control, that always succeeds in rousing him out of his paralyzing apathy (163). His plans to end his boredom in suicide were first disrupted by "a *piggery* which I wanted to see finished," his faint spark of interest lighting on a project dependent on others for completion. He then delays his suicide until an Egyptian statue he has ordered arrives, a decision that suggests the time before delivery is more interesting than the statue itself. That the statue arrives with a thumb broken "by the awkwardness of the unpacker" is the twist of fate to which he attributes his survival until his twenty-fifth birthday: "I had now something to complain of, and I was happy" (170).

These small episodes of loss of control are almost the only moments of specificity in his early narration. Glenthorn skims over his education, travels, bankruptcy, and marriage with a preoccupied carelessness, lingering more on the details of his profound dissatisfaction than on any one event. The arrival of his Irish nurse, an occasion of profound loss of control, marks the first scene of specificity in the text, as if the novelty of loss has jarred Glenthorn into the proper realm of the novel. We first read dialogue from a named character when the nurse's warm greetings, and her embrace of Glenthorn's horse, cause him to be thrown. Now paralyzed physically instead of mentally, Glenthorn learns what he has already lost—the loyalty of his servants, who hope for his death, and the affections of his wife, who plans to marry his right-hand man regardless of whether Glenthorn lives or dies. Glenthorn finds such losses salutary, noting "the interest which I perceived others had in getting rid of me increased my desire to recover" (174).

Despite the invigorating effects of loss, it is yet another promise of palpable ownership that lures Glenthorn to Ireland. His nurse notes that while he was "only a lord" in England, he could be "as a king in Ireland," and Glenthorn admits himself seduced by "the idea of the sort of feudal power I should possess in my vast territory, over tenants who were almost vassals" (175). Yet Ireland cannot deliver on the promise of absolute ownership either. Glenthorn discovers that the reported vastness of his Irish estate is due not to size but to diminutive proportions in Ireland, where "one or two houses together" are considered towns. While Glenthorn's English estate eluded his grasp by failing to rouse his interest, the Irish estate holds his interest by more actively resisting ownership. He perceives M'Loed's impersonal efficiency in running the estate as undermining Glenthorn's title. Even the natural landscape defies proprietary authority. Glenthorn notes that on his first tour of his estate, "the rabbits, sitting quietly at the entrance of their holes, seemed to consider themselves as proprietors of the soil, and me and my horse as intruders" (196). To these encounters with resistant property are added his run-ins with mobs of alternately grateful and hostile tenants who disabuse him of any remaining illusions he has about his "nearly despotic power" in Ireland (247).

The revelation that Glenthorn has no title at all to the property that so actively resists his control comes as the culmination of these encounters. It also constitutes a moment of complete amnesia for Glenthorn, effectively erasing the first 30 years of a life wasted in fidgeting, yawning and nodding off. No longer does he remember himself as the anesthetized owner, so secured to property that its experience was unavailable to him. Instead, he decides that he must transfer the estate to Christy because "unlawful possession of the wealth I enjoyed could not . . . satisfy my own mind" self-righteously ignoring his own lifelong failure to enjoy the possession of wealth (272). Glenthorn's acute misery as property owner makes his eagerness to do right by Christy an act more ominous than generous. He reflects philosophically on the limited power material goods have for conferring happiness, and recognizes that Christy, "with his education and habits . . . must be happier working in his forge than he could be as lord of Glenthorn Castle." Yet he follows this observation up not with apprehension but with a declaration of self-satisfaction: "I was not dismayed by the idea of losing my wealth and rank; I was pleased with myself for my honest conduct, and conscious of a degree of pleasure from my own approbation, superior to what my riches had ever procured" (276). To gain such pleasure, Glenthorn robs Christy of the opportunity to procure satisfaction through self-denial.

Glenthorn's smug pleasure in his own virtue and the admiration that his new circle of friends express for his act contrast starkly with the results of that act: the extravagant foolishness of the new lady of the castle and the tragic death of the blacksmith's son. Glenthorn's account of his success at the study of law—underwritten by Christy's generous gift of the Castle's stock of law books—is interrupted by a letter describing the disarray of the castle under its new lord, and of Christy's increasing sense of powerless misery. As if to make amends for causing trouble, Glenthorn sends back advice based on his own experience as the unhappy, inadequately educated lord with a disloyal wife and a declining estate. These disasters—not Glenthorn's current experience working diligently and rationally at a profession—signal his ascendancy over Christy. The natural heir's claim to the land is trumped by a superior claim based not on education, not on hard work, but on acknowledged illegitimacy. Glenthorn's prior dissolution and lack of self-control are the authority on which he comes to claim the estate. While he technically returns to the estate as Cecelia De la Mere's husband, his public disavowal of his right to the estate is the act that first draws her to esteem him.

This conclusion partakes of the Rackrentian logic of bonds persisting long after the identity of that which is bound has completely changed. Glenthorn enthusiastically adopts his new wife's name, De la Mere. And, of course, the estate to which he returns is not the same property he had left, the house having burnt to the ground. Edgeworth's other Irish novels feature similar endings, returning characters, renamed and often repositioned in relation to their national affiliations, to Irish estates defaced or renovated. Owner and owned both evolve beyond any connection to their initial identity, even as they remain oddly bonded to each other. Kiberd calls Edgeworth's creation of this series of succeeding and not entirely classifiable identities a defensive ploy, "a mimicry of mimicry" in a country he sees as "an echo chamber of competing mimicries" (245). His verdict depends on Homi Bhabha's notion of mimicry, a form of colonial discourse whose ambivalence ultimately disrupts and destroys the "civil discourse" of colonization. But Kiberd's reading of *Rackrent* as ultimately subversive to the colonizer depends, like Bhabha's idea of mimicry, on a colonizing power that believes itself strictly faithful to the abstract principles of rationality.[18] In their characterization of colonial mimicry both Kiberd and Bhabha underestimate the persistent value to the nineteenth-century British imagination of the idea of English rights of prescription. The British valued their self-image as a political body ruled by a constitution evolved out of time immemorial, whose legitimacy could never be contested because it could never be located in any specific set of texts at any specific time. The British understood their constitution to signify a set of unwritten practices and procedures that had been fashioned from past precedents, whose repeated applications legitimated those precedents but also imperceptibly changed them over time. The heart of British legitimacy, much like Edgeworth's whimsical vision of Ireland, was itself an echo chamber created by inexact repetitions.

Edgeworth's plots of changing identities and properties enact a national affiliation that in Edmund Burke's words constitutes "the great mysterious incorporation of the human race . . . in a condition of unchangeable constancy, mov[ing] on through the varied tenor of perpetual decay, fall, renovation, and progression" (34). Edgeworth's failure to sue for Anglo-Irish legitimacy is neither a subversive act nor a symptom of an inevitably self-destructing colonial discourse. Rather, Edgeworth follows Burke and the debates on Union in conceiving of Ireland's and Britain's unity as more secure when its incorporation is, indeed, "the great *mysterious* incorporation" and its legitimacy cannot be articulated. The landlords of Edgeworth's novels gladly acknowledge the illegitimacy of their ownership, paradoxically secure in their ascendancy because they cannot renounce their own false claims.

Ormond and the End of Illegitimacy

In *Castle Rackrent* and *Ennui*, illegitimacy guarantees inalienable attachment to property. In Edgeworth's scheme, property whose title can be traced back to no root can never be given up, and thus is secure. The gradual accumulation of long history that erases the roots of the title is also what facilitates the slow but steady incorporation of disparate identities into one collective. In at least two of her Irish tales, Edgeworth fashions from Ireland property that is collective, inalienable, entirely free from the state, and yet not incompatible with a free-market economy, property that both Irish and Anglo-Irish can call theirs.[19] Yet as the state grew more interventionist in nature in Ireland, her vision of a united nation emerging out of irreducibly thick layers of history became less tenable. In this section I will trace how the development of the state in Ireland changed Edgeworth's strategy for imagining the nation's property.

Published in 1817, *Ormond* appeared five years after the end of the Napoleonic Wars, five years that saw an unprecedented degree of government intervention in Irish affairs. After the end of the war, agricultural prices in the United Kingdom had plummeted, hitting Ireland's primarily agricultural economy far harder than it had even Britain. The austerity measures undertaken by Irish landlords in response caused widespread agrarian unrest. As a result, Chief Irish Secretary Robert Peel (a future British prime minister) instituted a centrally controlled police force in Ireland that could be deployed nationally to wherever unrest was the greatest. The months of *Ormond*'s composition were also months of severe food shortage, which in some Irish counties reached famine conditions. This too was met with an unprecedented degree of centralized relief. Peel appointed commissioners to dispense funds across Ireland to build up national infrastructure—especially the construction of roadways and canals—which might allow those most affected to earn money for food.[20] The Ireland Edgeworth had known, one in which major landowners like her father had been solely responsible for law enforcement (her father had raised his own corps of yeoman for protection during the 1798 rebellion) and for doling out relief, was rapidly becoming a thing of the past. And the initial optimism about the improvement of Ireland that had accompanied the Union was rapidly fading.

Yet in the face of economic woes and social unrest, Edgeworth's novel hints that it will continue the elaboration of the attachments forged by dispossession. Its eponymous hero's resolution, "to shine forth as an Irish Tom Jones," in fact seems to promise it (62). While not strictly illegitimate, Ormond shares a similarly tenuous position as the orphan taken in by an avuncular figure. Also like Tom Jones—as well as *Rackrent*'s widows, Jason M'Quirk, and the confusingly identity-free Glenthorn—Ormond starts with a title to nothing and by the end of the book is the only heir apparent left standing. In fact, he does all the once-illegitimate owners one better by having his choice of two estates.

But unlike these owners, Ormond's status is never independent of the state. Where Ormond is concerned, the idea of a national character composed from a gradual familial blending of Irish and British identities featured in Edgeworth's earlier novels is canceled out by state connections. As an orphaned infant he is taken out of the hands of a poor Irish nurse by his patron, Sir Ulick, because he is "the son of an officer who had served in the same regiment with [Ulick] in his first campaign" (10). While his fortunes change, Ormond's essential identity as the orphaned son of a soldier never does. The state seems to serve as foster-parent when Ormond loses the protection of Ulick and is also unfriended by the death of Ulick's cousin, King Corny. Left without an anchor, Ormond is aided by Dr. Cambray, an Anglican minister appointed to his neighborhood by the government—a state intervention made much of in the novel when Ulick protests the appointment, angry that he was not allowed as a landlord to choose for himself.

This new attention to state intervention means that when Edgeworth's book weaves its playful paradoxes of how one comes by a title to anything, the picture is never one of property emerging out of long tradition but, instead, of property whose definition and allotment might always be in the hands of the state. An early conversation between Sir Ulick, the corrupt and jobbing member of the Irish Protestant parliament, and his cousin, King Corny, a self-styled Gaelic king of a feudally structured island, is equal to the most dizzying paradoxes of ownership ever spun by Edgeworth. King Corny, congratulating Sir Ulick on his recent acquisition of a baronetage, says, "I hope they did not make you pay, now, too much" for the honor. Ulick defensively responds to what he interprets as an implication that his title was got by illegitimate means: "These things are not always a matter of bargain and sale—mine was quite an unsolicited honour, a mark of approbation and acceptance of my poor services . . . believe me, it was not, if I may use so coarse an expression, *paid for.*" (49).

Corny responds to this explanation with a playful refusal to understand the category of civic honor, pretending only to understand acquisition as a matter of buying and selling. First he expresses shock to find the title has not been paid for: "What, then, it's owing?" Then he waxes indignant at the unfair exchange. Ulick has worked hard for no reward: "To be paid for still? Well, that's too hard, after all you've done for them." Finally, he questions that Ulick even completed the necessary paperwork for the title, saying, "At least, I hope you paid the fees." Ulick, rather than have Corny question that the process of conferring the title is over, admits to having paid the fees, allowing Corny to carry his implicit point: the title, since it is paid for, cannot legitimately be Ulick's. Of course, the method Corny has used to establish this leaves no room for Ulick to claim any sort of legitimacy. Corny's initial question, implying a doubt that money can legitimately secure a title, easily morphs into other questions that reveal not paying to be just as illegitimate as paying.

This play on titles departs from the paradoxes surrounding Lady Rackrent's linens and Glenthorn's estate, however, not just by flirting with the changing definitions of what makes property legitimately one's own but also by tangling with a form of property that can be invented out of thin air. Sir Ulick's title of baronet, as the lowest rung of the peerage, is synonymous with the British crown's fund-raising activities. After all, it is a property that can be multiplied at will by a cash-poor treasury. Ulick's title points toward the power of the state, not just to corruptly buy and sell what should be awarded only on merit, but to invent property altogether. Edgeworth's identification of Ulick with an entire repertoire of investments in canals, mines, and, finally and most prominently, banking points toward a similar power. Able to find investments for his money because of his connections in government, Ulick is in a position of using state power to create property—shares, notes—from which he might profit. This means he also has the power to destroy the same property, even when it is in others' hands. The book's climax, with the run on Ulick's bank, drives this point home, leaving Ulick's note-holders scrambling to redeem their notes for half to ten percent of their original value.

The figure of King Corny would seem to be Edgeworth's antidote to the arbitrary creation and destruction of state-manufactured property embodied in Ulick's jobbing and corruption. Corny lives on the far periphery of any na-

tional network of state property, the feudal sovereign of a string of islands off
the coast of Ireland. Edgeworth describes the Black Islands as operating independently—in both culture and politics—from Ireland, much in the manner of
the Aran Islands in the far west of Ireland. With his own prime minister and
his own ragged court, Corny acknowledges no political connection to Ireland.
" 'Tis generally considered as a punishment in the Black Islands to be banished
to Ireland," he tells Ormond (42). He also acknowledges no economic connection to Ireland—or to anyone. Acting as his own architect, doctor, and lawyer,
he has also "with his own hands made a violin and a rat-trap; and had made the
best coat, and the best pair of shoes, and the best pair of boots, and the best
hat; and had knit the best pair of stockings and had made the best dunghill in
his dominions; and had made a quarter of a yard of fine lace, and had painted a
panorama" (43–44). In Corny's self-enclosed world, the manufacturing of property is always a material process, one free even of the division of labor.

Edgeworth ends her novel with Ormond able to choose between Sir Ulick's
and Sir Corny's land as his own permanent estate. His choice of Corny's lands—
an estate coextensive with what seems to be the sovereign domain of the Black
Islands—signals Edgeworth's departure from the comedy of illegitimate ownership. Rather than basking in the contradictions of Ulick's ill-gotten baronetage, Ormond is made rightful owner of Corny's estate four times over. He is
made lord by inheritance at the outset of the novel, during the public ceremonies in which King Corny declares him Prince Harry, heir to the throne. He
then becomes owner by purchase, when he uses his fortune to buy the islands
from Black Connal, the legal heir. The islands are secured to him by consent
of the inhabitants, who "actually offered up prayers for his coming again to reign
over them again" (297). Finally, the narrator implies that Ormond's choice of
the Black Islands is no more than a reclaiming of what has become internal to
him by virtue of his education: "To those who think that the mind is a kingdom
of yet more consequence than even that of the Black Islands, it may be agreeable
to hear, that Ormond continued to enjoy the empire which he had gained over
himself" (400). In learning to be a gentleman, Ormond has also internalized the
role of the owner.

This new adherence to a surplus of legitimacy comes with what seems to be
a new isolationism. That this chosen estate is King Corny's Black Islands, on
the very edge of the Irish world, and that King Corny is the father figure after
whom Ormond assumes dominion both would seem to prefigure Edgeworth's
late-life conservatism, which Thomas Flanagan categorizes as a choice, after

her father's death, to "cultivate snug cottages" away from "the warring Ireland of the Agitation and the Tithe War" (102).[21] Ormond's choice of the Black Islands because "he should hurt no one's feelings by this purchase—and he might do a great deal of good, by carrying on his old friend's improvements, and by farther civilizing the people of the Islands, all of whom were warmly attached to him" (297) definitely seems a shrinking from anything that might disrupt tradition or inspire rebellion. But the shrinking might have just as much to do with Edgeworth's ambivalence about an increasingly centralized post-Union government as it does with her later contempt for the violence of peasant insurgency.[22]

Her turn to a surplus of legitimate channels by which Ormond's title to the Black Islands is secured to him is a symptom of this ambivalence. Rather than entirely acknowledging and endorsing one source of legitimacy for property—an acknowledgement that might bring with it Ulick's corrupt powers of defining property—Edgeworth overloads the property with a surplus of legitimation. Ormond's final estate is not simply granted to him by the legalities of inheritance or the economics of purchase but by both those things and more. This surplus of legitimation operates similar to the complete delegitimation of property. In both cases, no single channel exists through which ties to the property can be cut. At the end of the novel, Edgeworth's hero would need to go bankrupt, alienate the affection of his tenants, somehow lose his personal education and moral development, and discover a competing heir in order to completely lose his property. Edgeworth's answer to the state's new role as centralized authority is not to directly refute it but to simply narrate it as just one among many other competing sources of authority.

This means that the novel is not so much a retreat from the idea of state power as the hypercontextualization of that power to the point where defining it as central makes no sense. Unlike Glenthorn, whose two poles of development were England and Ireland, Ormond's development unfolds around multiple sites. He experiences life on the completely self-authorized and self-contained estate of King Corny and also at Sir Ulick's estate, the Hermitage, a property entirely too enmeshed in the fluctuating values of a wider economy and the changing rules of property dictated by the state. He finishes his education in prerevolutionary Paris, where a decadent, too-absolutist distribution of property teeters on the brink of being entirely—and violently—redefined by the new national assembly, which Burke described as dictating that "possession is nothing; law and usage are nothing" and which installed "a currency of their own fiction in the place of that which is real" (153).

Were the novel limited only to Corny's Black Islands and Ulick's Hermitage, Ormond's education would be a rather straightforward survey of the advantages and disadvantages of, on the one hand, a government that is the product of tradition (the Black Islands) and, on the other hand, government by legislation (the Hermitage). However, Edgeworth's addition of France to the mix implies that each new system of government unsettles the centrality of ones previously introduced. Every new political culture Ormond encounters in his progress reframes the central authority of the culture he has already experienced. Edgeworth's conceit of the Black Islands as run with all the pomp and trappings of its own kingdom skews any clear understanding of Ireland's place in the international European scene. As the Gaelic periphery to Ulick's Anglo-Irish world, the Black Islands maintain a relationship with mainland Ireland that is analogous to Ireland's own relationship to Britain. Yet this analogy is disturbed by another analogy. King Corny calls Ulick's political concerns "[c]ontinental policies" and mentions that his daughter is away taking lessons in dancing and deportment, "gone off to the continent, to the continent of Ireland, that is" (48, 42). Corny's vision of the Black Islands' relationship to Ireland reflects Britain's peripheral position in relation to Europe. By invoking his kingdom's hyperperipheral status, he stresses not just Ireland's marginalized position in the British Isles but also Britain's own status as the parochial, unpolished country on the periphery of a cosmopolitan, French-dominated continent. The Black Islands stand for a chain of periphery-to-metropolitan relationships in which every metropole is peripheral to some other larger metropole.

The Black Islands also suggest the possibility of collapsing that hierarchy, at least where the metropole of England and the periphery of Ireland are concerned. In insisting that his kingdom is no part of a modern Protestant Ireland, King Corny has his daughter Dora educated in France, under the tutelage of a half-French aunt. Dora eventually marries another "Frenchified" Black Islander, Black Connal. Their subsequent emigration to Paris affords them a unique vantage in which England lies at the unmappable edge of the world. They introduce Ormond to French culture and scoff at "the Vandals they send us from England . . . barbarians who can neither sit, stand, nor speak" (250). At the same time, they acknowledge or ignore differences between English and Irish culture as it suits them, implying that there is no substantial difference between the two. Referring fondly to their shared childhood on the Black Islands, Dora calls Ormond "mon bel Irlandoise" while her husband introduces Ormond into French society as "le bel Angloise" (254). This disregard for difference within the British Isles turns back onto a British audience their own disregard of Irish heterogeneity. Edgeworth implies that a Briton who cannot distinguish between the tribal custom of the Black Islands and the cosmopolitan hub of Sir Ulick's hermitage will be subject to the same ignorance from a European perspective that lumps him with the Irish.

Edgeworth carries out her strategy of overloading the plot with competing sources of collective authority both geographically, toying with center and periphery in her play with the Black Islands, Ireland, and France, and chronologically. Her decision to set the story in the heyday of Grattan's parliament, well before Union, makes even the state Sir Ulick stands for uncertain. On the one hand, the setting of the novel positions the Protestant Irish parliament as the corrupt and incompetent central source of power. On the other hand, the political situation contemporary to Edgeworth's composition of the novel would imply that Ulick stands for an overreaching but ineffective Westminster parliament. Ulick, with his constant diversion of public funds into his own private enterprise, his canals and silver mines and banks gained through his special government connections, simultaneously stands for the corruption under which Ireland suffered until Westminster intervened with Union *and* for the meddling potential of a too-interventionist post-Union parliament.

In this world, the estate ordered by the Anglo-Irish landlord is vulnerable to outside interference. Trouble comes not only from above, from a top-down style of state governance, and below, from informal economies and governments adhered to *sub rosa* by the peasants, but also from right next door. In *Ormond* the individual estate has no autonomous status. It always suffers the effects of what is immediately beyond its boundaries. In contrast to the agricultural activities of Edgeworth's earlier landlords, Herbert Annaly, the pattern landlord on whom Ormond seeks to model himself, spends most of his time dealing with tenants who are "idle fishermen . . . , illicit distillers—smugglers—and miscreants who lived by waifs and strays; in fact by the pillage of vessels on the coast" (203). Rather than existing safely within the domain of one property, these tenants exist at its edges—on the coastline and in the sea, where they treat all property as up for grabs. Like Irish landlords during the 1816–17 food crisis, Herbert tries to remedy the situation by looking to the state for funds that would employ his tenants in building a lighthouse. But state intervention has only limited power in the intertwined economy of this novel. Herbert's reforms are "impeded by the effects of the bad example of his neighbours on Sir Ulick's estate," who offer leases to the worst offenders on the Annaly estate and thus keep them close by

(203). The power of the landlord is equally limited. In the end, Herbert dies from exertion while returning stolen and shipwrecked property to its rightful owners.

Only Ormond, occupying the far periphery of the web of competing power relations can be sure of always having the same position, no matter how often structures of authority are swallowed up by other structures of authority. When the center does not hold, very little changes in the Black Islands, which has always defined itself as the opposite of the center. With only one significant revision, Ormond's story bears out Burke's point in his *Reflections:* the stability of the nation is the stability of property, and both work in harmony to create a fixed order of people and things. Yet *Ormond*'s revision of Burke's message is unsettling: the colony, not the nation, becomes the only site—and form—of utterly secure property. The Black Islands form the only endpoint in the web of centers and peripheries. At the edge of an Ireland perceived as peripheral to Britain, which itself is perceived as peripheral to Europe, the Black Islands offer the most stability of title because they are at the furthest remove of the chain.

The contrast between Edgeworth's earlier Irish tales and her last one yields a surprising equation. When Edgeworth felt more assured in envisioning Ireland as a society woven from the fabric of independent landed estates, ones whose rights and responsibilities arose from their own particular histories and cultural contexts, she was also offering a model in which the Anglicization of Ireland was inevitable and the Irish were sure to "gradually lose attachment to their own identity" (*Rackrent* 7). However, as the apparatus of the British state developed in Ireland, with all of its policing and pedagogical force, Edgeworth became more invested in the importance of an Irish culture whose uniqueness existed beyond the reaches of any particular state. For Edgeworth, a colonizing attitude, which she did express, was hardly coextensive with a controlling state structure. Instead, it depended on the decentered, autonomous, but culturally embedded powers of the landlord of a large estate. By the time she writes *Ormond*, Edgeworth is as invested in the cultural specificity of property as Irish nationalists will become over the course of the nineteenth century. And just as they will, she sees Irish property as a site from which one might challenge the power of the British state.

In my next chapter I examine John Stuart Mill's writings on Ireland, writings that constitute almost the polar opposite of Edgeworth's dislike for state interference. Mill championed an interventionist state, vigorously advocating for the state-sponsored creation of peasant proprietorships—small plots of land farmed by their owners, rather than by leaseholders or by hired labor. But Mill's vision of the state whose power extends to the creation of smallholders contains a notion similar to Edgeworth's Black Islands: both the islands and the peasant proprietor's plot are spaces independent of state interference with their own highly specific cultures. The difference between the two is that while Edgeworth has to contextualize the Black Islands within multiple state systems in order to imagine them as free of the intervention of any one state, Mill imagines that the British state itself has the power to create such autonomous spaces, paradoxically drawing owners into a closer relationship with the state by creating a zone in which it was to leave them entirely alone.

CHAPTER TWO

The Forbearance of the State
John Stuart Mill and the Promise of Irish Property

Outside of a shared interest in thinking about property relations in Ireland, John Stuart Mill bears at least one other resemblance to Maria Edgeworth. Like Edgeworth he voiced doubts about the extent to which he might be seen as having produced his own writing. In his *Autobiography* (1873), Mill emphasizes the exceptional nature of his intellectual development, which leaves him unsure of the degree to which he really might take credit for subsequent accomplishments. His father started teaching him Greek at age three, moved his son through the classics normally reserved for an Oxbridge education by his fourteenth birthday, and added to that a rigorous training in classical logic and classical economics. The result left Mill with the feeling that his own education, as his father had told him, could not be ascribed to any effort on his own part but rather to "the very unusual advantage which had fallen to my lot" (22). Mill expressed similar reservations about the extent to which he might take credit for his accomplishments after he met Harriet Taylor, the woman who was to become his wife. He wrote that, given the extent to which the couple held "their thoughts and speculations completely in common," it would be fruitless to claim anything but that "all my published writings were as much her work as mine" (145).

Despite his unwillingness to claim the entire property of his own work, Mill also stands accused, like Edgeworth, of representing an imperialist sense of entitlement.[1] A champion of individual liberty for British subjects, Mill attracts this criticism because of his belief that cultural limits should be placed on such liberty. Arguing for the value of individual development, he famously cautioned that "we may leave out of consideration those backward states of society in which the race itself may be considered in its nonage." He implies that in cases such as these, entire races might be considered mere children, and despotism would be justified on the same grounds that justify parental authority (*On Liberty* 14). Like Edgeworth, Mill defended colonizing projects in the name of improvement. He argued that outsiders might have the authority to interfere with indigenous populations so long as their intention was to leave the populations better off than before.

Despite their common faith in the improving endeavors of a civilized people, there remains an enormous difference in social position between the two writers. Edgeworth aligned herself with the long tradition of British landholding as stewardship. In her novels she depended on the length of the tradition to depict landlord and tenants as hopelessly enmeshed in a history of ownership and dispossession. Mill, however, made his name jousting at the traditional ascendancy of landed property. The two writers differed entirely as to how property even originates. Edgeworth's Burkean conception of landownership assumes that land handed down over countless generations is a transmission that ensures the safe transmission of national heritage itself. Even at its most ironic, Edgeworth's vision of the landlord still holds the landed estates as a basic building block of the nation, and thus a social arrangement that precedes the establishment of any state.

Mill disdained this vision of a national character preserved in the vast estates of the aristocracy, a class whose outdated political and economic privileges he felt blocked England's much-needed legal and social reform. However, in his 1840 essays on Jeremy Bentham and Samuel Taylor Coleridge, Mill is careful not to dismiss as useless the national heritage which such traditional property was supposed to preserve. Bentham's shortcoming, Mill notes, lay in his failure to understand the importance of national character. In seeking to dismantle outdated traditions, Mill suggests, Bentham underestimated the irreducible specificity of the group of people who had held them. Mill praises Coleridge's grasp on the importance of national character but suggests that Coleridge's sense that landed property serves as vessel to this national disposition necessarily compromises the idea that an owner of land can be considered autonomous. If national heritage is guarded by the landed estate as Coleridge says it is, Mill argues, then the state always has cause to interfere in landed property. From Coleridge's writing he draws the conclusion that if the state fails to ensure that the cultivation and distribution of land promotes the happiness of the greatest number, then "the State fails in one of its highest obligations" (158).

Mill's perverse reading of Coleridge emerges out of his own utilitarian education which implanted in him a strong doubt that property could be considered to exist prior to the formation of government. Bentham, after all, had famously rejected the idea that property existed outside of political systems. "Property and law are born together, and die together," Bentham maintained. "Before laws there were no property; take away laws, and property ceases" (*Theory of Legislation* 138). It is because Mill subscribed to a utilitarian notion that political systems legislated the rights of property rather than property legitimating political systems that he was such an outspoken critic of the British government's dominance by landowners. An animus against a government run by those with landed property glimmers through all of his writing, where he routinely portrays aristocratic owners of land as unmotivated to improve their properties and hostile to commercial and political innovations. *On Liberty* (1859) and *Considerations on Representative Government* (1861) both advocate for a government built on the basis of individual merit. A government should be designed, Mill argues, to train its citizenry in thinking of the common good and thus should be composed of those whose "individual intellect and virtue" has already allowed them to achieve such habits of thought (*Considerations* 228). For Mill, a person's political qualifications were always grounded not in property but in personal qualities—forethought, industry, rationality, and an ability to keep in mind the varied and often competing interests of a wider public. Mill celebrates local government, service on juries, debating societies, and workers' cooperatives for their potential to develop an individual's civic capacities, independently of that person's prior possession of property. The shape of a government, he argues, should always be oriented toward developing such capacities.

The keynote in Mill's theories of political personhood is experience. A person can have no capacity for reason if he or she (and Mill stands out in Victorian England for his consideration that such a person might be female) is not placed in an environment where experiences are available that might develop such a capacity. Educational processes, not status, structure Mill's ideal society. Yet, as this chapter argues, Mill's emphasis leads him right back to the property whose current arrangement he so disdains. In his long-term commitment to land reform and his celebration of peasant proprietorship—an arrangement in which small plots of land are farmed by owners, who draw the bulk of their subsistence from their modest properties—Mill repeatedly implies that owning property in land is one of the most complete experiences through which one might develop an appropriately rational and individual personality.

While Mill imagines a range of environments into which one might be put in order to be educated, the experience of owning property in land stands out as the one model Mill fully articulates across a range of his writing. From his writings on Ireland in the late 1840s, which assert property to be the key motivating factor in developing an owner's forethought, self-control, and even affections, to his 1873 articles for the Land Tenure Reform Association that again celebrate small landholders as unparalleled for their "ungrudging and assiduous application of their own labour and care, and . . . attention to small gains and petty savings," Mill's conviction held steady that small agricultural holdings reliably developed their owners' capabilities ("The Right of Property in Land" 1242). But this valorization of the smallholder does not precisely accord with a narrative of possessive individualism. Instead, Mill's vision of the self developed by proprietary experience tends to unsettle both the dynamics traditionally associated with property and the dynamics traditionally associated with the self.

In his writing on peasant proprietorship, Mill imagines property in terms not entirely dissimilar from aristocratic terms. Like the aristocratic narrative of land as a property over which one's control is limited because it was inherited from forefathers with certain expectations and because it is already entailed to descendants to whom one owes a certain stability, Mill tends to see property in land as always owed to future generations. Far from imagining property as that over which one has complete control, Mill sees land as enmeshing an owner in generational commitments. But Mill adds to that an awareness of land's biological animation. In the place of an aristocratic discourse in which one draws political power from the land, Mill constructs a narrative of property as animated by its agricultural specificity, with soil, topography, and climate dictating the owner's behavior rather than the owner imposing his will upon the land. In Mill's writing, the net effect is one in which property might exert more control over the owner than the owner exerts over it.

This chapter offers an extended analysis of how Mill in his writings on Ireland in the 1840s advocates for this form of property—not entirely fungible, not entirely individual, not even entirely under the control of its proprietor. It then demonstrates that these same proprietary dynamics structure the description of the properly cultivated individual Mill esteems in his later political writings. Mill also draws on the model of the proprietor of a small plot of land to imagine a relationship between the state and its citizens that might be properly mediated by a space neither entirely enmeshed within the state nor entirely free from reference to it. In this version of property ownership, despite Mill's routine insistence that property only comes into being through the power of the state, it is the material of land itself that provides the beneficial experience of property. This means that, in Mill's writing, property in land retains some of the aura of complete autonomy with which the British political tradition endows it. But like so many of the writers in this book, he finds this autonomy not in British land but in the Irish proprietary landscape. In the final pages of this chapter I briefly consider how Mill's understanding of land ownership's relationship to the state changed when historicist ideas came into vogue that saw property arrangements as always culturally determined.

Reworking Locke

In both *On Liberty* and *Considerations on Representative Government*, John Stuart Mill explicitly argues that an older model of political consequence founded in ownership of property needed to be replaced by a more modern model of political consequence grounded in reflective and educated individuality. Mill fleshes out the modern conditions that call for this newer model in the opening paragraphs of *On Liberty*. The age in which propertied individuals were forced to use their domains as protection from an absolutist state is over, Mill asserts. It used to be that liberty meant "protection against the tyranny of the political rulers" (5). But with the rise of "elective and temporary rulers," the rulers became identified with the people. "Their power was but the nation's own power, concentrated," Mill argues. "The nation did not need to be protected against its own will" (7). Obliquely referencing Tocqueville's description of a "tyranny of the majority" in the young United States, Mill contends that the global spread of democracy has made it clear that even elective governments might be monopolized by a group smaller than the whole nation. After all, he notes, "The will of the people . . . means the will of the most numerous or the most active *part* of the people." Such a situation might call for the restraint of government, since the government in this situation would be only the expression of a certain segment of society, not its entirety. Mill's assumption is that a zone of personal property has little relevance to such restraint. And his interest lies more fundamentally with the modern condition in which "society is itself the tyrant" (8). This is the situation he sees as especially pertinent to England, where he claims that "the yoke of opinion is perhaps heavier, and that of law lighter than in most other countries of Europe" (12).

In formulating his thesis for the liberty of the individual under such circumstances, Mill imports into individual bodies the credo of property's absolute nature. Selves, rather than property lines, mark out the conceptual space he describes as "the part which merely concerns himself [ie, the individual]." Within that part, the rules of absolute property still apply: "Over himself, over his own body and mind, the individual is sovereign" (14). In attributing spatial qualities to this "region" of human liberty, Mill changes little from the theorems about the limits of government that he had formulated in *Principles of Political Economy* (1848): "Under whatever political institution we live, there is a circle around every individual human being which no government, be it that of one, of a few, or of the many, ought to be permitted to overstep" (*On Liberty* 16; *Principles* 5.11.4).

The "reserved territory" and "domain of inward consciousness" that Mill discusses in *Principles* emerge in *On Liberty* as the internal holding tank for individual opinion, which, according to Mill, should supersede property in political consequence. Yet in positing this supercession of property by the domain of individual opinion, Mill is haunted by the possibility that his readers will merely equate opinion and property. He reminds his readers that an opinion merits expression not because it is the property of the person who expresses it but because it is so much more than "a personal possession of no value" (21). For Mill, while a personal possession exists with no reference to the larger community, opinion is of intrinsic value to the social whole. But in his emphasis on the exclusivity and unassailability of individual opinion, it is hard for Mill to escape the language of property in describing this inner domain. In explaining that religious views cannot be adequate justification for silencing dissenting opinions, Mill reverts back to proprietary analogies: "There is no parity between the feeling of a person for his own opinion and the feeling of another who is offended at his holding it; no more than between the desire of a thief to take a purse and the desire of the right owner to keep it" (93).

It is this recourse back to property in order to describe what constitutes the true condition of individual liberty that leads Elaine Hadley to position Mill at

the forefront of a general liberal tendency to think about character as possession, and thus to use the category of character to reproduce the very hierarchy
that liberalism would seem to challenge. In Mill, in Samuel Smiles's best-selling
Self-Help (1859), and elsewhere in liberal discourse, she finds that "character is
asserted to be, in what seems a willed blindness of the greatest magnitude, prior
to and independent of property, even if the language one uses and the logic one
employs suggest otherwise" ("The Past" 10).[2] For Hadley, this tendency serves
the bad-faith purpose of making liberal citizenship seem a condition attainable
regardless of class or even race or gender, while still tending to couple traits
that are male, white, Protestant, and middle class with the qualifying definition
of character. It also drains property's alienating threats from liberal citizenship
by declining to name what operates as mental property—professional skills,
knowledge, reflective capacities—as subject to sale in the free market.

Hadley is in good company in her suspicion that a liberal rhetoric claiming
to shake off a hierarchy of wealth might actually be reproducing that hierarchy
all the same. C. B. Macpherson's thesis of self-possessed individualism argues
that such a contradiction persists through a line of liberal philosophers following
Hobbes and Locke. Nonetheless, as Lauren Goodlad points out, Hadley's use
of Mill as a leading example risks flattening out some of the complexity Mill
brings to his particular version of liberal selfhood. For Mill, Goodlad argues,
the self at liberty might very well be experienced as property but also could be
experienced as "practice or exercise, to be cultivated within a particular spatial
imagining of modern society" ("Character Worth Speaking Of" 11). In this
critique, Goodlad's specific concern is that Mill's attempt to think of selfhood
as always cultivated in reference to a wider social life is not entirely accounted
for by the model of the self-possessed individual, who, especially in Macpherson's formulation, is considered to owe nothing to society for his own capacities
and thus is seen as bearing no natural connections to a broader society. Goodlad's attempt to articulate more precisely the dynamics surrounding Mill's version of the self involves an appeal to spatialization as a model supplementary to
property. "On the one hand, individuals required spaces of development in
which to exercise their faculties untrammeled by conformist pressures," Goodlad
comments, echoing both Mill's explicit beliefs and the traditional republican
view of how private property fosters selfhood. But she sees something more in
Mill, where "since development was a deeply social and often public endeavor,
such spaces had to be porous, embedded, and dialogical" (23).

What Goodlad sets up as opposed—cultivated selfhood as a form of property versus cultivation as a "practice or exercise" within a developmental space that is "porous, embedded and dialogical"—is an opposition Mill repeatedly collapses when he writes on the experience of property for the peasant proprietor. Property for the peasant proprietor is, Mill asserts, first of all a genuinely possessive experience; it simply is not the sort of possessing that involves the owner's total control. Secondly, Mill sees the experience of owning for the peasant proprietor as the habitation of a highly particular space of development that opens out into a wider social world. This connective potential is especially important since Mill develops most of his thinking on peasant property in a larger argument about how the British state can securely attach Ireland to itself. It is this model of property that shapes the conceptual space he envisions as fostering both individual development and community connection in *On Liberty*.

This connection becomes apparent when we consider Mill's strong, if intermittent, interest in the economics of Ireland as a major part of his intellectual development.[3] In the rhetoric Mill employs in his writings on Ireland concerning the individuality of the peasant proprietor, the setting of the small agricultural property allows Mill to develop the idea of an energetic and civically engaged individual more completely than he is able to do in equivalent writing on workers' cooperative companies or on local government—the two non-land-based options he presents as available to the British for cultivating their selves and expanding their sense of identification with a broader public. For Mill, property in land allows the development of forethought, industry, prudence, and individuality while encouraging civic-mindedness. This is because he sees the exceptional status of property in the land automatically enmeshing every landowner—and even potential landowners—into a relationship with the state whose task it is to act as trustee, and possibly as landlord, for the soil, that one form of property that Mill insists can never be absolute and must always be considered "the inheritance of the human race" (*Principles* 5.1.5).

For Mill, the landowner's relation to the state is always one of enjoying the state's forbearance. In both his economic writing and his writing on Ireland, Mill argues that the state has the right to reassign property rights in land, should expedience call for such reassignment. In Mill's writing, the legitimate state might at any moment invade landed property. It allows owners of land to exist only by its own restraint. In outlining this dynamic, he imagines the relationship between the state and the citizen that is neither coercive nor paternalist in a classical sense. Instead, a citizen's relationship to the state might be catalyzed by a state's refusing to exercise some of the power it legitimately has. In this, Mill's conception of state power accords well with the Foucauldian model of a modern governmentality, in which to govern at all means to identify those sites from which governing must be restrained.[4] At the same time, because Mill conceives of land as a space whose biological and organic irreducibility endow it with a life of its own, the space in which the state leaves the owner entirely alone is never a space fully under the control of the owner.

On Liberty and the Individualizing Rhetoric of the Peasant Proprietor

Mill's skepticism about a wholly fungible, wholly individualized, universal form of property has its most canonical formulation in his definitive text, *Principles of Political Economy*, which underwent six revisions from its appearance in 1848 to its last edition in 1865. Before Mill wrote his best-known works on liberal political theory, he had already established himself as the pre-eminent spokesman for classical political economy. But the text he wrote on the subject does not bear out the stereotype of classical economics as sternly universalizing in its proclamation of iron-clad market rules. The first book of the volume, on production, he presents as describing phenomena "partak[ing] of the character of physical truths. There is nothing optional or arbitrary in them" (2.1.1). However, the second book, devoted to distribution, he qualifies as a different matter entirely. The distribution of wealth "depends on the laws and customs of society," which his work can only describe, not rationalize into a coherent theory (2.1.2).

His distinction between the universals of production and the culturally determined factors that influence distribution led to an innovation that set *Principles* apart from earlier canonical texts on classical political economy: where previous works had assumed that "property" was a phenomenon so universally recognizable as to need no foundational explanation or elaboration, Mill provides multiple chapters on the nature of all property and on cultural variations in the arrangements of property in the land.[5] The result is not only a detailed analysis of the origins and theory of property but also descriptions of several different types of property and the theories of distribution implied by them. Mill dismisses the Lockean idea that government was first formed by property owners to protect their property. "Enough is known of rude ages," he scoffs, to show that "tribunals (which always precede laws) were originally established, not to determine rights, but to repress violence and terminate quarrel" (2.1.2). He argues that the utility most people attribute to property is actually the utility of not disturbing long-established property rights. The only universal property right, Mill argues, consists in "the right of each to his (or her) own faculties, to what he can produce by them, and to whatever he can get for them in a fair market; together with his right to give this to any other person" (2.2.6).

What cannot be universalized takes up a significant portion of his discussion on the distribution of resources. Following the acknowledged lead of William Thornton and the implicit lead of political economist Richard Jones, Mill surveys various arrangements between landlords and tenants in which rights and responsibilities are defined differently, from the metayer rents of Italy, in which peasants pay for use of the land with a portion of the produce they raise, to the cottier rents of Ireland, where peasants rent directly from a landlord, rather than a capitalist farmer, and often rent properties too small for even subsistence.[6] He also writes at length about the peasant proprietors of central and northern Europe. Mill introduces peasant proprietors by noting that they, like slaves, participate in a system of production that assigns "the whole produce . . . to a single owner." In slavery, that produce goes to the master. In a peasant proprietorship, it goes entirely to the peasant. Thus, the peasant owner's "unwearied assiduity" is made the polar opposite of the slave's ceaseless labor by the peasant's "affectionate interest in the soil" (2.6.1). Ownership for the peasant proprietor, in Mill's formulation, is aligned both with slavery and monopolistic control. It is a connection in which legal bond and affectionate feelings merge. It is this relationship to property that Mill has in mind when the status of property owner shapes *On Liberty*'s notion of the cultivated individual.

After all, Mill's *Autobiography* suggests that he saw his work on the *Principles* to be of a piece with his later endeavors in *On Liberty* and *Considerations of Representative Government* and that the problem of ownership was a driving force behind them all. Mill names as an epoch "the third period of my mental progress," a period he dates as beginning both with his intellectual collaboration with Harriet Taylor and his drafting of the *Principles of Political Economy* (begun in 1845 and first published in 1848), and culminating in the publication of *On Liberty*, which he predicts is "likely to survive longer than anything else I have written" (150). Mill describes this period as one in which the central problem he and Taylor worked on together was "how to unite the greatest individual liberty of action with a common ownership in the raw material of the globe, and an equal participation of all in the benefits of combined labour" (138). Such a description ascribes a prominent place to the problem of property and suggests even the slight predominance of land—"the raw material of the globe"— over other types of property. *Principles'* chapters on the promise of socialist cooperatives for workers, and its repeated insistence that property in land required principles of distribution that upheld the widest public good stand as a monument to such thinking. But this thinking was first developed in Mill's series of 1846 *Morning Chronicle* articles on Ireland.

That Mill turned to journalism on Ireland in the middle of his composition of *Principles* makes his interest in Ireland seem somewhat opportunistic, an implication he does not duck in his *Autobiography*. He explains that he laid aside his work on political economy to write on the condition of Ireland and the work "unexpectedly entered warmly into my purpose," allowing him to advocate for "the formation of peasant properties on the waste lands of Ireland" (*Autobiography* 140). Exactly how warmly the articles fit into his larger purpose of composing an authoritative text on political economy can be read in *Principles'* multiple chapters on property, on cottier and peasant proprietor economies, on wages and overpopulation, and on the proper sphere of the government, all of which repeat arguments—often verbatim—that Mill first presented in the *Morning Chronicle*. But the immediate result of Mill's political economic agenda is a group of articles that can be breathtakingly oblivious to actual conditions in Ireland. Referring to the potato blight in 1846, which would unfold into famine conditions for the next two years, Mill comments that he wrote because "the stern necessities of the time seemed to afford a chance of gaining attention" for his plan of both providing relief and improving the permanent condition of Ireland (140). Yet the articles do not read as if they were written by someone acutely aware of the "stern necessities" involved in a famine whose aftermath would cut Ireland's population by a quarter within a handful of years.

Instead, each of the forty-three articles Mill wrote for the *Morning Chronicle* offers a somewhat freestanding argument for the reclamation of wasteland in Ireland that could be sold, rented, or distributed by the government as small plots for peasant proprietors, who would then undertake the land's improvement. In article after article, he argues that Ireland's economic and moral regeneration depends on closely following such a plan, and that to undertake the former without the latter would be to accomplish nothing of permanence.

He repeatedly attacks possible alternative plans for relieving Ireland's distress, even when those alternatives differ very little in substance from his own plan. As the mass exodus, deadly epidemics, and starvation attendant on the potato blight of 1846 became more general, Mill quibbled with those who wanted landlords or the state to oversee wasteland property (the peasants, he argued, should do as much as they could themselves), with those who advocated an Irish Poor Law as a stopgap measure until wasteland reclamation could have effect, and with those who advocated any other sort of relief project to address the immediate needs of the starving poor of Ireland.

The zeal with which Mill defended his highly specific program, rigidly fending off all challengers, suggests that when he talks about the simultaneous moral and economic benefits that property can offer the Irish peasant, such benefits inhere in property only under certain circumstances. For Mill those circumstances involve the government buying unused and uncultivated land at a fair market value from Anglo-Irish landlords of large estates. The state would then divide the lots into "portions of the most convenient size" and assign them to appropriately industrious peasants for improvement. Mill hedges about the exact extent of the government's involvement; it might need to offer a small advance to peasants who need to buy basic tools to begin the work of improvement, and it might continue to charge a fixed rent to the improving peasants. He is nonetheless clear that state involvement should be kept to a minimum, with the peasant proprietors themselves performing all the labor. The very act of granting them title to the land in perpetuity will do all that needs to be done toward making sure the work will be completed. "The whole efficacy depends," Mill stresses, on "the perpetuity." He explains, "It is not paying no rent that makes the peasant proprietor industrious; it is that the land is his own" (1004). For Mill, the most salutary rights of property are entirely encompassed by fixity of tenure, the guarantee that one can stay in one spot indefinitely and even ensure that one's children and grandchildren might do the same.

Mill's fixation on small properties as the key to changing the character of Ireland is in keeping with his general philosophy—consistent from his writing on Ireland all the way through to the end of his career—that "what shapes the character is . . . the unintentional teachings of institutions and social relations." While a strong believer in educating the public through traditional literacy, he argues that this method has its limits: "the real effective education of a people is given them by the circumstances which they are surrounded" (955). Thus, changing the property relations of Ireland will prove a more substantial moral improvement for the proprietor than would mere sermons or lessons because property itself, at least for the peasant proprietor, is always a process and a social relation for its owner.

But if this is the condition of the liberal individual, always implicitly propertied, Mill's rhetoric infuses the propertied condition with an involuntary quality, one in which the possession of property controls the individual as much as the individual controls the property. The condition of knowing one might remain on a given piece of land and derive profit from its improvement inevitably leads to action that, in the language Mill uses to describe the benefits of peasant proprietorship, often seems independent even of the owner's conscious will. Mill suggests that assigning property rights will in itself generate an animated relationship between proprietor and soil, a relationship whose origins do not lie properly with either party. His Irish articles power through aphorism after aphorism about property's inspiriting power: "Property in the soil has a sort of magic power of engendering industry, perseverance, forethought, in an agricultural people" (898). "Here is the secret for converting an indolent and reckless into a laborious, provident and careful people. It is a secret which never fails" (897). Mill quotes and requotes Arthur Young on the surprisingly lifelike powers of property: "Give a man the secure possession of a bleak rock, and he will turn it into a garden; give him a nine years' lease on a garden, and he will convert it into a desert." All that Mill wants his readers to believe about property can be summed up in Young's own slogan, which Mill repeats several times, that "[t]he magic of property turns sand into gold" (957).[7]

In all these epigrams, the qualities that plant life derives from the soil are shifted to the imagined proprietor, who is cultivated by the relationship with property much in the same way he is supposed to be cultivating his plot of land. Just as the assiduous small farmer will coax sprouts and blooms from the most inhospitable ground, so too will proprietary rights coax hard work from even the least likely of laborers. So effectively does this equation work that in the end it may be property itself that cultivates both owner and thing owned, turning "sand into gold." Mill quotes Arthur Young in a typical passage in which property bypasses all agents to become the prime mover of the sentence: "I know no way so sure of carrying tillage to a mountain top . . . as by permitting the adjoining villagers to acquire it in property" (958). The magic of property that turns sand into gold also, apparently, makes manure climb mountains.

The owner never seems entirely in charge of this property's cultivation. Instead, the condition of owning always seems to be a cultivation of the owner-cultivator.

The slippage in this proprietary rhetoric, in which the power of animation is located uncertainly in the type of property (a garden springing to life), the actual relationship *of* property (perpetuity rather than a nine-years' lease), and only lastly in the proprietor himself, is a slippage that also takes hold in Mill's conceit, in *On Liberty*, of the individual self as both owner and thing owned. Mill makes it clear that mere possession of qualities does not make for an individualized self; nor does complete self-policing of all one's actions. Instead, it is the combination of the two that make a true individual. It might be part of common wisdom, Mill concedes, "that our understanding should be our own," but it is less commonly asserted that "to possess impulses of our own, and of any strength, is anything but a peril and a snare. Yet desires and impulses are as much a part of a perfect human being, as beliefs and restraints" (66). His model of selfhood in this particular passage is one of self-division: a person with desires can only be truly individual when he develops the self-control to counter—but not to kill—those same desires. To be fully free from the oppression of society is fundamentally to wage a low-grade and unending war with oneself. And both sides in this self-war must remain perpetually opposed, perpetually undefeated, according to Mill: "The same strong susceptibilities which make the personal impulses vivid and powerful, are also the source from whence are generated the most passionate love of virtue, and the sternest self-control" (67).

In this dynamic, that which Mill advocates the possession of—impulses— is also that which creates the force that limits, directs, and subordinates the possession—"the sternest self-control." The condition of having one brings the other into being in a way that, much like his descriptions of peasant property, seems to bypass the actual agent experiencing them. Mill convicts his contemporaries of being too focused on self-control when the real danger is not one of failing to command oneself; the real danger is having no self at all. What threatens modern society, Mill insists, is "the deficiency of personal impulses and preferences." The result is the production of modern subjects who "become incapable of any strong wishes or native pleasures, and are generally without either opinions or feelings of home growth, or properly their own" (68).

Mill's disappointment about the lack of "home growth" opens onto a series of images in which he describes the self-division he sees as necessary for true individuality in almost agricultural terms: "It is not by wearing down into uniformity all that is individual in themselves, but by cultivating it and calling it forth, within the limits imposed by the rights and interests of others, that human beings become a noble and beautiful object of contemplation; and as the works partake the character of those who do them, by the same process human life also becomes rich, diversified, and animating, furnishing more abundant aliment to high thoughts and elevating feelings, and strengthening the tie which binds every individual to the race, by making the race infinitely better worth belonging to" (70).

This imagery—of the "cultivation" and "calling forth" of individuality "within limits" that yields beauty, diversity, and, finally, community—can already be found in the physical descriptions and the proprietary dynamics that Mill relied on so heavily in his repeated arguments for the virtue of a peasant proprietary system, arguments where "home growth" and "native pleasures" are central. In his series of *Morning Chronicle* articles on the condition of Ireland—and again in repeated editions of *Principles of Political Economy*, in sections that echo his articles almost verbatim—Mill provides a concrete illustration of what it means to have property that in resisting control elicits controlling impulses from its owner, much as he will later claim that individuality is an experience of having both strong impulses and the self-control elicited by those strong impulses. Over the course of his series of *Morning Chronicle* articles, Mill offers up a picture of the peasant proprietor as fulfilling all the qualities necessary for individuality—motion rather than rest, rich diversity rather than sameness, a property perpetually resisting the owner, and an owner perpetually studying the property in order to craft the proper response to its irreducible specificity.

In his *Morning Chronicle* series, Mill selects passages from other agricultural writers and travelers to create a rhetoric of the peasant proprietor that contains the nascent outline of the individual he celebrates in *On Liberty*. This rhetoric is characterized by the small, the diverse, and the continual staging of an ownerly dynamic in which the unruliness of property elicits a strong controlling response from the proprietor. Quoting from Henry Inglis's travels in central Europe, Mill focuses on peasant property whose very smallness stages both the liveliness of what grows in the ground and the exertions an owner takes to contain such impulses: "If, for example, a path leads through, or by the side of a field of grain, the corn is not, as in England, permitted to hang over the path, exposed to, pulled or trodden down by every passer by; it is everywhere bounded by a fence, stakes are placed at intervals of about a yard and, about two and four feet from the ground, boughs of trees are passed longitudinally along. . . . The vegetables are planted with seemingly mathematical accuracy; not a single weed is to be seen, nor a single stone. . . . every shrub, every flower is tied to a stake, and where there is a wall-fruit a trellice is erected against the wall, to which the boughs are fastened and there is not a single twig that has not its appropriate resting place" (985).

Inglis's picture of the intensively pruned, trimmed, staked, and fenced agricultural property provides the visual emblem of property-inspired control that has its parallel in Mill's belief that the combined pride, comfort, and forethought generated by ownership of property would inevitably result in the owner's sexual self-control, a quality he obliquely refers to as "providence" and "prudence." Drawn from William Thornton's work on overpopulation, one element of Mill's argument for small peasant-cultivated holdings is the idea that those who have property to lose will be unwilling to compromise their material stability with too many children. The explicit discussion of practices in controlling agricultural fecundity stands in for the other implied practice of controlling human fecundity.

In Mill's rhetoric, the hypercontrol of potentially unruly growth, both human and agricultural, inevitably yields both plenitude and diversity—two qualities Mill highlights as characteristics of peasant properties. Despite the limited space of the newspaper article, Mill goes out of his way to quote long lists from other sources that emphasize the range both of the peasant proprietor's labor and of that labor's products. Mill copies a passage from William Howitt's *Rural and Domestic Life of Germany* (1842) exemplary in this tendency:

> Here they are everywhere and for ever, hoeing and mowing, planting and cutting, weeding and gathering. They have a succession of crops. . . . They have their carrots, poppies, hemp, flax, saintfoin, Lucerne, rape, colewort, cabbage, rutabaga, black turnips, Swedish and white turnips, teazles, Jerusalem artichokes, mangel-wurzel, parsnips, kidney beans, field beans and peas, vetches, India corn, buckwheat, madder for the manufacturer, potatoes, their great crop of tobacco, millet. . . . They have had these things first to sow, many of them to transplant; to hoe, to weed, to clear off insects, to top; many of them to mow and gather in successive crops. They have their water meadows . . . to flood, to mow, and reflood; . . . their early fruits to gather, to bring to market with their green crops of vegetables; their cattle, sheep, calves, foals and poultry to look after; their vines, as they shoot rampantly in the summer heat, to prune and thin out the leaves where they are too thick; and any one may imagine what a scene of incessant labour it is. (970)

Quotes of this nature and length from Arthur Young, German professor Karl Rau, French economist Simonde de Sismondi, and traveler Samuel Laing punctuate Mill's articles on Ireland, and almost all appear again in Mill's discussion of landed property in *Principles of Political Economy*. Their recitations of diversity in occupation and harvests were an oblique response to the argument made by advocates of large-scale farming that farmers of small estates were dull, with limited experience and even more limited imagination. Mill's selection of testimony emphasizes instead that the very smallness of the holdings render them so diverse and the peasant proprietor such a jack of all trades. In a quotation from Inglis, Mill presents a picture of a property whose idiomatic arrangements maximize the scarce space: "Wherever grass will grow, there it is; wherever a rock will bear a blade, verdure is seen upon it; wherever rye will succeed, there it is cultivated" (986).

Contrasted with the monoculture of large English farms and the alienated labor of the English wage worker, the smallholdings Mill presents as the solution to Irish poverty offer a rich training ground in a diversity of experience and an individuality in habitual practice that he also advocates in *On Liberty*. In Inglis's and Young's and Howitt's renderings of the peasant proprietor there is surely enough variety to meet the criteria Mill quotes from Wilhelm Von Humboldt on the requisites for the development of originality—"individual vigour and manifold diversity" (64). Conversely, in writing on the potential of peasant property in Ireland, Mill suggests that it is the man who works for a wage who can never cultivate individuality. While the wage worker can only "become a good artificer in his particular manual operation," the peasant proprietor is able to thrive "in sagacity, in thoughtfulness, in power to judge of consequences and connect means with ends" (975).

This type of peasant education is based on rationality and forethought, but it is a training that involves the heart as much as the mind. Where the small proprietor is concerned, Mill asserts, "Their labour must not be for wages only, it must be a labour of love—the love which the peasant feels for the spot of land from which no man's pleasure can expel him, . . . and in which every improvement which his labour can effect belongs to his family as their permanent inheritance" (916). It is the sense of connection with future generations inherent in dynastic owning that fuels the peasant's feeling. The peasant loves his land because in part it is not his—it is already owed to heirs that he also loves. But at other times Mill classifies the peasant proprietor's industry as a literal love of the land itself, "what may almost be called affectionate interest in the land" (985). By the time this argument makes its way into *Principles of Political Economy*, this affectionate interest takes on a strikingly literal quality. Mill quotes

Jules Michelet's *Le Peuple* (1846) as an authority on the thought processes of the French peasant proprietor who can be found visiting "his mistress" on a Sunday: "What mistress? His land." In the quote, Michelet details a scene of industry—the peasant finds himself lapsing into weeding and clearing stones despite being dressed in his Sunday best—but it is more fundamentally a scene of intimate emotion: "If he sees a passer-by, he moves slowly away. Thirty paces off he stops, turns round, and casts on his land a last look; somber and profound, but to those who can see it, the look is full of passion, of heart, of devotion" (n 2.7.19).

Such an affectionate relationship hints that Mill's repetitive celebration of the "magic of property" applies to only a very narrowly defined type of property, one small enough to be known and even loved in all of its intimate details by one cultivator. Mill's treatment of the smallholding as naturally calling forth the industry, and sexual continence, of its owner—and having the power to morally and economically transform an entire nation—contrasts sharply with the striking lack of power Mill sees in aristocratic estates to command any attachment from their owners at all. He attacks one critical letter writer to the *Morning Chronicle* for suggesting that the land has, for the landlord, a *"pretium affectionis,"* the legal term for the value put on a thing by the fancy of its owner. "Who ever heard of *pretium affectionis* in an Irish bog?" Mill scoffs. "If any man has a satisfaction in calling himself lord of so many thousand barren acres, he has a sufficient equivalent if he receives their money value" (1002). For Mill, only an intimate knowledge of the minutiae and diversity of a smallholding can make a proprietary attachment secure. The fact that no such cultivation can be found in the aristocratically held wasteland Mill is so eager for Irish peasants to reclaim is proof that no ownership has ever really taken place there. Improved wasteland can not be offered back to its "original proprietor," he insists, if by that label is meant the landlord. "The 'original proprietor' is the person whose ancestor had the land granted to him in the days of Tyrone or of Cromwell" and whose family since that time could not be said to have "exercised any one of the attributes of ownership over the land, but that of preventing other people from making use of it" (961).

And the "attribute" of exclusion is for Mill the most pernicious aspect of ownership. In his later political writing, Mill treats the privacy enabled by private property as always at odds with the development of a healthy civic-mindedness. Mill worries, in *Considerations on Representative Government*, that "private persons, in no eminent social situation" have no sense of broader duty that would help them develop an "unselfish sentiment of identification with the public.

Every thought or feeling either of interest or of duty, is absorbed in the individual and in the family. The man never thinks of any collective interest" (255). Property's status as "private" also leads Mill to devalue it in *On Liberty*. He concludes that an opinion must always be valued higher than "a personal possession" because while theft of the possession might be "a private injury," the suppression of an opinion "is robbing the human race, posterity as well as the existing generation" (21). In this passage, Mill values opinions more than personal property because opinion for him is always public; in fact, he groups "absolute freedom of opinion and sentiment on all subjects" as inseparable from "the liberty of expressing and publishing opinion" (16). But the possession of a peasant proprietorship turns out to be a lot like the expression of an opinion in that it also might be considered to be already owed to someone else. And prohibiting the sort of relationship to property that constitutes the peasant proprietorship may itself be akin to "the peculiar evil of silencing the expression of an opinion" because both might very well be "robbing the human race" (21). While an environment that encourages varied opinions might shape the public as a whole, an environment that fosters the diversity of cultivation found on small properties is one in which public-mindedness also thrives. In *Principles of Political Economy*, Mill quotes Laing's descriptions of small owner-occupied farms in Scotland as exemplary in their public-mindedness, arguing that "[t]he excellent state of the roads and bridges is another proof that the country is inhabited by people who have a common interest to keep them under repair" (2.6.14). He adds that peasant proprietors in Flanders and Switzerland have often led the way in cooperative movements, banding together for economies of scale and mutual insurance of property against natural disasters (2.6.16). In fact, peasant proprietorship might be the very condition of even imagining such possible bonds. The German peasant, Mill quotes Howitt as asserting, "has a stake in the country, as good as that of the bulk of his neighbors" (969). Such a boon for the Irish peasant, Mill predicts, would yield similarly assimilative results, "It would make him an orderly citizen. It would make him a supporter of the law" (974).

Landed Property and the Forbearance of the State

In arguing for the advantages of peasant proprietorship, Mill also described land's surprising autonomy in developing its owner. Land becomes a sort of agent in Mill's writing, putting things into action that the state itself cannot. Mill's emphasis on the autonomy of land in the experience of land ownership far outstrips his precision in explaining exactly how the state might be involved in creating such conditions of proprietorship.

Mill's imprecision as to how the state should help to start an Irish class of peasant proprietors carries with it one surprisingly consistent message: that the state has the power to create and destroy property rights, but forbears from doing so in order to create a relationship with property owners. Mill sees the state's quarantine of its powers from the spaces of property as creating a more durable relationship with the Irish than could any positive interference with their lives. Only by drawing away can Mill's state draw the Irish to itself.

Mill remains adamant throughout all his *Morning Chronicle* pieces that the state should obtain the unimproved land from the landlords who now hold it and that beyond granting it to the peasants who will improve it, the state should have little active role in the management of the land. But his insistence that he advocates no spoliation of landlords' property and would have nothing removed from them without proper compensation is constantly undermined by his expositions of the perfect right a state has to take such property from landlords without offering them compensation. And his disdain for state intervention in the lives of the Irish poor—he is eloquent in his disapproval of the way the Irish Poor Law has left peasants too used to the idea that they can depend on the state for wages—seems somewhat compromised by his admission that a class of peasant proprietors might pay rent to the state for their holdings and still be considered proprietors.

What comes off as carelessness and occasional contradiction in the details nonetheless resolves into a remarkably consistent concept of the role the state plays in maintaining property in the land. No fan of any Lockean theory of a right to property in land that precedes the state, Mill challenges what he calls the "superstition" and "religion" of property by reiterating "the moral and social basis of the right of property": "the right of the labourer to the fruits of his labor. All other proprietary rights exist for this one" (908). But Mill points out that land is the exception to this rule since "[l]and is not the product of labor. No landlord's ancestor made the land" (908). For that reason, he insists that the state has the mandate to interfere when proprietary rights to land become deranged. With their repeated references to this mandate, his articles on Ireland create a picture of a state that has unassailable title to the land so long as it uses that title for the public good. Mill also presents the effective state as one that excuses itself from interfering in property for the sake of the public good. Rather than being the space that preserves independent subjectivity by keeping the government out, property in land is the publicly allotted space the government reserves for the development of individual subjectivities.

Mill's vagueness on precisely whether land is to be taken from landlords under legal compulsion or willingly sold for fair compensation allows him the leeway both to assert the right of the government to appropriate property for the public good and to celebrate its forbearance in not doing so. He responds indignantly to a letter-writer's accusation that his proposed plan of peasant proprietorship amounts to "the doctrine of general spoliation" by detailing exactly how and for what he would compensate the landlord whose wastelands would be reclaimed for the project. After laying out the plan for compensation, he then adds that a more imperious government takeover of land would still not amount to "plunder, and spoliation, and confiscation" because to give someone money for their land in order to use that land for a public good is the right of the state. "The Legislature of the country can deal with the property of the country as expediency requires, making compensation to the owners," Mill asserts, citing English railway bills that authorized rail lines on private property as his precedent. But he is quick to add that he is not yet calling for a measure that extreme. "Milder remedies are possible. This is the point we are laboring to prove" (906).

He repeats this pattern of distinguishing his plan from a government confiscation of land and then asserting that such a move is nonetheless well within the right of the state in imagining Dublin Castle's objections to his plan. The Irish administration, he anticipates, "will sound the alarm in defense of an imaginary idol called rights of property" when they hear of his suggestion to make "the six millions of acres [of wasteland] useful, for the benefit of any persons other than those who have so fully exercised the right of *not* using them" (920). He once again goes through the reasoning of distinguishing his plan from full confiscation, only this time, rather than defending his plan against charges that it amounts to confiscation, he rushes at the accusation, threatening to do exactly that. He is fully able to concede, he says, that cultivated land might exist as property "so that gentlemen in superfine coats who inhabit large houses in Ireland . . . may be supported in elegant leisure" (921). However, landlords can claim no such property in land they have not improved for cultivation, and so, Mill concludes quite menacingly, in direct address to such hypothetical landlords, "the time is now come when a public necessity requires that what you have omitted to do should be done for the general good by the representative and organ of the general good—the State. We are going to take the land from you; to enter it and do as we please with it, for the purpose of rendering it productive, whether with your leave or without" (921).

In this series of articles, then, Mill fluidly categorizes his plan as falling far short of the state's rightful powers, as conforming with the accepted practices of the state's rightful powers, and as constituting an unprecedented practice that nonetheless is entirely in keeping with already-existing state powers. But he makes it quite clear that the state has to be careful to avoid catalyzing the wrong sort of relationship with its subjects. His condemnation of the Irish poor law suggests that land reform might be the necessary prophylactic to avoid creating an inappropriately enmeshed relationship between the Irish people and the British state. Mill repeatedly takes on George Poulett Scrope, a member of parliament whose utilitarian sympathies were quite closely aligned with his own. Scrope's error, for Mill, was in advocating for an Irish poor law that would *guarantee* impoverished Irish a *right* to relief. Repeating rumors that Irishmen were declining to farm at all, preferring to live off the wages they made laboring on government-sponsored relief projects, Mill presented the nominal wages of a government relief program as instilling a permanent sense of title in those who receive it, creating in them a sense of property in the state itself, rather than in the separate material of the land. "The wages bestowed [on the Irish] in charity they already look upon as a right, and what the Irish peasant considers his right, he enforces by a penal code of his own; already the officers of the Board of Works are assaulted and fired at for withholding employment" (992). Mill blames the government for creating a system in which the Irish might grow to feel about wages how he believes it will be most salutary for them to feel about land.

This particular attribution of blame is one of the most unstable moments in Mill's extended argument that the Irish are what the misgovernment of the British have made them and not by nature an inferior race. Earlier, Mill had argued that the Irish peasant's defects were due almost entirely to the moral and economic evils of the cottier system, which gives holders of land no hope for permanence even in an economy where possession of land is the means to survival. He defends them against charges of intrinsic lawlessness, explaining "Rockism and Whiteboyism" not as "qualities of his nature, but hard consequences of his desperate situation" (956). To then suggest, less than a month later, that "the Whiteboy and the Rock system" are now concerned with shaking the poor relief system down for wages that are becoming felt as an Irish right would seem to overturn Mill's earlier plea for Irish lawlessness as a mere consequence of hard circumstance. It is instabilities like these that lead Janice Carlisle to conclude that Mill's early ambition to create a science of how characters—both national and individual—are formed never amounted to more than "a chance to parade one's own prejudices and presuppositions" (156).[8] But his distinction between a peasant guerilla insurgency he can excuse—the Rockites and White-boys engaged in attempts to keep peasants on land—and one he cannot—the alleged Rockite and Whiteboy violence to defend a right to poor relief—shows that his narrative of the interdependence of government and property has a clear line of demarcation. His version of bad Rockite rebellion is rebellion for a right to property that is in essence a part of the state rather than for property from which the state has excused itself.

The Role of the State in "The Probable Futurity of the Labouring Classes"

So far I have been arguing that Mill's most sustained example of the fully individualized self such as he celebrates in *On Liberty* emerges in his recommendations that a disaffected Ireland be reconciled to the British state through the creation of a class of Irish peasant proprietors. In imagining the land to mediate a relationship between the Irish subject and the state, Mill also imagines Irish peasants as able to inhabit a space and an experience that reforms them while keeping them at a remove from a state power that might otherwise be crippling or coercive. In this section I solidify this claim by contrasting the owning self Mill imagines in his writing on the peasant proprietorship with the owning self he tends not to articulate in his next most sustained example of a subject reformed by a reformed distribution of property: his discussion of the possibility of British workers' cooperatives. What this comparison yields is the sharp contrast between the fully fleshed-out experience of the connective, even affective, ownership Mill provides in his examination of an Irish peasant proprietorship and his depopulated and emotionally flat descriptions of the collectives that might make up British workers' cooperatives. Composed without the backdrop of a physical plot of land, his narrative of the rise of workers' cooperatives lacks the substantiating details that make his writing on peasant proprietorship so forceful. When faced with what he classifies as the exceptional development of the British working classes, Mill fails to sustain a concrete model of self-cultivation. He also has difficulty imagining a cultivated self safely removed from the influence of the state.

In *Principles of Political Economy* Mill devotes a chapter to imagining the process by which class divisions in Britain might gradually be eroded into non-existence by the formation of workers' cooperatives, which would erase the difference between owners of capital and performers of labor. Mill predicts that this future will emerge from a spontaneous process, one in which the state will not have to take into its own hands a socialist redistribution of property. He also imagines it as an arrangement uniquely suited for the British working classes. Because of the length of the discussions he has devoted to peasant proprietorship, he allows that he has given his reader reason to anticipate that his recommendation for the improvement of the British working classes will involve the allotment of small agricultural properties as well. But he outlines what he imagines instead in a chapter—"On the Probable Futurity of the Labouring Classes"—that is more prophetic in its conviction of what *will* happen than it is prescriptive of what *ought to* happen. For Britain, he predicts, there will be a gradual transformation of all production away from capitalist-owned companies staffed with wage laborers and toward cooperatives in which workers are both laborers and owners. Mill presents almost the inverse of his plan for bringing the Irish into civilization. Rather than requiring a rearrangement of property so that the institution might serve as a civilizing influence on them, the English working class, he suggests, has already attained such a high level of civilization that a corresponding rearrangement in property is inevitable. Because he believes that in Britain property will merely follow a civilization already in place rather than create it, he never offers a description of the experience of being attached to property. Such an experience, in the British case, will simply be a manifestation of who the British workers already are.

In an argument that contradicts some of his earlier claims about peasant proprietaries, Mill belatedly crafts a hierarchy in which holders of small agricultural properties must always trail in civilization behind participants in more complex economies. Only in his discussion of workers' cooperatives does Mill expose problems with peasant proprietorship, even problems that up until this time he has argued are not inherent in a system of small properties held by individual cultivators. Such a system first and foremost is unsuitable for the British working classes because once large-scale production has been adopted as a mode of production, Mill argues, the people who have adopted it cannot go back to a smaller scale. He lays aside all of the arguments he has made up until this point about the super-human efficiency of the hypermotivated peasant proprietor, as well as the arguments he has made about peasant proprietors who, exiled from economies of scale, must strike up their own alliances to get done what large-scale farmers accomplish with no spirit of cooperation. Instead, he argues that peasant proprietorship is never the best that human society can achieve. Mill concedes that "as a step out of the merely animal state into the human, out of reckless abandonment to brute instincts into prudential foresight and self-government," peasant proprietorship serves a valuable purpose. But in order to make this argument, he frames peasant proprietorship as the state of profound absorption in an isolating property, a result he repeatedly refuted in both his articles in the *Morning Chronicle* and in the second book of *Principles*. Peasant proprietorship simply will not work for the British working class because "something better should be aimed at . . . than to disperse mankind over the earth in single families . . . having scarcely any community of interest, or necessary mental communion with other human beings" (4.7.14).

This is an abrupt about-face from his articles on Ireland, in which he argued that the peasant proprietor is better off than the wage-laborer for a social education. "A day-labourer who earns his wages by mere obedience to orders, may become a good artificer in his particular manual operation," Mill concedes, but "in sagacity, in thoughtfulness, in power to judge of consequences . . . in every intellectual faculty which it ought to be the object of popular education to cherish and improve," the truly educated man is the peasant proprietor. After all, his is the "agreeable" task "of finding every way of improving and making valuable a small farm, of which the whole produce is his own, and which is the permanent inheritance of his children" (975). But Mill now announces that the sort of property that joins the peasant proprietor to future generations is superseded in sociability by the sort of relationships available in workers' cooperative associations. He argues that cooperative ownership offers the most perfect form of social institution in which "each human being's daily occupation" enrolls him or her in "a school of the social sympathies and the practical intelligence" (4.7.59).

In Mill's eyes, the British working classes do not need the more elementary instruction available in the possession of property because their civic education has already been under way, informed by newspapers, pamphlets, working-class institutes, and the education of the collective bargaining of labor unions and the collective politics of chartist agitation. For such people, Mill insists, "if public spirit, generous sentiments, or true justice and equality are desired, association, not isolation, of interests, is the school in which these excellences are nurtured. The aim of improvement should be not solely to place human beings in a condition in which they will be able to do without one another, but to enable them to work with or for one another in relations not involving dependence" (4.7.14). Mill sees this ideal relationship best embodied in associations of operatives, who, combining their scant resources, start a business from which all workers can profit and to whose steering all workers might contribute.

Such associations will contribute to an overall increase in the productivity of the economy, Mill argues, because in vertically integrating both manufacturing and distribution, they eliminate the drain on profits that separate distribution can cause. Even more importantly, the associations will increase productivity because a worker will always work more efficiently where he perceives his own interests are served. But such economic benefits are nothing compared to the "moral revolution" that workers' cooperative associations would effect. The spontaneous growth of workers' cooperatives, Mill anticipates, will amount to no less than the complete erasure of class rivalry, "the transformation of human life from a conflict of classes struggling for opposite interests, to a friendly rivalry in the pursuit of a good common to all" (4.7.59). With class warfare ended, all workers will be able to claim a part in the planning and deliberations involved in their daily labor, having had a civic education that has bypassed private property entirely.

But in contrast to his writing on peasant proprietorship in *Principles of Political Economy*, Mill's positing of worker's cooperatives as "the most beneficial ordering of industrial affairs for the universal good which it is possible at present to foresee" feels hasty. Most strikingly, the narrative strategies he undertakes to sketch out the operations of a workers' association offers no picture of individuality that might be seen as a prototype of the political individual he celebrates in *On Liberty*, one whose individuality is protected from the tyranny of the majority but still safely engaged with the common good. Instead, his description of cooperatives offers almost no glimpse of individuals at all, presenting the organizations themselves as the basic unit of narration.

Nevertheless, Mill maintains that the transformation of the economic landscape into cooperatives is inevitable because cooperatives offer the most compelling advantage—"the common interest of all the workers in the work" (4.7.60). Mill's chapter on workers' cooperatives is free of any maxims about the improving power of this common interest. All that his readers know of the instructive power of working in one's own interest, in fact, has already come from the chapters he has written on property. And because Mill asserts that the working class in Britain has already had an education in their common interest, there is less room in his narrative for discussing the educational value that workers' coopera-tives *might additionally* bring. To write on the inevitable attractions and trans-forming powers of cooperative movements would be to undermine his empha-sis on the civic education that the British workers have already had. "There is a spontaneous education going on in the minds of the multitude," he asserts, in arguing that the British will never return to a golden age of a deferential working class and a paternal upper class. But it is a spontaneity in tension with the con-scious deliberation he claims it produces: "The institutions for lectures and discussion, the collective deliberations on questions of common interest, the trade unions, the political agitation, all serve to awaken public spirit, to diffuse variety of ideas among the mass, and to excite thought and reflection in the more intelligent" (4.7.9).

As detailed as it is, this narration of a civic education lapses into tautology. In contrast to his clear-cut claims for the improving force of peasant propri-etorship, Mill offers a far more fluid picture of British working-class educa-tion. The gradual freedoms attained by the lowest social classes—taught to read, allowed to choose their religion, granted mobility in occupations—will generate an ability to handle such freedoms and a desire for more, he predicts. His explanation of working-class progress encompasses more interrelated in-fluences than do any of his discussions of peasant proprietorship. But it also has a circular logic: the development of the intelligence of the working classes is the key to developing the intelligence of the working classes. Without the pithy explanatory power of the magic of property, even the inevitable rise of workers' associations comes from a tautology. Such associations, Mill asserts, might "by the very process of their success" be "a course of education in those moral and active qualities by which alone success can be either deserved or attained" (4.7.62). Because they succeed, cooperatives will teach workers how to be successful, although the associations' success depends on the workers knowing that very thing.

Mill's tautologies underline the fact that spontaneity is a key characteristic of the workers' cooperative movement, a characteristic he makes central when he distinguishes his vision of a class utopia from those of earlier theorists of communal property, like Robert Owen. It might have seemed before the work-ers' cooperative movement, Mill argues, that such experiments weren't likely to be carried out unless the capital for them was "seiz[ed]" and "confiscate[ed]" "for the benefit of the labourers" (4.7.21). But in Mill's vision of the future, workers will pool their own meager savings, motivated by the example other cooperatives and the potential rewards of working for their own interests. In one of the most laissez-faire accounts of business in a volume far from consistently laissez-faire, Mill presents the inevitable cooperatives of the future as the spontaneous movement of society toward equality, independent of government interference.

But a careful reading of Mill's plan shows that spontaneity to have begun somewhere, and much as with his discussion of the peasant proprietor, that origin ultimately lies with the state. "There is a capacity of self-exertion and denial in the masses of mankind, which is never known but on the rare occasion when it is appealed to in the name of some great idea," Mill states. The explanation resembles his claims that the promise of property in perpetuity called forth extraordinary efforts from the peasant proprietor. Only, instead of property, it is the influence of "some great idea." For Mill, the French Revolution of 1848 presented such an idea because it convinced the working classes of France that they had obtained "a government who sincerely desired the freedom and dignity of the many" and who did not look upon the natural role of the working classes as "instruments of production." Convinced of the government's care, Mill explains that French workers "came to the resolution" that they would work for no master but themselves and do so "not by robbing the capitalists . . . but by honestly acquiring capital for themselves" (4.7.21). Mill sees the example of these self-helping French cooperatives as spreading contagiously across the English channel. While he emphasizes the material independence of these workers, scraping together their initial capital through much self-sacrifice, Mill quite literally does not see them as individuals owing nothing to society for their capacities. To the contrary, they owe their own virtues to the catalyzing example of the state.

While for the Francophile Mill this British indebtedness to the French state is relatively unproblematic, to his readers it might have suggested something other than "a government who sincerely desired the freedom and dignity of the many." After all, the reach of French influence across the channel carried with it in the nineteenth century the threat of invasion by a state the British disdained as too absolutist in both its republican and imperial incarnations. The French state's invasion of Britain with its cooperative-inspiring sincerity points up one more way that Mill's vision of a peasant proprietorship for Ireland more fully allows its beneficiaries an involved but noncoercive relationship with the British state. The peasant attached to his land might transfer his loyalty from one state to another, but such transferences never require him to transfer his affections away from the "home" that his property also is.

"England and Ireland" and Mill's Historicism

Mill's interest in Ireland informed his political philosophy in the 1860s, even as his concrete attention to Irish politics ebbed during those same years. In *Considerations on Representative Government* (1861) he cavalierly referred to Irish problems as in the past. While conceding that British misgovernment had once barred Irishmen from considering themselves members of a British nationality, Mill claims that the most recent Irish generation has been able to develop "the consciousness of being at last treated not only with equal justice, but with equal consideration" by the British (433). Yet even Mill could not sustain such sunny views of British-Irish amity in the face of the Fenian violence later in the decade, in which Irish separatists carried out raids in Canada and on British soil in the name of ending Union. The most notable of these, the explosion at Clerkenwell Prison, was carried out by Fenians to free Fenian prisoners but had the unintended consequence of killing several people living near the jail and injuring scores more. The event set Mill back to writing on Ireland. His pamphlet "England and Ireland," written in the last months of 1867, renewed his project of demanding a program of land reform for Ireland, but with a sense of urgency even more palpable than the famine generated in his earlier writing.

Mill does not mention by name any Fenian undertakings as prompting him to write. Instead, he paints the moment as one of crisis because almost all chance of conciliating Ireland with measures that the state might generate has passed. At this delicate moment, Irish rebellion no longer looks like "one of grievance or suffering; it is rebellion for an idea," Mill warns, offering this maxim: "Rebellions are never really unconquerable until they have become rebellions for an idea" (7). The real danger of the moment is that "this desperate form of disaffection . . . does not demand to be better governed, . . . asks us for no benefit, no redress of grievances, not even any reparation for injuries," because its entire motive and aim is "mere nationality" (8). His recommendation for action, now that the British find themselves on such a precipice in Irish relations, is the strategy of making the government a benefactor to the Irish nation once again, of giving it something material and concrete: "The rule of Ireland now rightfully belongs to those who by means consistent with justice, will make the cultivators of the soil of Ireland the owners of it; and the English nation has got to decide whether it will be that just ruler or not" (23).

In the remainder of his pamphlet, Mill argues from familiar premises that a permanent attachment to the soil will prove most salutary for small cultivators and that the state can legitimately reassign property rights in land where it is expedient. However, "England and Ireland" is free of Mill's earlier waffling about the role of the state in remedying the situation. No longer just suggesting that the state has a *right* to reassign property, Mill instead prescribes for it a central role in the upheaval of an entire system of landed property. In his plan the state must establish a commission for valuing all the land in Ireland and for fixing it as a perpetual rent price for the tenant. The state should collect this rent, he argues, and transmit it to the landlords. The landlords might choose to sever their connection with the soil altogether, taking their rent as a government pension without any involvement with the actual land of Ireland.

The extent to which this plan marked an entirely new line of thinking on Ireland for Mill is subject to debate. The historian E. D. Steele, in two successive *Historical Journal* articles, argues that "England and Ireland" was an abrupt and radical departure for Mill from a line of thinking that otherwise insisted on the absolute security of private property. Bruce Kinzer argues that "England and Ireland" was a culmination of thought Mill had already worked out in the *Morning Chronicle* articles, noting his many arguments against the immutability of landed property and his routine championing of the morally improving qualities of small freehold properties.[9] Like Kinzer, I see much continuity between the earlier articles and the later pamphlet; they advocate similar plans and even draw on the same vocabulary to do so. But without question, Mill shakes off the indeterminacy that riddled his *Morning Chronicle* articles about the precise role of the state in arbitrating property relations. This very concrete departure from his earlier writings is underwritten by a second departure apparent in his pamphlet: an embrace of a proprietary historicism, newly available to those thinking about questions of property in the land.

In "England and Ireland" a new type of historicism informs the assertiveness with which Mill argued for the power of the state to rearrange property rights. This historicism originated with Henry Sumner Maine's publication of *Ancient Law* in 1861. The Lockean view that property allocated individuals a space of sovereignty remained basic to Victorian conceptions of property, but by the 1860s writers also routinely drew upon Maine's historicist view of property law's evolution. Maine expressed his theory with the maxim that all property evolved from "status"—in which identity, kinship, and occupation all merged with proprietary powers—to "contract"—in which an individual, through his powers alone, could acquire and alienate property. Property thus became a power separate from the domains of family authority or political power. In this thesis,

Maine revived the scientific stature of stadial theories of historical development, arguing that it was relationships to property—and not to production, as Adam Smith's hunters and gatherers, farmers, and merchants suggested—that dictated a society's place in the long evolution toward advanced civilization. His idea proved a weighty alternative to a more abstract and universalized understanding of property.

In this historical view of property that starts out as communal and gradually evolves toward the individual, Mill found a sympathetic framework through which to imagine private property that might function to unite a common public. More importantly, Maine's ideas allowed Mill to argue for the involvement of the state from a stance that was essentially conservative, a call for the restoration of old conditions rather than an insistence on new ones. Maine provided Mill with a convenient backstory to property that Maine argued had once been owned in common by primitive societies who joined together in village communities. The village community provided a model of trusteeship that the state could emulate in taking back control of the land for the sake of the common good. In fact, the notion of the primeval village community suggested that communal control of the land was the norm from which modernity had deviated. It provided a conservative veneer for what were otherwise labeled radical ideas about property. In reviewing Maine's subsequent work, *Village Communities* (1871), Mill shows himself emboldened by this conservative logic to imagine a more active role for the whole community in determining the rights of property. One of the inferences that can be drawn from Maine's work, Mill argues in his review, is that "[i]f the nation were to decide, after deliberation, that this transmutation of collective landed ownership into individual shall proceed no further, . . . the nation, in so deciding, would not overpass the limits of its moral right" (549).

With the influence of Maine, Mill's thinking on Ireland takes a longer historical view. In his *Morning Chronicle* pieces and the multiple editions of *Principles of Political Economy*, Mill had used only recent history to explain the character of the Irish people, arguing that "Rockism and Whiteboyism are not qualities of [Irish] nature, but hard consequences of his desperate situation," a situation created by recent acts of British misrule (955). In "England and Ireland" Mill looks to a different—and much older—historical context: the native memory of Irish tradition. The notion of a landlord with absolute rights to the soil, he asserts, is entirely contrary to Irish ideas "and has never to this day been recognized by the moral sentiments of the people." This is because "before the

Conquest, the Irish people knew nothing of absolute property in land. The land virtually belonged to the entire sept; the chief was little more than the managing member of the association" (11). Drawing on a vision of ancient Irish society, Mill changed his understanding of the environment that contributed to Irish character from one in which the British figured prominently to a native memory in which the British barely figured at all.[10]

Mill's adoption of this sort of historicism in his pamphlet at first seems largely cosmetic. After gesturing toward this native memory in the first couple of pages, Mill says little more of it, proceeding to outline his recommendation for a state valuation of all the land in Ireland, followed by the legal assignment of permanent tenurial rights to all tenants willing to pay the assessed rent. The plan was radical in assigning to the state, and not the free market, the determination of the economic value of land. It was equally radical in dictating that the state, not the owner, should determine who might stay on the land. In reactions to Mill's pamphlet, what struck the press as most shocking was the plan's disregard for the landlord, who would continue to receive rent but would no longer be able to choose his tenants. Such an approach was seen as antithetical to the entire social order in Britain. Following up its review of Mill's pamphlet, the *Times* editorialized that, in considering the case of Ireland, "Every man should make up his mind whether the received laws of property are to be upheld in the United Kingdom; or whether, beginning first with Ireland, we are to establish principles which would unsettle our whole social fabric" (qtd in Steele, "Reform" 439).

The *Times*'s panic registers what was radically new about Mill's position. There remained no trace of his *Morning Chronicle* vision of a state that might justifiably invade the rights of landed property and simply chooses not to. But those early articles' implicit theme of forbearance persists even in this later and more radical piece. In place of a state drawing its citizens to it by refusing to interfere with landed property rights, Mill offers a vision of a state first of all forbearing to use violence to keep Ireland in the union. Should the British decline to address the Irish land issue and instead "attempt to hold Ireland by force," Mill predicts, "it will be at the expense of all the character we possess as lovers and maintainers of free government, or respecters of any rights except our own" (45). His equation implicitly acknowledges that the state *might* hold Ireland by force; such a thing is possible. The reason to refuse such a course has to do with taking the higher moral ground.

More significantly, "England and Ireland" imagines a new sort of state forbearance where national culture is concerned. Mill imagines the state as withholding its power of imposing one cultural norm of ownership onto an inappropriate cultural situation. The British erroneously have thought "that there could be no boon to any country equal to that of imparting [British] institutions" on it, and since the benefit of British institutions had been generously showered on Ireland, "Ireland, it seemed, could have nothing more to desire" (8). Mill sees such a mindset as being at the heart of Britain's Irish failures. Outside of Britain, "there is no other civilized nation which is so conceited of its own institutions." At the same time, where Britain is concerned, "there is no other civilized nation which is so far apart from Ireland in the character of its history, or so unlike it in the whole constitution of its social economy" (9). The reform most necessary for the British state to undertake, Mill concludes, is one in which the British refrain from imposing their norms on Ireland.

In this vision of cultural forbearance, Mill is joined by many of the major players involved in passing the Irish Land Acts, which assigned responsibility to the British government for assessing the value of land, for enforcing fair rents, and ultimately for keeping Irish tenants on the land they tilled. William Gladstone, in proposing the first Irish Land Act in 1870, argued for it on the premise that "[a]ll the circumstances, all the associations, and all the accretions that have grown around the native ideas are different in the one country from what they are in the other. We cannot name a point in which the relation of landlord and tenant in Ireland and Great Britain are the same" (Healy 115). Even J. A. Froude, a vociferously pro-Union, anti-Catholic, pro-coercion historian blamed the troubles of Ireland on a failure of the state to withhold its own cultural institutions: "Of all the fatal gifts which we bestowed on our unhappy possession [the worst] was the English system of owning land" (qtd in Solow 9).

This idea that the English relation to property was a culturally specific institution that could be imposed—and imposed inappropriately—marked a change from Mill's ahistorical and a-cultural imagination of the "magic of property." While, in *Principles of Political Economy*, Mill had consistently acknowledged that the distribution of property was a product of cultural custom, he had never treated any of those customs as in danger of invasion or compromise. His presentation of Ireland as a fragile proprietary ecosystem, one threatened by nonnative British ideas of ownership, marks a new way of thinking, one underwritten by nothing less than a sea-change in the theoretical underpinnings of property's origins.

But his was not the only source that claimed for Ireland not just native rights to the land but an indigenous way of owning not equivalent to English modes of owning. Irish nationalists in the 1840s and 1850s also claimed that the Irish experienced ownership in ways the British did not. And as I argue in the next chapter, the model of indigenous owning they offered, and the British accepted, reconciled some of the worst contradictions that riddled modern British property.

CHAPTER THREE

Native Property

Young Ireland and the Irish Land Acts
in the Victorian Proprietary Landscape

Both Mill and Edgeworth used the specificity of the Irish situation to imagine how property in Irish land might come to be a unifying rather than an atomizing force, a force that would bring people together even as it barred the state from its precincts. But they employed two competing narratives of property, whose radically different implications made the concept of property itself unstable in nineteenth-century Britain. Edgeworth was working with a model of property as an estate, a model that accommodated a sense of community; the owner of an estate was connected by mutual ties to his dependents and had responsibilities to them, not just rights to his property. The paradigm of property at which Edgeworth aims her comedy is similar to Samuel Coleridge's understanding of the landed estate as the connective tissue of a national community—those "fastenings and radical fibres . . . by which the Citizen inheres in and belongs to the Commonwealth" (199). When Edgeworth wrote tales that emphasized the uncertain title to any property, hidden in the forgotten past, she worked to undermine the sense of hierarchy such a community implied, but she did so with the aim of keeping a sense of communal connection intact. Landlord and tenant might be interchangeable in the dim mists of a property's history, but they were irreducibly tied together.

Mill aimed to revise a much different narrative of property, one that emphasized not interconnections underwritten by property but the absolute individual nature of such property. Mill critiqued a paradigm of property more aligned with jurist William Blackstone's eighteenth-century celebration of property as "that sole and despotic dominion which one man claims and exercises over the external things of the world, in total exclusion of the right of any other individual in the universe" (2). This definition of property as absolute control over a concrete thing emphasizes exclusivity as the central experience of being an owner. Mill's vision of Irish land ownership as creating community connections was one that challenged property's attributes of complete isolation and control.

The two models of property Edgeworth and Mill critiqued were perhaps the two most prominent ways of thinking about property during the nineteenth century, even though they emphasized almost opposing characteristics. The Coleridgean paradigm highlights property's capacity for holding together a social order while the Blackstonian definition holds individual autonomy above all else. Nonetheless, both paradigms served equally well as imaginative bulwarks against the threats of an increasingly market-driven society. The notion that property in land was the basis of community among the classes suggested that at least some forms of property might be safe from the isolating effects of the marketplace and from a myopic absorption in individual interests. Conversely, the idea that property in land marks out the space in which an individual might exercise complete control provided a reassuring means to safeguard individual agency at a time when an increasingly complex and overdetermined economy made such agency less available.

The fact that landed property appeared to offer simultaneously the experience of community and the experience of individual agency made the experiences themselves seem less contradictory. Yet fault lines between these two versions of proprietary power often caused tension in nineteenth-century British narratives of property. This friction was compounded by yet another development in proprietary thinking, one that framed property rights as competing claims among people rather than as person-thing relationships. The first part of this chapter dwells on how these conflicted conceptions of property were never quite resolved in nineteenth-century literature and culture. British thought about property in land was not a coherent, unified whole beside which the more localized practices of traditional Irish society looked fragmentary and irrational.

The second part of the chapter argues that Irish celebrations of localized practices might have attracted Britons troubled by their own culture's proprietary paradoxes. Focusing on the rhetoric surrounding the midcentury Young Ireland nationalist movement and on the subsequent passage of the Irish Land Acts of 1871 and 1881, this chapter shows that British commentators perceived Ireland as a more elegant and unified proprietary terrain than Britain. For them, property in Ireland united, rather than divided, its owners, and Irish proprietary rights might be discerned simply by paying attention to the authentic emotions of those who felt themselves to be owners. This perception of Irish property has complex roots and even more complex consequences. On the one hand, this was a vision of Irish property crafted by Irish nationalists who advocated for an independent Irish nation-state. On the other hand, the vision strongly attracted the British politicians most responsible for crafting a means to keep Ireland and Britain united.

The Problems with British Property

In order to understand some of the problems with British property, it helps to go back to the father of modern thought regarding property. In his second *Treatise on Government*, John Locke crafted a theory about the origin of government in the consent of the governed that conflated the moral, economic, and political functions of property. "Every Man has a *Property* in his own *Person*," Locke's familiar assertion runs. "This no Body has any Right to but himself. . . . *Labour* being the unquestionable Property of the Labourer, no Man but he can have a right to what that is once joined to" (287–88). From this premise he draws the conclusion that men's interest in preserving their property led them to voluntarily subject themselves to the authority of a government. Such a government necessarily saw property owners as the only persons who counted, since it had been called into being exclusively to serve them. The Lockean government formed by consenting property owners also had a clear and obvious limit on its own power. Because its entire purpose was the preservation of property, it could not take property away from those it governed. Property necessarily marked out a space where the subject was free from government interference.

Locke's famous line of reasoning, in which personhood leads to property and property leads to community, gave rise to a tradition of political theory in which political power, economic wealth, and personhood all operate along similar lines. This conflation became disturbing in the face of an increasingly pervasive concept of property as freely circulating and fully alienable. Suddenly, personhood and community seemed subject to the fungibility of commercial property. Political theorist C. B. MacPherson offers perhaps the most famous formulation of modern property's disruption of community ties when he observes that beginning with Locke's theories, the English political subject was conceived as a person fully self-possessed—one who might think of himself as "proprietor of his own person or capacities, owing nothing to society for them" and thus "free inasmuch as he is proprietor of his person and capacities" (3). Conceiving of their personhood as property entirely theirs, these subjects have no reason to understand themselves to be under any permanent social ties or obligations.

MacPherson's critique suggests that modern concepts of property attenuate community ties. An equally familiar critique of modern property's role in political and economic thought indicts it for the effect it has on modern selfhood. In a world where relationships are determined by temporary market relationships of exchange, this critique points out, having a propertylike self is not necessarily an advantage. Formulating what she sees as "the paradox at the heart of liberal property ideology," legal theorist Margaret Radin observes that in a commercial economy, "To consider him/herself free and autonomous, a person must be free to sell his/her property, but property is necessarily identified with the person, so that alienation breaks the link between the property and the person, which breakage threatens to transform 'freedom' into 'estrangement'" (197).[1] For Karl Marx, the estrangement of one's identity, along with the alienation of the property in one's labor, is the founding injury of an industrialized capitalism. Subdividing each worker's contribution to the making of a commodity, capitalism dims the worker's recognition of what is his own. The worker thus cannot recognize that society's wealth is of his own making. Such a state of estrangement unmoors the worker's true identity.

Anxiety about property's disruption of community and its threat to a stable selfhood plagued the nineteenth century. Their appearance together, however, suggests one more problem with property: the impossibility of clearly conceptualizing property's boundaries. Anxieties about private property's socially disintegrating effects and its potential to alienate even the self were, at root, anxieties about the power of property as a bounded entity. The fear of social atomization in a world of absolute property was a fear that the boundaries of property worked entirely too well, that private owners absorbed in their private property would be sealed off forever from concerns with, or obligations toward, anything beyond the boundaries of that property. At the same time, fear that dealing in a world of alienable property might result in the alienation even of one's self was a fear that the boundaries of property could never be established, that there could be no part of the self or identity marked off for privacy and safekeeping that would not, in the end, also be subject to the rules of alienable property. The possibility that property might be too easily and fully controlled by individuals *and* the possibility that individuals might never be able to control even the property they claimed in themselves seemed equally likely. Clear boundaries around property and their absence appeared equally poised to do damage.

This situation was created by two competing narratives about property's boundaries, yet the British drew from both as if there were no substantial difference between them. For centuries the British looked to the English tradition of property as a zone of complete liberty for an owner. This narrative, best characterized by Blackstone's definitions, might be invoked against the threat that property no longer was a stable enough entity to shield its owner from the wider world. But even as this idea persisted into the nineteenth century, Victorians also embraced a competing narrative in which property in land acted as the repository of communal and eternal traditions immune to the encroachments of a market culture. This narrative of property, one I associate with Coleridge and Burke, was a favorite defense against the fear that property's strict boundaries ultimately filtered out even the possibility of community ties.

In what follows I outline the basic features of both of these narratives of property, emphasizing their fundamental differences and examining how Victorian culture tried to manage those differences. I then turn to one substantial commonality: both narratives depended on property in land as the archetype of property. With land as their model of all property, Victorians could assume property rights always to be anchored in material and in space. As a result, both also occluded the development of more modern paradigms of property as a mere matter of rights and expectations, agreed on and subject to revision among a limited group of owners.

Blackstone's Autonomous Zone

Blackstone's conception of property as the zone of exclusive control has a genealogy that stretches back to before the English Civil War. Along with their estates, Victorian landowners inherited a legal narrative from the pre–Civil War era in which landed property imparted rights of resistance against a feudal and absolutist monarchy. By the 1700s, this anti-Royalist assumption took on more classical tones, drawing on republican thinking that celebrated landed ownership as the necessary condition for the development of an independent personality. This republican ideal cast landowners as the exemplary leaders of society. The estate from which the landowner drew his living guaranteed him both the leisure to become engaged in larger political affairs and the opportunity to develop the free will that would qualify him for public service.[2]

This zone of autonomy was not necessarily the large landed estate. Alongside the ideal of the large-scale landowner as citizen-leader flourished the similar ideal of the English yeoman, the sturdy freeholder of a small estate, beholden to no one. Radicals toward the end of the eighteenth century incorporated the yeoman ideal into their campaign for an increased political franchise. They argued that the independent personality and civic responsibility that the large landowner cultivated could also be cultivated in the more limited spaces of the small freehold. But just as often, conservatives used the republican ideal to defend the status quo of the English constitution, which, they pointed out, allotted exemplary independence to both large and small owners. This conservative rhetoric treated the individualizing power of property as allowing all property holders to partake in the same identity. If the freedom of the Englishman consisted of the right to have everyone leave him alone on his own property, then it was a right that made every individually owned property in England, in effect, a smaller England; each landowner was connected to the nation through his ability to represent the freedom of the entire nation in microcosm.

In this model of property as autonomous zone, property existed to foster the individual owner's development of an independent will. The absolute nature of this independence can be read in jurist William Blackstone's eighteenth-century celebration of property as "that sole and despotic dominion which one man claims and exercises over the external things of the world, in total exclusion of the right of any other individual in the universe" (2.2). While Blackstone's *Commentaries* (1766) showed the laws of real property to be anything but absolute and perfectly under the control of one individual, his assertion of its powers of total control ("sole and despotic dominion") over objects of a concrete nature ("the external things of the world") reflects the strong influence the narrative of property as zone of autonomy had over the eighteenth-century legal thinking he summarized. In reconciling the intricacies of English law to the paradigm of property as absolute control over an external thing, Blackstone encountered all sorts of property—a right to appoint a parish clergyman or the right to draw water from a stream—that was far from concrete and that imposed limitations on others' rights to their own property. He remedied these inconsistencies by treating that right like a thing in itself, an *imaginary* thing over which the identified owner was said to have complete control. For instance, the scenario in which one man held a right of easement to cross another man's field would be treated as a scenario involving two owners of separate property—one the absolute owner of an easement, the other the absolute owner of the field.[3]

While Blackstone's account of English property was not the Lockean narrative of primordial first owners, banding together to form a government, it nonetheless imagined the current state of English law to affirm Locke's vision of government with naturally built-in limits, formed by and for property owners. Blackstone's emphasis in the *Commentaries* on the easing of older feudal structures and his sparse reference to English legislative interventions into the laws of property made his narrative one of an oppressive government power that had gradually withdrawn in order to let owners enjoy their natural liberty. One of Blackstone's major accomplishments in crafting the *Commentaries*, in fact, was his ability to marry a constitutionalist vision of a historically and culturally determined English law with a more theoretical, liberal account of law. What Locke had offered as an account of the state of nature, Blackstone offered as an account of the organically emerging logic of the English law.[4]

But whether constitutionalist or liberal, the freedom from interference that property guaranteed depended on property's thinglike quality, its quality of having clear boundaries. This was not just Blackstone's innovation. As legal theorist Jennifer Nedelsky points out, property's persistent rhetorical character as "specific, identifiable, knowable" goes hand in hand with a modern liberal political theory in which "individual autonomy was conceived of as protected by a bounded sphere—defined primarily by property—into which the state could not enter" (qtd in Underkuffler 132). Recognizable boundaries play a major role in this equation. After all, one holds no rights good against all the world—either to personal autonomy or to property—unless all the world can easily recognize those rights and understand their corollary duty not to trespass upon what is clearly privately controlled.[5] Justice Joseph Yates rejected an author's entitlement to perpetual copyright reasoning from a spatial premise: because ideas "have no bounds or marks whatever, nothing that is capable of visible possession," they thus have "nothing that can sustain any one of the qualities or incidents of property" (qtd in Rose, "Author as Proprietor" 60). This eighteenth-century pronouncement sounds to the modern ear like a hopelessly naïve inability to imagine property as anything other than corporeal. But in refusing to entertain the idea of property without bounds, Yates hews closely to the principle that liberty itself might be outlined by the spatial boundaries of property.

In the narrative of property as zone of autonomy, then, landed property operated as an archetype of all property, marking out the coherent selfhood of its owner through its demarcation of space over which the owner might be understood to have complete control. But, in the eighteenth century at least, what the owner claimed that control *against* was the state, not the alienating and atomizing forces of the market. J. G. A. Pocock argues convincingly that property's politically crucial separation in the eighteenth century was not the separation of owner from marketplace but the separation of owner from too much dependence on the centralized government and its system of patronage (51–72). Raymond Williams also points out that far from celebrating the estate as refuge from the market, country house poems of the eighteenth century are often forthcoming about their involvement in a broader economy and not shy about mentioning the breaks in lineage and commercial transfers of property that united an owner with a particular estate (56–57).

When Victorians inherited this narrative of property from the eighteenth century, they inherited it from a culture less troubled by Radin's paradox of liberal ideology—in which a person must be free to sell property, but in doing so risks losing all claim to personhood. The autonomous landowner's liberty was not dependent on his insulation from the free market. It rested instead on his freedom from dependence on the state. Thus, instead of mourning the loss of personhood involved in commerce, Adam Smith's *Theory of Moral Sentiments* (1759) celebrates commercial culture as allowing for the development of a broadly sympathetic personhood. Much as one borrows and trades on the market, Smith's commercial subject expands his powers of sympathy through the temporary borrowing of other mindsets and the ability to imaginatively observe oneself as if from the outside. Such practices did not require a self to operate according to the model of the spatially bounded subject of Nedelsky's liberal ideal.[6]

However, in the last third of the century a new discourse emerged that framed land as a space that insulated its owner from the market. Agricultural writers saw estate owners as trapped by tradition, barred from applying capitalist principles to their estates. Evangelizing the idea that land should be treated like any other resource whose productivity ought to be maximized for the general good, writers on agricultural improvement suggested that owners needed to break free from practices specific to their own estates. In his survey of Suffolk, commissioned by the Board of Agriculture, improving writer Arthur Young notes that his purpose is to describe "the most interesting features of the local practices" as well as "the most remarkable deficiencies" so that the productive practices might be introduced elsewhere, while the deficiencies might be corrected by practices originating elsewhere (vii). In his tours of agriculture in England, Ireland and Scotland, Young treated all manner of customary practices surrounding the land not as evidence of a tradition of perfect liberty but as interfering with the landowner's freedom to maximize his wealth. In his estimation, land was too isolated from a wider commercial culture, an isolation that needed to be overcome to allow the owner the exercise of complete freedom. For many writers on agricultural improvement, the eighteenth century's vision of the landowner's perfect liberty was a myth that needed actualization in the free market—a market from which owners' land separated them, saddled as it was by long leases, entails, and the accretion of traditional practices.

Burke's and Coleridge's Space of Communal Inheritance

In the limited context of eighteenth-century improving agriculture, then, the landed estate's status within a long English tradition was no longer one of underwriting individual power that could be exercised against the state. Instead, owning land began to symbolize being tied to the past, being committed to practices one did not create and could not destroy or control, and thus being isolated from the market. Landed property became the site on which an owner experienced obligations to a cultural heritage, rather than his own perfect control and freedom. And while within the limited discourse of improving agriculture this meaning was decidedly negative, the twin calamities of the French Revolution and the Napoleonic wars generalized the communal connotations of land to the wider culture and gave it a more positive valence. With these two events, land's role as symbolic guarantor of individual liberty was gradually upstaged by its symbolic function as the material that ensured communal and historic ties. First the French Revolution's upheavals came to associate the rhetoric of liberty with a violence far from English notions of respect for property. Next the severe food shortages Britain suffered during the blockades of the

Napoleonic wars changed improving agriculture from a moneymaking tactic for individually ambitious farmers to a patriotic duty to maximize food production to feed the nation.[7]

Edmund Burke led the charge in reconnecting the ideas of property and liberty in a way that might be both exclusively English and explicitly antirevolutionary. The result was something other than Blackstone's imagination of all property as a "complete and despotic dominion." Sidestepping the idea of individual property altogether, Burke connected a specifically collective English liberty to the inalienable traits of the landed estate: "It has been the uniform policy of our constitution to claim and assert our liberties, as an *entailed inheritance* derived to us from our forefathers and transmitted to our posterity; as an estate specially belonging to the people of this kingdom" (33). In Burke's scheme, property becomes less an enabling platform for individual ownerly liberty than a solemn duty and prescripted role for an entire people. The principles on which the laws of the commonwealth are based, he claims, are fashioned to make sure that "the temporary possessors and life-renters in it [are not] unmindful of what they have received from their ancestors, or of what is due to their posterity" and thus be led to act "as if they were the entire masters; . . . think[ing] it amongst their rights to cut off the entail, or commit waste [ie, permanently change the land] on the inheritance" (95). Of course, these are the very actions improving agriculturalists felt should be open to improving landlords if land was to be made more productive.

Burke's vision of a national heritage that operated like an estate influenced those looking for a way to mitigate the social upheavals of industrialization. They attributed industrialization's disintegrating social effects to what they now saw as a relatively recent rejection of the old model of inalienable and communal ties modeled by property in the land—the same rejections that in the eighteenth century had been celebrated as marking the death of a patently unEnglish feudalism. Thomas Carlyle denies any validity to the Scottish Enlightenment's concept of benevolent commerce as a potentially sympathetic medium. His thunderous declaration in *Past and Present* (1843)—"Love of men cannot be bought by cash-payment; and without love, men cannot endure to be together"—indicts market society for its atomizing effects (269). Carlyle's workers are a far cry from the mercantile subjects of Adam Smith's philosophy of moral sentiments, gaining in experience and sympathy as they circulate cheerfully in the marketplace. While Smith's subjects acquire a broader ability to understand those who they encounter, participants in Carlyle's "cash nexus" lose basic skills of distinguishing inner essence from outer appearance. Convinced that money is property without understanding the source of its value, Carlyle's industrial citizens mistake the sign of currency for the essence of human well-being. Their mistake can only be corrected, Carlyle implies, by the less mediated subsistence offered through property in the land. In his essay "Chartism" Carlyle argues that before "the Supreme triumph of cash," the low and high were intertwined "[n]ot as buyer and seller alone, of land or what else it might be, but in many senses still as soldier and captain, as clansman and head, as loyal subject and guiding king" (58). Without such feudal connections underwritten by the landed estate, Carlyle sees all of society as operating according to the aloof principles of laissez-faire political economics, free only for the purposes of leaving each other alone.

Carlyle was in good company when imagining forms of landed property outside of commercial exchange as the antidote to a completely atomized market society. The years after the 1832 Reform Bill, when questions about competing interests among the classes were at their most intense, saw Benjamin Disraeli's unabashed nostalgia for a church and aristocratic property that he imagined to have been always communally beneficial, and the Young Englanders' nostalgia for a class-inclusive "Merry Olde England" of maypole dances on the commons and Christmas celebrations in aristocratic great halls. Joseph Nash's fashionable *Mansions of England in the Olden Times*, serialized throughout the 1840s, offered engraving after engraving of such scenes, reiterating literal landed property as central to the interconnection of the classes.[8] Meanwhile, John Clare's poetry and John Constable's etchings celebrated the communal country life of an agrarian village.[9] A capitalist society in which individual owners controlled their individual property was, according to these texts, an impoverishment of an earlier social order in which social interconnectedness was underwritten by tangible property in the land.[10]

This change in symbolic registers can be detected even in the analogies made between literary property and landed property during debates about copyright law. Exactly contemporaneous with Smith's and Blackstone's works, the 1774 court case of *Millar v. Taylor* ruled against a previously established law that had made copyright perpetual. The debates leading up to the decision hinged on how rights might be recognized in a property that was by its nature so easily copied and disseminated. In arguing that original ideas and style were the readily recognizable property in a literary work, Blackstone refuted the assumption that consent to publication was consent to permanent alienation. Rather, he argued, permission to publish "is more like making a way through a man's own private grounds, which he may stop at pleasure; he may give out a number of keys, by publishing a number of copies; but no man who receives a key, has thereby a right to forge others, and sell them to other people" (qtd in Rose, "Author as Proprietor" 64). Edward Young's *Conjectures on Original Composition* (1759) bears a similar understanding of property as always about bounded space when he claims that the writer committed to original ideas will have "the sole Property of them," the writing of which he can consider as "not only a noble Amusement, but a sweet Refuge" (qtd in Ross 14–15).

These analogies attribute qualities of total privacy and right to absolute and even whimsical control to both landed and literary property. Such notions are missing from similar analogies made during the copyright debates in the nineteenth century. In these debates literary property is once again compared to land, but this time land that, like Burkean property, is more held in trust than owned. William Dougal Christie's 1840 *A Plea for Perpetual Copyright* imagines that the recognition of an author's permanent right in his work will result in a situation in which "[t]he child [of the author] with filial reverence will guard the sacred bequest [of the copyright], and transmit it uninjured to his child. . . . there will exist a class of men holding their hereditary estates not in broad lands but in books" (qtd in Vanden Bossche 60). Chris Vanden Bossche and Mary Poovey both argue that these debates employ the rhetoric of the landed estate to claim for the author a sort of property that is organically interwoven with the national culture.[11] That the authors could use the example of the landed estate to make such claims reflects a shift from an eighteenth-century understanding of Britain as composed of individual landed properties that might microcosmically mimic the totality of the nation in their independent operations to an understanding of the landed estate as those Coleridgean "fastenings and radical fibres . . . by which the Citizen inheres in and belongs to the Commonwealth" (199.)

Such shifts in landed property's symbolic register were not the product of substantial alterations in real property law. With the exception of the spate of enclosure acts in the late eighteenth and early nineteenth centuries, which gave landowners total individual control over land previously open to usage by locals, very little about landownership changed from the eighteenth century to the mid-1880s. The complicated logistics behind the alienation of land stayed the same between the eighteenth century and the bulk of the nineteenth century. In both centuries, however, those who made fortunes in commercial endeavors were motivated to and succeeded in removing those obstacles in order to become proprietors of great estates. In both centuries, too, all landowners enjoyed much the same political influence because of their property. Despite the nineteenth century's dramatic expansion of the franchise, those who owned land continued to hold the majority of elected positions in rural local government and in both houses of Parliament.

Paradoxically, the rise of free-trade activism at midcentury amplified land's cultural status as the type of property that protected ancient custom and inalienable interconnections, even though the movement was wholly opposed to the idea that a stable community depended on a special status for landed property. Advocates of free trade saw themselves as battling for individual liberty guaranteed by the free market against landed opponents protected by deeply entrenched legal structures that made the transfer of land rare or impossible. In this battle, free traders tended to exaggerate the legal barriers to land's alienability when they castigated landowners as opponents of individually owned, fully marketable property. In their repeated introduction of bills to revoke the laws of entail and primogeniture, free traders contributed to a public perception that land was bound in the protective web of legal inalienability far more tightly than it in fact was, since both entail and primogeniture were voluntary practices, which landowners could choose to end at will.[12]

Proprietary Dissonance and the Problem of Thingness in the Victorian Novel

The fact that landed property appeared to offer a means both for catalyzing community in the Burkean and Coleridgean frame and for exercising total individual control in the Blackstonian paradigm made these goals themselves seem less than contradictory. The Victorian cult of domesticity, itself dependent on the idea of a space that at least operated like property, even if it was not in fact owned, might be seen as drawing on both these narratives, ignoring their contradictions. On the one hand, domesticity's powers aligned with the narrative of property as autonomous zone, and the home was celebrated as a space of separation and privacy. On the other hand, domesticity's powers aligned with the narrative of property as communal heritage, and the home was seen as a unique space that generated the spirit of generosity, self-sacrifice, and intergenerational connection. When Victorians spoke about domesticity, they often contrasted it with the alienating and atomizing powers of the market, thus making it seem as if domesticity itself operated in one unified way against the market's encroaching ethic of selfishness and self-division.

But evidence that the two narratives of property did not precisely dovetail with one another can be traced in the small plot tics that shape the Victorian novel's narration of a character's progress toward something that might be called home. *Jane Eyre*'s (1847) archetypal narrative of its heroine's journey toward property allows its heroine to experience home both as a space of communal connectedness and as a zone of autonomy, but it allots those experiences serially rather than simultaneously. The novel furnishes Jane with two sites where she might experience attachment to property. At the Rivers's cottage, Moor House, Jane grounds her inheritance in rent and furniture, creating a house where she might coax her cousins to be her siblings and family connections for life. As if to make amends for the atomistic self-possession she has practiced up to that point—contracting for her own labor, coldly controlling her desire for companionship—she insists on giving one-fourth of her inheritance to each cousin, keeping only a fourth for herself: "I am not brutally selfish, blindly unjust, or fiendishly ungrateful," she explains to St. John in a litany of possible accusations leveled against the propertied at the time. "I am resolved I will have a home and connections" (391).

But if the moral of Moor House is that property is only good for connecting you to others and saving you from a life of isolated self-interest, a different lesson takes hold at Thornfield. Jane's proposal to her cousins inaugurates a type of affiliation less hierarchical in nature than the gothic feudalism that broods over Rochester's estate, but the logic of the plot does not directly replace an old patriarchal control with this new, more egalitarian model of connection. Instead, Rochester, the character who suffers most from the limits that family property and prestige place on individual autonomy, is healed by a completely isolating form of individual property, separated from all communal ties. When we are introduced to Rochester, we are given to understand that his own lack of self-discipline stems from his father's tragic manipulation of his life, all in the name of keeping up the family estate. The book clearly offers Jane's example of independent self-possession as the model for Rochester's reform. In fact, so clearly does it prescribe an autonomous self-possession as the source of his reform that it ultimately removes Jane from the scene of her sibling affiliations in order to achieve it. Burned out of the family estate, Rochester is reunited with Jane at the hunting lodge of Ferndean, "deep buried in a wood," where Rochester's property features no apparent tenants and no family ties of any sort (435).

The novel, then, reveals a split consciousness about what property in land does for its owner, even as Brontë's work manages the split by supplying Jane with two properties. That management, however, depends on the novel's vision of property as a spatialized object. The *Jane Eyre* two-estate solution solves none of the complications introduced by a new paradigm that rejected property's conceptualization as a material thing. In this new paradigm, frequently called the "bundle of rights" paradigm of property, property shed its associations with the physical bounds of space and its "natural" existence came to appear much less sure. As a result, the state's intervention came to seem much more necessary. Additionally, with the normalization of the idea that property was no longer a thing, the physical objects of property took on new and dangerous fetish-like qualities.

At the opening of the nineteenth century, utilitarian discourse issued a high-profile challenge to the notion that property marked out a recognizable zone that either all of the world was obligated to leave solely to its owner or that might act as a vessel of communal culture. Instead, utilitarians attacked the idea that property could ever be instantly recognizable at all. Jeremy Bentham saw in metaphors of property's thingness a denial that humans had the power to create and revise rights of property. In his *Theory of Legislation* (1789), Bentham begins his discussion of property by insisting, "Property is nothing but a basis of expectation. . . . There is no image, no painting, no visible trait, which can express the relation that constitutes property. It is not material, it is metaphysical: it is a mere conception of the mind" (137). While his brief sketch of property still hews closely to the notion of property as absolutely under the control of one owner, Bentham implied that even this trait was up for grabs in his categorical rejection of the notion that a right to property was available to humans in the state of nature. "Property and law are born together, and die together," he maintained. "Before laws there were no property; take away laws, and property ceases" (138).

Bentham's argument that property was brought into being entirely by human legislation, rather than the Lockean theoretical model in which legislation was brought into being to protect preexisting bonds of property, paved the way for a legal and political paradigm of property that was on the rise as the century progressed. In this paradigm, property was not distinguished by its resemblance to a thing. Instead, it was seen as a modular "bundle of rights," whose exact configuration could vary greatly according to the wishes of those involved in its contractual definition. Conceived as a bundle of rights, property's nature is no longer absolute and good against all the world. Instead, it becomes a set of variables open to negotiation.[13] The relationship of owner to thing owned—indeed, the identification of any absolute owner at all—is secondary to sorting out different claims and uses whose existence might not be grounded clearly in a "thing."

Thus, Bentham's attack struck two deeply interwoven assumptions about property. The first, which Bentham attacked explicitly, was the notion of a natural law of property that allotted inalienable rights to individuals and that a state must respect in order to be legitimate. Bentham's insistence that no property existed prior to law invoked a positivist conception of law as a mere construction of human legislation, a construction that can always be altered by legitimate governments. But a second assumption also came under attack as a result of Bentham's dismissal of a natural rights version of property: the conventional English conception of property as a relationship between a person and a thing, a notion Bentham wanted to replace with the idea of property as a relationship among people. This replacement would come to dephysicalize the concept of property, making it an affair of rights and expectations. This model of property also made it extremely difficult to imagine property as existing independently of the state. Discarding the idea that property is universally recognizable, the bundle-of-rights model of property leaves open the question of how one might enforce rights that are not instantly apparent to all the world.

The spatial model of property, after all, helped naturalize the notion that property would be an instantly recognizable right. The freedom from interference that property guaranteed depended on property's quality of having clear boundaries. After all, one holds no rights good against all the world—either to personal autonomy or to property—unless all the world can easily recognize those rights and understand their corollary duty not to trespass on what is clearly privately controlled. Bentham challenged this implicit link between spatial models and individual liberty with his objection to the thingness of property. In fact, his dismissal of the "visible traits" of property raised the possibility that conceiving of proprietary attachments as attachments to a thing might reveal ownership to be not the subjection of a thing to a person but instead the subjection of a person to the power of a thing—in essence, a fetish. In this line of thinking Bentham had a surprising ally: Thomas Paine, the radical committed to the argument that property in one's labor was itself a natural right. Paine's earlier radical indignation—that an English appeal to traditional symbols assigns to things the rights that properly belong to people— aimed directly at Burke and his defense of English liberty as an estate. Arguing that the right to engage in war and declare peace rests in the nation's body of people, not in the constitutional entity referred to as "the Crown," Paine rages that "this right is said to reside in a *metaphor*, shewn at the Tower for sixpence or a shilling a-piece" (*Rights of Man* 128). To imagine a right to be inherent in a thing is to fail to imagine a person as the rights holder. To imagine a right to inhere in landed property, for Paine, is equally a failure to acknowledge a wider population's claim to it. Paine rails against the irregular English system of granting parliamentary representation on different conditions to towns, universities, and all manner of rotten boroughs. "The custom of attaching rights to *place*, or in other words, to inanimate matter, instead of to the *person*, independently of place, is too absurd to make any part of a rational argument" (qtd in Rickman 258).

For Paine, if property is attachment to a thing, there always lurks the possibility that the thing is actually the powerful party in the relationship. This possibility looms larger to more people as the century wears on and full mastery over an object of property becomes more thoroughly equated with the power to alienate it. Inalienable property gradually became that which controlled its owner, rather than yielding to ownerly control. In their wariness of property's thingness, both Bentham and Paine suggest a property fetishism different from Marx's commodity fetishism. In Marx's fundamentally economic vision of the fetishized commodity, objects made by humans take on their own agency in the marketplace, acquiring value that appears independent of the labor that went into their manufacture, of the usefulness they offer to society, and even of their material existence in the world. But Paine and Bentham offer primarily political critiques of English property law. For them, the fetishization of property attaches rights to physical space, deanimating the humans who hold the rights and instead animating the object with political agency.

While the Victorian novel is preoccupied with commodity fetishism, routinely pointing out the strange control commodities exercise over their own value in a world of mass production, it is equally preoccupied with this other type of fetishism, the fetishism that animates property that cannot be alienated and that subordinates owners, turning them into mere attachments to the more permanent thing. Following Paine and Bentham, Victorian authors understood this sort of ownership to be the opposite of autonomy. Property in an object offered two equally undesirable possibilities. Either one's power and identity, once embedded in material, would be alienated in the market, or one's power and identity, as derived from a piece of property, left one hopelessly subjected to an inanimate object. To have alienable property and to have inalienable property were two equally undesirable prospects. Thus, the true and oft-repeated tale of the Victorians' horror that the market might alienate even their property in their selves often leaves out the equally true tale that inalienable property might also threaten an owner's sense of stable and autonomous selfhood. Even imagining oneself as inalienably possessed by oneself posed this threat. To imagine oneself without recurring to the model of landed property, as both Carlyle and Marx imply, is to lose oneself in a complex economy where one's claims can never be clear. But to imagine a self as holding property that *does* operate according to such metaphors of property in land is no clear guarantee of stability. As the vehicle in a metaphor expressing the tenor of selfhood, landed property points in more than one direction: toward clearly demarcated ownerly liberty and also toward a communally available enduring tradition of which an owner can be only guardian.

Writers in the nineteenth century rarely succeeded in characterizing property as a mere incorporeal right, but they were also wary that treating the powers of property as anchored in a thing might be a primitive habit that placed owners in subordination to the thing they owned. Thus, landed estates also begin to show up in Victorian novels as sources of constraint rather than platforms for agency. In *Middlemarch* (1871), Dorothea Brooke's inability to do almost anything useful with her late husband's estate is matched in restrictiveness by the rider in his will that forbids her marriage to Will Ladislaw. In *Our Mutual Friend* (1865), John Harmon finds himself the heir to a dustheap estate only on the condition that he marry the woman his father has picked out for him. Faced with such an inheritance, he pretends he has drowned, preferring to shed his own identity rather than be owner to such an agency-compromising piece of property.

In this environment, in which the thing one owns just might own the owner and even full inalienable self-possession posed threats of instability, the interference of the state in property comes to look more desirable. This is a lesson brought home by Mr. Wemmick, in *Great Expectations* (1860), whose pride in ownership and belief in the powers of property are unparalleled among Victorian characters. In fact, it is an index of the threats of property-owning at midcentury that the character so clearly marked out as the archetypal owner is already reduced to minor status in the novel, playing only a supporting role in the more central plot of the hero's radical loss of self-possession. Pip, at the center of the novel, is a character who not only has no clear claim on any property, he also has no clear claim on himself. Appropriated first by Miss Havisham, who seeks him out as a plaything for her adopted daughter, Pip finds himself forever estranged from the rural yeomanlike roots of his brother-in-law Joe's iron forge. His deracination is only intensified when he is moved to London by an unknown patron. Controlled by a benefactor's whims, Pip's gain in property is a loss of agency, leaving him incapable of acting in accordance with his own will. In London he proves unable to stick with his moral resolutions to be decent to Joe or with his financial resolutions to keep his expenditure within his budget. His lack of self-possession is compounded when the basis of his expectations turns out to be not property but theft—a theft that might be repeated on his own self. When the felon Magwitch reveals himself as Pip's patron, he makes it clear that he is a patron who genuinely believes he has taken possession of his beneficiary. Congratulating himself on his creation of Pip, Magwitch crows, "If I ain't a gentleman . . . I'm the owner of such" (339).

In contrast, the clerk Wemmick would seem to offer the clear lines of self-possessive boundedness that Pip lacks. The deep divides between Wemmick's work life and home life promise recognizable bounds of privacy marked off by property. At the office, he is a "harder and dryer" man. At home he undertakes the rituals of tea and toast, and caring for his father, the Aged Parent. Wemmick insists that "the office is one thing, and private life is another" and "they must not be confounded together" (231, 310). As if to invoke the lineage of the privacy his property affords, he marks off the literal borders of his home with all the accoutrements of the English aristocracy. His house literalizes the maxim that a man's home is his castle with its false roof "painted like a battery mounted with guns," "decorated with the queerest gothic windows," and surrounded by a miniature moat whose drawbridge Wemmick raises every night. Showing Pip the kitchen gardens and poultry, Wemmick suggests "If you can suppose the little place besieged, it would hold out a devil of a time in point of provisions" (229).

But the deranged scale of Wemmick's property suggests Dickens's uneasy awareness of property as fetish, not power. Indeed, the fact that it seems to be a home the son has secured for the father's comfort, rather than a home established for Wemmick's dynastic future, suggests a certain backwardness to the whole space. Like a man driven by compulsion, not an agent acting from independent will, Wemmick performs a myriad of repetitive rituals that suggest him to be more slave to his property than free agent dwelling in it. In fact, he seems a lot like Mill's peasant proprietor, animated into action by his property, capable of intensive attention to small spaces out of which he can coax a surprising productivity.

Also like the peasant proprietor, Wemmick's status as owner places him in a relationship with the state that intervenes to insure the legitimacy of even his most curious property. He is, after all, a man dedicated to the gradual accumulation of "portable property." He accepts payment in all forms—roasted hens, carrier pigeons, brooches—from the clients he deals with at the law offices. "I always take 'em" he explains. "They may not be worth much, but, after all, they're property and portable." His fidelity to this "guiding-star" results in his transformation of criminally tainted objects into the upstanding domesticity of the house he calls "the Castle." But the nature of the items Wemmick considers property—mourning rings are mentioned prominently in this category—are often identified with the personality from which they have been taken, suggesting that rather than being a bastion against the alienated self, a domestic property such as Wemmick's might just be an accumulation of other alienated selves, a process the former owners' larcenous careers firmly associate with theft.[14]

What absolves Wemmick from the possibility that his property is actually theft is his involvement with the law. The personalities and crimes that might cling to stolen property as it wends its way through market exchanges are evacuated from the objects by the operations of the state, which has the power to deem an object to be either a piece of property or a stolen good. Wemmick's status as a clerk in service of the law, rather than as an entrepreneur in service of the market, suggests that the state plays a major role in legitimizing his property. While few characters perform the rigid separation of work and home as thoroughly as Wemmick, he does not seem able to keep the state separate from either side of his life. Like "the proprietor of a museum," he showcases to his domestic guests the criminal confessions and locks of hair that are souvenirs of his career. And just as the state seems responsible for legitimizing his claims to his property, the state appears ready to intervene and relieve him of a too permanent attachment to it. At least that is what Wemmick's Aged P anticipates when he informs Pip that his son's home is "a pretty pleasure ground" that "ought to be kept together by the Nation, after my son's time, for the people's enjoyment" (231). In this, Wemmick's servitude to the rituals of his own property might have the same escape valve Pip ultimately has when his enjoyment of Maggs's property threatens to turn him into a criminal himself: state intervention stands ready for both men should their property prove too overwhelming.

In his reading of *Great Expectations*, Bruce Robbins argues that the novel makes the most sense to readers when read through the filter of the modern welfare state, whose bureaucracy of distributive justice was barely embryonic at the book's publication. Robbins argues that it is through this filter that Pip's act of using his "expectations" to buy his friend Herbert Pocket a living makes the most sense. Pip, like the welfare state after him, engages in the redistribution of funds that are not technically his own, in the name of a more just distribution of opportunity among the deserving population. Pip's "property" and Wemmick's "property" both ward off the incursions of the market by providing a home for those—Herbert and the Aged P—who might otherwise be at the mercy of an unfair capitalism. What I would add to Robbins's argument is that a redistribution of property might serve more than just those left dispossessed by the uneven development of capitalism. State redistribution might be necessary to ward off what would otherwise be property's agency-draining potential of a too-secure ownership.[15]

Property, Land, and the State: Chartists and Land Reformers

Dickens is not the only Victorian who began imagining new relationships between property and the state, especially when that property was land. The long process of franchise reform in the nineteenth century gradually dislodged the right to participate in national politics from its imagined location in the substance of the land. Rotten boroughs, controlled by single property owners, were eliminated, and elective districts were redrawn based on census reports so that equal populations might receive equal representation. Each reform moved the state closer to Paine's and Bentham's vision of a government that resisted territorial models of a nation, recognizing rights in people rather than property. Michel Foucault argues that such a turn is characteristic of the development of a modern governmentality. The premodern ruling power, once conceived of as a one-on-one relationship of prince to principality, was replaced by a modernity in which state power constituted itself primarily through population ("Governmentality"). With the widening circle of men to whom the right to vote was granted, political power came to be located not in estates but in persons. But once the idea of a franchise was detached from territory, it became much less clear what a nation's proper relationship to the actual material of the land was.

A quick examination of the competing Chartist plans for restoring the working class to the land illustrates Victorians' confusion about the relationship between land and state. In challenging the current distribution of political power according to landed property, the Chartists retained the centrality of the category of property by describing their fitness for participation in government in terms of their own property—property in their own labor. This insistence on property as the category that legitimized participation in the government generated many of the same confusions about the powers and genealogy of property made apparent by Brontë and Dickens. In suggesting that the aristocracy had created "artificial" rights by legislating power only to those who owned land, Chartists also raised the question of what could ever be imagined as a "natural" right to property, a question that persisted in the second half of the century in a series of land reform proposals and campaigns.

Chartists based their claims to political rights on the argument that property in one's own labor was a natural right, in contrast to the more artificial property of land. Labor, after all, a writer in the Chartist paper the *Northern Star* argued, was the source from which "every description of property arose, and therefore, . . . the only property of real value."[16] But because Chartist understandings of property were founded ambivalently on arguments both about natural rights and about traditional rights guaranteed by the English Constitution, they were always grappling with questions of government's role in making property in one's own labor manifest through property in the land. William Cobbett's pro-working-class constitutionalist claim that "there is no principle, no precedent, no regulations . . . favourable to freedom, which is not to be found in the Laws of England, or in the example of our Ancestors" was echoed decades later by Chartist leader Feargus O'Connor's assertion that universal male suffrage was "formerly a portion of the boasted constitution of our country" (both qtd in Epstein 556). But this constitutionalist interpretation required the rejection of huge swaths of constitutional history. Workers' constitutional equality, Chartists argued, had been disrupted by an aristocratic monopoly of property in the land that was at root an "artificial" type landowners had legislated into being according to their own biased inclinations. But if legislation produced an artificial type of property for the upper-class members of parliament, it remained unclear what guarantee existed that Chartist participation in legislation would produce any more natural property. Such questions were difficult to settle without at least an implicit appeal to the idea of a natural, and not merely traditional, right to property.

The disparity between the plans of Chartist leaders Feargus O'Connor and Bronterre O'Brien to restore the working class to the land provides an index of a Chartist failure to concoct a unified theory of what might characterize artificially constructed property, in contrast to natural property. O'Connor told his audiences that all agitation for the Charter would be useless "if we [are] not prepared with a solid social system to take the place of the artificial one we mean to destroy" (qtd in Armitage 93). For him, the less artificial system involved returning to a society of landed owners of small plots, where their individual self-control and political worth might be made apparent through their independent cultivation of the soil. This recognition of their consequence, he believed, could be brought about, not through government intervention, but through private initiatives such as his own idealistic Chartist Land Company. That O'Connor proved disastrously unable to understand the abstract financial calculations and expectations involved in his own operation is perhaps fitting given his fixation on land as the instantly recognizable medium that would persuasively establish to the world the working man's natural rights in property. Urging his audience to rid their heads of theories of property that justified the status quo, he instead urged them to keep their minds focused on the spatial and thinglike reality of property. He warned the Land Company's first cottagers that "A foolish reliance upon those fascinating principles has diverted your mind from the reality—THE ACTUAL POSSESSION OF THE THING ITSELF" (qtd in Howkins 13, capitalized in original).

O'Connor gravitated toward the idea of natural rights in property that were visible, obvious, and tied to an owner by labor and private enterprise, not by government intervention. This was a concept entirely at odds with Bronterre O'Brien's advocacy of land nationalization. In O'Brien's plan, the state would act as trustee, guarding property in the land that belonged to a whole people, not to individual owners. For O'Connor, natural rights in property were given their freest expression in the relationship between owners and their small freeholds. For O'Brien, property was naturally a relationship among people, not a relationship between owner and thing owned. Natural property in land could only be collective; what was artificial was not the current arrangement of property but the idea that the land of a just society could belong to individuals at all. O'Brien argued that only the collective intervention of "a just and enlightened Legislature" could correct the artificiality of individual property (qtd in Plummer 79).

O'Connor's and O'Brien's competing notions about the proper way to restore a natural order in landed property prefigured the next half century of
debate about precisely how property in the land should work in a society that
aspired to distribute more widely the political prerogatives once reserved for
landowners alone. In some sense, they also initiated a conversation explicitly
recognizing that state power could potentially define, and possibly even redistribute, property in land, rather than merely protecting a preexisting natural
right. Proposals for land nationalization, laws enabling the freer alienation of
land, laws forbidding the transfer of land to anyone but the state, privately funded
cooperatives to aid individuals in purchasing small freeholds, government-
subsidized loans to those purchasing small freeholds, restoration of commons
rights, and a blanket tax on the profit a landlord realized in rising property
values all circulated as possibilities for land reform in the second half of the
century. These proposals had roots that went as far back as the Levellers of the
seventeenth century. They drew on Robert Owen's socialist experiments and
Thomas Spence's plans for land communally owned and controlled at the level
of the parish. But as the century progressed, schemes for land reform changed
from utopian plans drawn up by disenfranchised radicals to serious plans proposed by parliamentary members as the basis for legislation. All were pitched
as possible solutions to something dimly perceived as "the land problem"—a
problem most apparent to urban, middle-class professionals of a reforming mindset who derived very little of their income directly from the British land.[17]

The profusion of these plans, and the frequency of their proposals in the
wake of the second reform bill, signaled the increasing confusion over property
caused by the widening of the franchise. A growing tendency to see property
in terms of rights rather than objects had given the ownership of objects a mildly
threatening quality. The Reform Acts worked similar effects on the land. Once
political participation was no longer pegged to landownership, it no longer was
clear how property in the land ought to be imagined. Land's aura of exceptionality persisted, but as the model of simple thing-ownership was contested by
the model of property as a bundle of rights, the nature of its exceptionality
changed. Free traders at midcentury had argued that land's exceptional status
as property was purely a product of artificial laws. But they were succeeded in
the 1860s by economic thinkers who now insisted that land was a property unlike any other because it was not, and never could be, artificial; it could not be
created through human labor. The spatial qualities that had made landed property the archetype of all property and personhood in the eighteenth century

came to be a hallmark of its exceptional status as property since a nation composed entirely of exclusive individual property in land could never provide for the whole population what Carlyle referred to in *Past and Present (1843)* as "Earthroom for this Nation" and what Herbert Spencer more prosaically called in *Social Statics* (1851) "room for the soles of their feet." As Great Britain began to think of itself in terms of population, statistics, and economic indicators rather than in terms of territory, landed property came to seem a stubborn trace of materiality that impeded conceptualizing the nation as a whole.

Irish Ownership

British property in land, then, was far from a settled concept in the nineteenth century. Property in land operated on two different models at once: first, a space of individual autonomy for the owner, a space into which the state could not penetrate, and second, a site of communal heritage, where local face-to-face relationships obviated the need for a more centralized or bureaucratized state system. Victorians relied on both of these concepts of property in land, often without acknowledging the difference between them, when they imagined land as a haven from market relations. The nineteenth century also witnessed a new tension in paradigms of property in land. The notion that property was a bundle of rights, a relationship among people rather than a relationship between person and thing, discredited Victorian habits of imagining all property to be defined in terms of space, universally recognizable and prior to the organization of any state. The paradigm of property as a bundle of rights challenged basic British assumptions that property was the fundamental natural right the state existed to protect. It also created a situation in which, when property was imagined to be a spatialized thing, property itself came to be the fetish that might control the owner, rather than something an owner could control.

Read against the backdrop of British confusion about property, Irish rhetoric concerning property rights emerges as less troubled. This claim is a bit counterintuitive, given the complicated proprietary landscape of Ireland. The main body of landowners were the Anglo-Irish, Protestant descendants of English conquerors. Their tenants were primarily Catholic Irish. Considered to be foreigners by their tenants and extravagant, irresponsible, and unreliable by the British state, landowners in Ireland fell wide of the mark as keepers of a communal heritage and were no better models of autonomous individuals whose experience in controlling their property empowered them for wider rule. But it is precisely for this reason that Irish nationalists were able to imagine that both roles might be filled instead, and without contradiction, by an Irish population whose national consciousness would be awakened through a proprietary relationship with the land. And in doing so, Irish nationalists conceptualized Ireland as potentially a more elegant proprietary landscape than Britain was.

For this reason the Irish nationalist view gained the attention of those at the very top of the British government. In 1870, William Gladstone, proposing to change the laws of landed property in Ireland, voiced a sentiment that was at that moment gaining ground among liberal politicians and thinkers. Property, he contended, meant something entirely different in Ireland and in Britain. "All the circumstances, all the associations, and all the accretions that have grown around the native ideas are different in the one country from what they are in the other" (qtd in Healy 115). Gladstone's assertion feels a bit disingenuous; given the gathering force of proposals for land reform in Britain, it was hard to ignore the fact that "all the circumstances, all the associations, and all the accretions" of native British ideas about property were hardly unified or settled. But in focusing on a need for Irish reform over a need for British reform in land, Gladstone described the Irish situation as one in which a form of property proved culturally resistant to state incursion—and thus was resistant to both the alienations of the market and the interference of the state. Irish property in land extended the promise that such property existed, in a way that found no analogy in British property in the land.

Even the briefest sketch of Irish history under English rule makes it clear that the conditions that gave rise to contradictory meanings of landed property in Britain simply did not exist in Ireland. In its centuries' long involvement with England, an involvement marked by violent conquest and draconian suppression of Irish political power and cultural identity, Ireland proved singularly exempt from any historic tradition that the natural rights of property had led to the formation of a state that guarded the liberty of its owners. Likewise, the upheavals in the distribution of property repeated by several English invasions made impossible any illusion that existing property relations manifested a uniquely Irish character. In successive English plantations, England sent settlers to Ireland to establish political and economic control over sections of northeastern Ireland. Cromwell's brutal conquest in the seventeenth century, his relocation of huge numbers of people to the west of Ireland, the subsequent reassignment of confiscated estates to English soldiers, and the next 200 years of penal laws that prevented Irish Catholics from holding significant amounts of property also merged property arrangements with the subjection of the native Irish in a way that accentuated Ireland's status as a conquered country.

Perhaps for this reason, commentators in the nineteenth century explained Irish character in terms of economic conditions. This was a logic that closely aligned national character with property, implying Ireland's material impoverishment to be its main cultural trait while Britishness was defined by a certain pride of ownership. In 1834 a writer in the conservative Protestant organ the *Dublin University Magazine* argued that within Ireland the Protestant population was "all on the side of England, and of property and law": "They have never forgotten that they are the descendants of the original English and Scottish settlers, inheriting their names, their language, their habits, and their religion, and they are, therefore, in all their feelings and interest, attached to British connections. . . . The Protestant requires decent clothing, good feeding, and a certain portion of education for his family. He cultivates cleanliness in his house and person and displays an independence of mind and conduct in all things" (qtd in Boyce, "Weary Patriots" 23).

The native Irish relationship to property was similarly an index of national character. Writing in the same publication in 1845, Samuel Sullivan argues that the Irish landlord cannot undertake his job as paternal guide of the Irish people because of a culture of absolute poverty. After a long history of possessing barely anything at all, such peasants do not even possess the inner self-respect necessary for improvement. He observes that "in many districts their only food is the potato, their only beverage water . . . a bed or a blanket is a rare luxury, and . . . their pig and manure heap constitute their only property" (477). Their lack of conventional outer property is evidence of an even greater inner lack. Sullivan contends, "Much of what is lamentable in their condition arises out of their insensibility to miseries which would be felt by the corresponding class in England or in Scotland." He concludes, "*the great want* in Ireland, as regards the labouring classes, is *the want of wants.*" If a landlord is to succeed at any improvement at all, he will have to "raise the standard of personal and domestic comfort in their own minds" (477–78, emphasis in original).

These oft-repeated "truths" about Irish and British character provided, in addition to an explanatory framework for Britain's treatment of Ireland as less than equal, a reassuring vision of property as visibly, recognizably, and meaningfully attached to a particular owner. Sullivan's estimation of the Irish peasant's inner poverty as marked by his outer lack of possessions appeals to the belief that outer possessions, even in the age of political economy's abstractions, still index an inner worth. That British writers made conventional the figure of the spiritually impoverished, materially bereft Irishman suggests that the presence of the Irish actually reinforced what was otherwise a waning belief in property's thinglike qualities. If the Irish were a dispossessed lot, the British encounter with Irish dispossession reassured the British of the visibility and irreducible correspondence between inner identity and outer property. The neat homes and clean clothes of the British working class might stand as proof of their respectable and propertied inner selves.

The Irish presence in England also sent commentators scrambling back to the idea of property in things as the basis of their economic analysis. This happens perhaps most famously in Friedrich Engels's *The Condition of the Working Class in England* (1845), which enumerates the outer signs of Irish dispossession in a list much like Sullivan's: "The worst dwellings are good enough for them; their clothing causes them little trouble, so long as it hold together by a single thread; shoes they know not; their food consists of potatoes and potatoes only . . . What does such a race want with high wages?" (102). Engels's analysis generalizes to a national level Sullivan's observations on Irish dispossession. He speculates that, on the whole, Irish labor power belongs not to Ireland but to England. After all, English industry could never have grown so quickly "if England had not possessed in the numerous and impoverished population of Ireland a reserve at command" (101). But if Irish labor is an English possession to be commanded, it is one that, like all objects of property, has the potential to change the character of the owner. Engels treats Irish poverty as dangerously contagious in the levels of dispossession it introduces into the general population of the industrial cities where the Irish flock for employment. Forced to compete with the Irish, whose inner lack of self-possession leaves them without a need to display their respectable selfhoods in material property, the English find themselves forced to adjust ever lower their own understanding of what subsistence-level wages are. As Engels observes: "The Irish have as Dr Kay says, discovered the minimum of the necessities of life, and are now making the English workers acquainted with it" (103).

The Property of Irish Nationalism

Already implicit in these negative assessment of Irish relationships with property was the sense of an astonishing Irish autonomy, resistant to outside interference.

Irish nationalists who aligned themselves with the Young Ireland movement honed in on British statements about Irish dispossession and exploited them for what they might prove about Irish autonomy. At midcentury, nationalists began to associate an Irish sense of dispossession with what they asserted to be a coherent and organically constituted Irish cultural character, the product of a collective, indigenous memory immediately palpable to the native Irish. This nationalist vision had the effect of making Irish dispossession paradoxically similar to the spatialized conception of property as a clearly recognizable relationship between person and thing.

The transition from the early-century Irish nationalism headed up by Daniel O'Connell to the more separatist rhetoric of the Young Ireland nationalists in the 1840s might be characterized as a transition whose more open resistance to the British state evolved with the state's increasing comprehensiveness. O'Connell, a devout Catholic landlord and fervent disciple of Jeremy Bentham, led a nationalist movement primarily geared toward increased civil rights for Irish Catholics, who he hoped might then integrate more fully into British politics and society. O'Connell coordinated large-scale campaigns for Irish Catholic political rights based on the idea that no profound cultural barrier existed that might bar them from full membership in the British state. While tirelessly advocating for increased political rights for Catholics—he headed the campaign that finally resulted in Catholic emancipation in 1828 and, as a result, was the first Catholic to take a seat in Parliament since the Civil War—O'Connell did so under the cloak of a utilitarianism that treated all men as equal, rather than as alienated by intractable cultural divides. His nationalism was geared toward concrete action for increased Irish civil liberties and away from the cultural associations that might suggest the Irish to be anything other than unmarked British citizens, equal to all others. His apathy toward any sort of cultural nationalism that might be used to exclude the Irish from a broader British public sphere can be read in his markedly unsentimental comment on the decline of the Irish language: "The superior utility of the English tongue, as the medium of all modern communication, is so great that I can witness without a sigh the gradual disuse of Irish."[18]

O'Connell's stance was almost the polar opposite of that taken in the 1840s by Young Ireland, a group of loosely associated Irish nationalists. Young Ireland espoused a more romantic vision of Irish culture and a more rigid rhetoric of separation from the British state. Its leaders were more comfortable invoking a unique Irish culture as the grounds of Irish agency, and they were able, surprisingly, to turn the stereotype of dispossession to good account. They were all at one time involved in writing for the *Nation*, a paper whose motto was "to create and foster public opinion, and to make it racy of the soil" (qtd in Duffy 63). But in imbuing their writing with the native flavor of Ireland, they implicitly agreed with critics like Engels and Sullivan, who imply that what the Irish do not have is what they are. The landlessness that signified Ireland's degeneration to the British was to Young Ireland a clear rallying point around which all the Irish could unite in a nationalist agenda. In fact, their sense of dispossession from the land allowed them to depend on its symbolic valences in ways that British land, with its nineteenth-century contradictions, could never be deployed. After all, with the British state distanced from the Anglo-Irish landowner whose legitimacy it called into question, land in Ireland stood neither for the individual liberty of its owners (who were often absent from it and disidentified with its locality) nor for the communal heritage of the nation. The split that had troubled the meaning of land in Britain never touched Irish land. Thus, Irish nationalists could do what no British writer could do unproblematically and assert land as the site of a national autonomy that gave liberty to individual owners but might also be shared nationally without any disruption of cultural unity or privacy.

Thomas Davis, one of the founding members of Young Ireland, adhered to a specifically Irish logic of property in land when he recommended acquisition of land as the measure that would restore a sense of collective national identity to the Irish. He condemns as fantasy those who imagine the absentee landlord returning to "deal out justice, economy, and seed oats to his wondering tenants who learn from him farming, quiet, loyalty, and Church-of-Englandism." All schemes for the improvement of Ireland are fruitless, he asserts, "while the very land, ay, *Ireland itself, belongs not to the people, is not tilled for the people!* Redress this and your palliatives will be needless, your projects will be realized" ("Udalism" 145, emphasis in original).

Even though he primarily addressed an urban middle class, he envisioned Ireland's true character as a self-sufficient agrarian culture able to resist integration into British economic and political networks, which worked in concert far more obviously in Ireland than they did in Britain. In the years before Union, England's prohibition on Irish exports to all but British ports and its systematic discouragement of the development of Irish manufacturing had made the Irish economy as much a matter of law as of political economy, and Young Ireland advocated a resistance to both. In his columns for the Young Ireland paper *The Nation*, Davis returns repeatedly to the virtues of home manufacture, both in the sense of goods produced in domestic privacy and in the sense of goods made and consumed within a national community whose economic boundaries are enforced by taxes on imports and exports. For Davis there is no difference. Davis's home can resist the well-integrated British state and market at once. Davis's focus on homes bounded by self-sufficiency and nations bounded by their own systems of exchange also emphasizes property's ability to signal to others where it begins and ends—and thus where it belongs. Even portable property made within the home space of Ireland can be a source of inalienable identity. Commending the textiles produced through "home industry," Davis contends, "Clothes manufactured by hand-work . . . are more natural and national than factory goods" ("Commercial" 135).

Davis's Young Ireland compatriots echoed this idea of an Ireland whose material products signal a national identity. If the Irish commodity could be properly recognized as a "home product," its theft could also be made recognizable. In his writing on the Irish midcentury famine, James Fintan Lalor assumes the possibility of such recognition, contending that the British "took the whole of the harvest and left hunger to those who raised it" ("Letter" 62). John Mitchel, who tirelessly propagated the thesis that the famine arose from Britain's conscious genocidal intention to wipe out the Irish, accused the British of perverting the circulation of Irish goods and thus making home products unrecognizable to the Irish: "Irishmen have been taught to look so long to England as the ruler and disposer and owner of all things Irish, that we scarce know our own plunder when the plunderers send a small pittance back to us in the form of alms" (*Last Conquest* 133).

Mitchel's scrutiny of the famine mirrors a Marxist analysis of the worker estranged from the product he has made, no longer able to recognize the rights he has to it. But this Irish version of consciousness-raising does not lead to global revolution—in fact, it leads nowhere. Irish property can only point back to a bounded Irish community whose attachment to it resists the chronology of either a Lockean narrative of the founding of the state or a Marxist vision of class warfare leading to the end of history. Mitchel's indictment of British relief efforts during the famine illustrates how Irish property could exist somewhat outside of history. "The reason why we want relief and they can give it," he argues, "is just that our substance has been carried away, and they have it" (133).

His evocative phrase—"our substance"—implies that the British have taken what belongs to the Irish, and that they have taken the essence of what the Irish are. That both are the same admits of no Lockean moment where a mixing of persons with the external world created property. And having been taken, it has not stopped being "our substance." The British, in his analysis, participate in an event in time—there clearly was a before and an after marked by the taking— but it is an entirely British event with no final impact on the Irish. Chartists might argue that they needed land to make them recognizable as persons of consequence deserving the same political rights as those who already held land. But Irish rhetoric of the same period resisted the Lockean timeline in which labor in one's self comes first and its mixture with the outer world comes next. Instead, Young Ireland fused Irish identity, Irish possession of the land, and even Irish dispossession from it into one irreducible bond.

Perhaps the most influential formulation of this idea came from Lalor during the high tide of the famine. Responding to members of Young Ireland who had grown impatient for the repeal of Union, Lalor argued that a "mightier question" than repeal loomed. For Lalor, the nationalist struggle was not about attending to history at all; instead it meant heeding the autonomy that was both property and nation. The fundamental struggle is about "Ireland her own— Ireland her own, and all therein, from the sod to the sky. The soil of Ireland for the people of Ireland, to have and to hold from God alone who gave it—to have and to hold to them and their heirs for ever, without suit or service, faith or fealty, rent or render, to any power under Heaven" ("To the Editor" 57). Without even the structure of subject and predicate, "Ireland her own" resists placement in time. Trading in the abstraction of "repeal" for the materiality of "soil," Lalor subordinates all political questions to an intense bond between Irish people and the land. His assertion of national autonomy refuses the disaggregation of powers that Irish landlords suffered, just as it refuses the notion that the state might define this property: "The entire ownership of Ireland, moral and material, up to the sun, and down to the center, is vested of right in the people of Ireland; . . . they and none but they are the land-owners and law-makers of this island; . . . all laws are null and void not made by them; and all titles to land invalid not conferred and confirmed by them" (60–61). His assertion also insists on the powerful thingness of property in Ireland, which foils even attempts to represent it with signs that substitute for its thingness. For Lalor, "the enjoyment of the people . . . of first ownership of the soil" is a more essential fact than the "mock freedom" promised by "constitutions, and charters and articles and franchises" whose substance is mere "paper and parchment"

(61). In establishing the organic interconnectedness of people, land, property, and language, Lalor emphatically denies that Ireland is subject to the complicated chain of market exchanges. In fact, he calls into question whether land can even be represented by linguistic signifiers at all.

Lalor's insistence on a rhetoric of landownership can in part be attributed to political strategizing. Young Ireland and the nationalists who followed them sought ways to merge the urban intelligentsia's concerns about self-government with the popular force of the more pragmatically minded rural population to whom questions of land were also questions of survival. Rural interest in repeal, Lalor argues, is not "native or spontaneous" and so a desire for it can not be naturally impressed on rural minds as desire for land can ("To the Irish Confederate" 72). Implicit in his assessment about what will work among the untaught Irish is an assumption about property's instant and universal recognizability. Property, always anchored in the thingness of the land, could be read and understood by the majority of the population, even if abstractions about political rights could not. For Lalor, this leads to a vision of government that always begins—in a fundamentally Lockean way—in the land.

But in imagining Irish land as outside of a chain of economic, legal, or linguistic signifiers, Lalor also taps into a nationalist logic that goes beyond mere strategic recruitment of rural constituents for the nationalist cause. His sense of how attachment to the land works—as a timeless and material fact unmolested by chains of economic or linguistic exchange—is a common motif in Irish nationalist discourse. Davis's essay on "Our National Language"—an essay whose advocacy for the use of the native Irish influenced Douglas Hyde's efforts to de-Anglicize Ireland later in the century—ties the irreducibility of Irish as native language to the Irish land's own self-referentiality. Urging his readers to recover the Irish language as a way to experience solidarity with the Irish nation, Davis equates the particularity of the Irish language with the particularity of land: "The hills, and lakes, and rivers, and forts and castles, the churches and parishes, the baronies and counties around you, have all Irish names—names which describe the nature of the scenery or ground, the name of founder, or chief, or priest, or the leading fact in the history of the place" (102). The complete coincidence of sign and signified, he argues, is in fact the nature of both language and land in Ireland. Referring to the Irish-language definitions that lurk within their names, he argues of the Irish landscape, "Meath tells its [own] flatness, Clonmel the abundant riches of its valleys, Fermanagh is the land of the Lakes" (103).

Davis associates a profound cultural self-referentiality with an autarkic national economy: both the intellectual and real property of such systems exclude outsiders. In other writing, he attributes this dual impenetrability to Norway, a nation of peasant proprietors that he sees as a potential model for an independent Irish nation. Norway, he argues, needs to be known by all who are interested in national systems of smallholding, but knowing Norway can be a challenge because its very system renders it nobly inaccessible: "Norway sits alone self-revering, not dependent on fame, nor urged to complain—nearly silent"—as silent as Davis saw the Irish land to those unacquainted with the Irish language ("Udalism" 138).

Inalienable Dispossession

Davis's vision of an entirely autonomous Ireland was a vision of property that was also culture. He imagined this property as resistant to a state whose control over both the economy and citizens' day-to-day lives was more absolute than the same state's control on British soil. There are two particularly relevant features of this imagined resistance of Irish property to the British state. The first lies in the fact that both Irish and British came to imagine Irish property to be secured as property through the feelings of its owners, independently of all law. This independence from law creates the second, more paradoxical, feature of Irish property—the fact that the British despoliation of Ireland created the occasion that allowed the Irish to assert their native attachment to the land to be more forceful and more enduring than a British attachment could ever be.

Young Ireland maintained they had property that gave them privacy from the state, as well as shelter from the endless circulation of the market. They did so in arguments in which the notion of cultural and economic autarky mattered more than the native status of those who enjoyed such autarky. They described Irish national property as one whose ownership was determined largely by what seemed to be self-willed affect. While they insisted that Irish property bore a meaningful relationship to its owner's identity, they also treated it as an identity that came, not from the owner's lineage, but from the owner's proprietary attitude toward the property. In the course of his revolutionary rhetoric, in which he threatens to strip landlords of their "robbers' rights," Lalor declares that all will be considered tenants of the nation so long as they "bear full, true, and undivided fealty, and allegiance to the nation, and the laws of the nation" ("To the Editor" 61). He declares that "to all who own land or are living in Ireland, Ireland henceforth must be the Queen-island" ("To the Irish Confederate" 17). The simultaneously absolute and action-free requirement of allegiance to a "Queen-island" by which all Irishmen must hold their land makes the condition of ownership a feeling, rather than a matter of entitlement assigned from an outside authority. And it is a feeling in no way biologically racial. Taking up this theme, Davis makes the very condition of being native depend on emotions: Landlords who make Ireland their queen can be sure that "Ireland is yours for ages" because they "will be Irishmen, in name, in faith, in fact" ("A New Nation" 38).

Lalor's and Davis's avoidance of racial or nativist rhetoric is of a piece with Young Ireland's cross-sectarian ambitions. They hoped to create a sense of Irish national character that transcended Catholic and Protestant divides; thus, they sought to avoid implying that the Catholic peasant might claim a more native status than could the Anglo-Irish landlord or members of the very small Catholic and Protestant urban middle class to which many of them belonged. In using the rhetoric of ownership, rather than the rhetoric of nativism, to imagine an Irish nation, Young Ireland does for the Irish nation what anthropologist Marilyn Strathern asserts all claims of ownership can do: "Ownership re-embeds ideas and products in an organism. . . . Ownership gathers things momentarily to a point by locating them in the owner, halting endless dissemination, effecting an identity" (177). In asserting "Ireland her own—Ireland her own, and all therein, from the sod to the sky," Lalor might be seen as calling Ireland into being, a ritual the patriots of the 1916 Easter uprising repeated when they announced, "We declare the right of the people of Ireland to the ownership of Ireland." Such an ownership was supposed to animate the people on whom it endowed identity, inspiring them to acts of martyrdom in its name. Framed in national terms, Irish property in land was far from the potentially agency-draining fetish that it was in mid-Victorian British novels. Instead, it was a genuinely life-sustaining property, animating its owners both physically through its agricultural powers and spiritually through its national powers.

In Young Ireland's account of the ownership of Ireland, what makes Irish property, nation, and people mutually self-generating, self-identifying, and resistant to all state and economic interference is the impenetrable nature of their attachment. Rather than being about deservingness proven over time or essential identity, Young Ireland depicted Irish property as a zone of fiercely deployed emotion, whose exact nature was opaque. Indeed, constant reference to Irish "native feeling" in the remainder of the nineteenth century dwelt on both the difficulty of interpreting it and the extent to which it determined a real Irish relationship with the land. But its opacity was also what made it such an inclusive criteria for imagining membership in a nation.

Possessive Irish native feelings were seen as organizing the social structure of the rural Irish peasantry. Ireland was often characterized in the press as a violent landscape of secret societies and grassroots associations that sprung up among the peasantry—White Boys, Ribbon Men, Rockites—who enforced through extralegal means a moral economy of Irish rights. Informal "soldiers" in the tithe wars made sure that fellow tenants collectively refused to pay tithes and that those who collected them would regret their cooperation with the National (Protestant) Church of Ireland. Secret brotherhoods resisted unfair rents with coordinated refusal to pay. Native feeling equaled native right in nineteenth-century Ireland, not just in nationalist rhetoric, but in the day-to-day resistance of Irish peasants to economic exploitation. That this resistance grew from the ground up, in secret, among men who were uneducated and often illiterate gave all nationalist assertions of Irish right and Irish feeling a durable aura. "Deep and dark in the inmost soul and in the inner life of the peasant," the Irish Protestant parliamentary member Isaac Butt says, "lies the ever present remembrance that the whole soil of Ireland was wrested from its rightful possessors" (*Land Tenure* 47). In the dim recesses of Irish memory, Butt imagines a landed inalienability that comes entirely from feelings.

Butt was hardly alone in this view of the Irish attachment to land through cultural memory. Lord John O'Hagan, who would later serve as a Gladstone-appointed head of the Irish Land Commissions, announced to the Social Science Association that the ancient Brehon laws of Ireland "manifest the principles and peculiar notions which guided the Irish in their dealings with the land, and which to this hour, have not ceased to operate, through dim tradition, on our actual state." Friedrich Engels, too, commented that the Irish system of law that had once been "forcibly broken up by the English" nonetheless "still lives today in the consciousness of the people" (both qtd in Laird 22). A writer for the *Fortnightly Review* categorized the condition of Ireland as a "chronic social war in which one side relied upon the letter and the power of the law, and the other upon an instinctive sense of justice" ("Irish Land Question" 393). Matthew Arnold echoed this sentiment that an instinctive memory of what came before conquest never precisely dissipated: "The sense of prescription, the true security of all property never arose. The angry memory of conquest and confiscation . . . have continued to irritate and inflame men's minds" ("Incompatibles" 279).

As Arnold's comment begins to suggest, this common wisdom about the persistence of Irish attachment to property through an internalized cultural memory, contains within it one of the most dizzying contradictions of Irish nationalism in the nineteenth century: the British conquest of Ireland came to prove the Irish possession of an inviolable national character. Located in a group folk memory, the sense of what the Irish might rightfully call theirs could not be addressed or dismantled with legal or economic precision. Instead, the persistent sense of having had something taken from them might outdo legal possession in sheer durability. It certainly allowed the Irish and British alike to imagine a bond indissoluble by state power. In fact, it was a bond that was only made more palpable by state power's repeated attempts to disrupt it. In defending the idea that "the ordinary Irish peasant is by no means an unhappy man," Anthony Trollope cites this superior Irish sense of ownership, made discernible through disruption: "[The Irish peasant's] cabin, small, smoky, ill-conditioned, is his own, with a feeling of ownership that rarely belongs to the English cottier. We know that he may be ejected,—and we know, too, what he may do when ejected; but the very violence of his proceedings in that emergency shows how strong within him was that sense of possession" ("What Does Ireland Want?" 287). Even in writings such as Trollope's, not fully sympathetic to Irish grievances, the respect for private property that was supposed to be the native characteristic of the English paled in comparison to the possessiveness of the Irish. Unlike the English vision of a constitution forever evolving toward a more perfect respect for private property, Young Ireland's vision of Irish national property depended on no history at all. The national character of Irish attachment to property variously called "Ireland," "the land," and "the soil" was perpetually present and perpetually made apparent by British attempts to pull Irish land into a history of conquest.

The Young Ireland formulation of Irish cultural property proved persuasive even to the British public, which after midcentury increasingly sympathized with legislative measures designed to legally restore what was assumed to be an Irish attachment to the Irish land. Abruptly reversing what had been a forty-year legislative trend toward making Irish land more alienable, the Irish Land Acts of 1871 and 1880 codified into law a "tenant right," also called "Ulster Custom," whose long persistence in custom, proponents of the Acts argued, aligned it with long-lived native sentiment. In the north of Ireland this tenant right was used routinely as security for loans to a tenant, and in many parts of Ireland, the right was willed to a tenant's survivors or auctioned to pay off a tenant's debts. Precisely what the right *was*, however, was a matter of controversy. Some said it was a transaction that ensured the incoming tenant had the neighbors' goodwill; some said it was compensation for improvements the outgoing tenant had made; some said it stood for the tenant's right to stay in that property undisturbed as long as he paid the rent. Its presence at least in the Ulster informal economy, however, suggested that customary arrangements recognized a tenant's right to his property to operate in at least an analogous fashion to the landlord's right. The tenant's ability to buy and sell some right associated with the property he rented signaled his status as a sort of co-owner of the land.[19]

In debating the measures contained in both Land Acts, legislators and nationalists alike dwelt on the difficulty of articulating the precise nature of the attachment, which seemed to be nourished in equal parts by both possession and dispossession. Documenting Irish agitation for land rights, the nationalist Charles Gavan Duffy explained the Irish Land League as the product of the peasantry's "living claim as the descendants of those who had owned the land in common with the Celtic chiefs and had been wrongfully deprived of their property" (qtd in Steele, *Irish Land* 19). Even Prime Minister William Gladstone, in proposing the bill that would change Irish land laws, proved confused about whether the British state had ever affected Irish property at all. In Ireland, he noted, "the old Irish ideas and customs were never supplanted except by the rude hand of violence and by laws written in the statute book, but never entering into the heart of the Irish people" (qtd in Steele, *Irish Land* 41).

In this emphasis on the impenetrable nature of the attachment that appears as both possession and dispossession, British and Irish alike imagined that rather than being about essential identity, Irish property was a zone of fiercely deployed emotion. Located in a group folk memory, the sense of what the Irish might rightfully call theirs could not be addressed or dismantled with legal or economic precision. However, the fact that British, Anglo-Irish, and Irish all understood an Irish sense of right to the land as founded in Irish dispossession from it also suggests a vision more complicated than raw native attachment. The British conquest of Ireland came to prove the Irish possessed an inviolable national character. It allowed for the imagination of a bond indissoluble by state power. In fact, it was a bond that was only made more palpable by state power's repeated attempts to disrupt it.

The Irish Land Acts and the British Advantages of Dual Ownership

At first glance the Irish Land Acts appear designed to shatter the absolute and thinglike nature of the ownership of Irish land that Young Ireland celebrated. After all, the staggered passage of the two bills formalized the different treatment of land in different parts of Ireland. The First Land Act of 1870 only affected a limited number of properties in the north, where Ulster Custom was already observed. The Second Land Act of 1881 extended the practice to all of Ireland. Together, the two acts emphasized property as a relation among people rather than a one-on-one relationship between owner and thing owned. They guaranteed tenants a right to remain at will on the land they rented, provided that they continued regular payments to the landlord. This recognition of a tenant's right to remain on property legally owned by someone else—and the accompanying acknowledgement that a tenant might also sell that right or even borrow against it—was understood as instituting a legal co-proprietorship of the land.[20] That commentators largely greeted the acts as a startling violation of a landowner's "sole and despotic dominion" in his estate suggests that the measures integrated Irish land into the "bundle of rights" model of property, in which different owners might have competing abstract rights. But the rhetoric the British used to describe their motives for passing the bills emphasized instead the holistic nature of Irish property and the policy of noninterference the new laws espoused.

Aware of the brewing demands for British land reform at home, Prime Minister William Gladstone sought a solution to the Irish land problem that would allow the state to intervene in Ireland without creating any sort of precedent for state interference with English property. He was particularly attentive to thinkers who argued that the precedent for allowing tenants the fixity of tenure that agrarian organizers were demanding lay in Ulster Tenant Right, a right bought from outgoing tenants by incoming tenants, without reference to the landlord.[21] It was the ostensible historical and cultural specificity of this arrangement that Gladstone latched onto in trying to allot fixed tenure to insecure Irish tenants, and he emphasized the acts' status as preservation and conservation, rather than innovation. The Bessborough commission, appointed in 1879 to investigate the workings of the 1870 Land Act, recommended its extension in the name of "giving legal recognition to the existing state of things" (qtd in Bull 89).

That the Land Acts even passed through Parliament was largely due to the rather new popularity gained by Henry Sumner Maine's historicist maxim that all property proceeded from status to contract. For the legal theorist Maine, the original unit of society was the family, not the Lockean man mixing his labor with the land: "ancient law knew nothing of individuals" (*Ancient* 214). The movement of history, he argued, gradually tended toward a more contractual model, in which individuals might exercise proprietary power independently of their political or family positions, but only in limited ways and over a limited category of things. The traces of more primitive property arrangements could still be found alive and well in cultures where the basic social unit is the village community, "an assemblage of co-proprietors" who assume themselves to share a common origin and who allot property rights to individual families only with the understanding that when families became extinct, their property would return to the village unit. Absolute property, controlled wholly by one individual without social interference, was entirely a modern invention, one that reached its fullest development in the feudal aftermath of modern England. And while Maine strongly felt that the attainment of a contract society was the apotheosis of civilization and a thing to be strongly desired, he pointed out that it was also rare enough to make British mercantilism the exception, not the rule.

John Stuart Mill and, even more prominently, the former Indian administrator George Campbell saw in Maine's theories an explanation for all of Ireland's ills. Maine's own investigation of the ancient Brehon laws of Ireland in the mid-1870s openly disputed the uses to which these men put his theories in regard to Ireland; in Maine's scholarly estimation, there had been no violent Norman imposition of absolute ownership onto an archaic communal Irish law and thus there existed no need for any return to less individuated forms of property.[22] But Mill and Campbell, and most importantly Gladstone, found explanatory powers in Maine's dual model of, on the one hand, an ancient society in which all powers of property had been aggregated in one communally defined unit and, on the other, an advanced society in which the functions of proprietary power had disaggregated across several domains (family, government, the marketplace) and into the hands of individuals. George Campbell, who had seen Maine's notions of a primitive "village community" style of ownership put to the purpose of land reform in India, argued extensively that in Ireland, too, native ideas of property had little resemblance to what the English meant by property. Exhorting his readers to remember Maine's maxim "that in certain stages of society things depend rather on 'status' than on contract," Campbell argued that "Great Britain is almost the only country in the world" that has brought the notion of contract to bear so extensively on land.

The Maine-ite analyses of Irish land by Campbell, Mill, and Gladstone won in the end, but the political effects of the Irish Land Acts were negligible. The acts did almost nothing to defuse an increasingly aggressive separatist sentiment in Ireland. By 1879 the Land League in Ireland had already launched its Land War to agitate for lower rents and occupier-owned farms. Headed by former Fenian Michael Davitt and leader of the Irish Parliamentary party Charles Parnell, the National Land League combined the Irish tradition of clandestine organized resistance with more official government channels to work toward their broadly stated goal of "[t]he land of Ireland for the people of Ireland." Buying and redistributing land, rather than sharing it, quickly took center stage in the Irish land question, and by the early 1880s the question of Irish Home Rule had upstaged even land agitation. The political climate in Ireland, especially after 1880, had little use for a rhetoric of shared ownership. Given this new direction in the nationalist agenda, the First Land Act stands as a historic milestone mainly for its Bright Clauses, which encouraged full tenant ownership through a government program that purchased land from the landlords and sold it to tenants at reasonable rates. This rather minor codicil took on retrospective importance as a faint forerunner of the 1903 Wyndham Acts, which made such programs the central administrative policy of Irish land.

But revisions in Irish land law hardly yield a straightforward history in which attempts in the 1870s and 1880s to appeal to customary law were inevitably overcome by the naturally more autonomous arrangement of absolute property in the land and its analog, an independent nation-state. Instead, the acts provided legal channels through which tenants could, and increasingly did, call on the state to intervene in rent disputes. The short-term outcome of the Land Acts' passage was that tenants became more immediately enmeshed in the apparatus of Union government in order to obtain individual property rights. For the Irish, wresting ownership away—stick by stick from the bundle, as it were—from the Anglo-Irish meant submitting to British-created land courts. Repeating the mantra that they had misunderstood the Irish cultural relationship to property, the British in the last three decades of the century established these courts to assign legal title to native claims. The land courts were set up to translate into law what a writer in *The Economist* called at the time "an undetermined sort of property" based in native feeling (qtd in Steele 263). The tenant under British law was treated as experiencing a deep ancestral attachment to the land, which the state would recognize in an imprecise translation into a right to what were called the 3 Fs—fixity of tenure, fair rent, and freedom to sell the right to the first two to another tenant. The establishment of the land courts enmeshed Irish subjects further into the British state, requiring Irish tenants to turn to the British state to make a legitimate title out of the possessive feelings they experienced. The emphasis on the impenetrable nature of Irish feelings, which proved the property's existence prior to state interference, also cleared a space for the relationship to proceed without any natural endpoint. Since both sides acknowledged that the legal language of Britain could only asymptotically approach the ineffable feeling of Irish right, the process would always be in need of revision and fine-tuning.

Such a situation falls wide of romantic interpretations of Irish history, in which nineteenth-century nationalism is seen as informed by a racial memory of tribal ownership, a memory that made contractual possessive individualism incoherent to most Irish. Such interpretations might be found in historian Oliver MacDonagh's assessment that "two world-pictures (or at least two societal pictures) of great power and range were in collision, whenever property[,] and in particular landed property, was being considered" (34). Drawing on Henry Sumner Maine's maxim that the progress of all societies moves from status to contract, MacDonagh argues that, having moved from status to contract, the British could only understand possession as "an absolute condition," whereas "the Irish tenant was pursuing a line of reasoning that never intersected the atomistic contractual" (34, 45). For MacDonagh, this rule of thumb explains the clash between Irish and British viewpoints; it also offers him the vantage from which to survey both the Irish tendency toward status and the British tendency toward contract. However, he fails to acknowledge that this rule was already available to those thinking on the Irish question. MacDonagh downplays the fact that the British administration called on Maine's authority to address British-Irish tensions. He only invokes Maine's notion of early societies dominated by status and late societies structured by contract to explain why there were tensions at all. Terry Eagleton's explanation of the First Land Act as "founded on a whole series of misreadings" between "two texts, the [English] one written and contractual, the [Irish] other tacit and traditional" similarly elides the long history that such theories had in dictating the official terms of the Irish debate. He recapitulates Campbell's announcement that "in Ireland a landlord is not a landlord and a tenant is not a tenant—in the English sense" without acknowledging that such an understanding was the instrument used by both Irish nationalists and the British state to think about ownership (*Heathcliff* 140; Campbell 5).[23]

MacDonagh's and Eagleton's accounts leave out the fact that Maine's was a form of cultural tolerance that came at a high cost. In imagining a natural Irish tendency toward group property, the British exempted themselves from accusations of infringement on Irish rights, since those rights were clearly not based on contract. Thus, even though Mill, Gladstone, and ultimately the British state used Maine's historicist explanation of property to recognize a significantly enhanced proprietary right for the Irish, proprietary historicism could be— and was—also used to excuse the British from any obligation to participate in fair and equal material dealings with the Irish because it treated ideas of individual contractual obligations as absent from Irish culture. Campbell's advocacy of Irish tenant right, like Maine's approach to theorizing and administering the law in India, removed the need to reconcile an external policy of rule by conquest with an internal policy of civil rule by consent. Through the logic of culturally relative degrees of ownership, a country could now be under British administration and simultaneously belong—in its own way—to its own people. One can see this in Campbell's vision of the Irish population as one that naturally craved only limited forms of dual ownership. Campbell contended that no Irish land purchase scheme was necessary since, as his exposition has shown, "[i]t really seems that the Irish peasantry scarcely desire to own land in our sense—it is contrary to the custom of the country" (75). Instead, he assures his readers that tenants prefer to hold their farms under customary tenures, when it is permitted. Such declarations add up to a narrative in which the British government can give up its desire to impose British ideas of property on Ireland and still not really lose anything at all. The Irish might own the land in their own way, and the British might go on controlling the same land in theirs.

Campbell's observations were marked by the same sense that the British government—both colonial and at home—needed to distinguish itself by its forbearance in imposing its norms on other cultures. George Campbell, much like John Stuart Mill, argues that "part of our own proper strength must be put aside to keep Ireland," including the proper strength of an English proprietary power (4). Part of the ease with which Campbell recommends such forbearance is due to his conviction that what the British surrender matters far more to the Irish than to the British. Because property for the Irish resembles British property in name only, Campbell predicts that "a reasonable surrender of some of the extreme legal rights of property" will affect Anglo-Irish landlords only as a matter of "sentiments" (15).

The idea that one might experience ownership as a sentiment rather than as a legally assigned right haunts not just the discourse most explicitly connected to the land acts but also fiction only loosely associated with it. My next chapter shows how Anthony Trollope divides the labor of ownership in the British Isles into legal ownership and affective enjoyment. His vision is haunted, I argue, by the structure of the Irish Land Acts, whose possible features were just beginning to be discussed in 1865, as he began his six-novel Palliser series, centered on the everyday lives of characters at the heart of the British state—in Parliament. It is Trollope who provides the most vivid redirection of the Irish Land Acts' scheme of Anglo-Irish landlord and the Irish tenant harmoniously dividing between them rights to, and feelings about, the same property in land. In the Palliser series, he takes this dynamic and projects it onto the entire structure of the British state.

CHAPTER FOUR

The Wife of State

Ireland and England's Vicarious Enjoyment
in Anthony Trollope's Palliser Novels

The famine that was so catastrophic for the Irish proved perversely fruitful for
the aspiring social commentator—especially the aspiring social commentator
on land ownership. Close to the same time when John Stuart Mill was pro-
pounding his theories about the need for peasant proprietorships in Ireland
and when Young Ireland were articulating their demands for a national ownership of Ireland, a surveyor's clerk for the Irish postal system wrote to the
London newspaper the *Examiner* elaborating on what he saw as the causes and
effects of the famine. Unlike Young Ireland, Anthony Trollope did not see the
British state as the force that Ireland needed to resist. Instead, he shared Mill's
faith in the ability of the British state to act effectively in the Irish crisis. His
faith, in fact, far outstripped Mill's. Free of Mill's nervous sense that state interference with Ireland could easily go awry, Trollope's letters enthusiastically
championed the British measures taken during the famine, even those with
immediate ill effects.

Trollope composed his letters as a response to those published in the *Times*
by philanthropist Sidney Godolphin Osborne condemning British state intervention in the famine. Such intervention, Osborne contended, was inefficient

and had produced a lazy and dependent Irish population that now expected to be fed by the government without any exertion on their part. In his response, Trollope defended even the moves of the state that produced bad consequences. He concedes that the public works undertaken were often useless and ineffi-cient. "Idle habits were engendered," he admits, "fraud was made easy, and . . . last and worst, the people were taught to know that if they do not work and feed themselves, others must work and feed them" ("Trollope's [Six] Letters" 83). Yet none of these consequences could have been avoided, given the magnitude of the task and the severity of the time constraints. Trollope holds firmly to his argument that "the salvation of life was the object, the ill effects were known to be unavoidable" (75).

Trollope's stance might seem surprising given his reputation for interpret-ing the famine in terms of strict classical economy. His best-known pronounce-ment on the famine comes ten years after his *Examiner* letters were written, in his novel *Castle Richmond* (1860). In the novel, which awkwardly joins the hor-rors of the famine to an upper-class plot of romance and family secrets, Trol-lope pronounces his verdict that the famine was a "mercy" in the Malthusian sense of wiping out an excess population and giving survivors better access to the limited resources available.[1] But in his letters written in the immediate after-math of famine, he instead emphasizes the fundamental goodness of a government that saved lives and held starvation at bay, and he imagines government interven-tion will continue to have the same power.

Trollope, like Mill, imagines that a positive government intervention would create owners who then might experience a direct relationship to the state. In his long exposition of the problems of Irish agriculture, Trollope names as most pernicious among the developments of the early-nineteenth-century Irish economy the development of a middle layer of land-letters between the land-lords and the tenants. Enabled by rapidly rising rent prices at the start of the century, this "race of landlords," as Trollope will later call them, "gave up their occupation, sublet their lands at a great profit, dubbed themselves estated gen-tlemen, and betook themselves to the race-course and the fox-covert" ("Trol-lope's [Six] Letters" 94, 78). Now, he contends, these same landlords, without capital of their own to invest in the land, separate the Irish from the state. They drive good tenants off the land and to America and force impoverished tenants into the workhouse, raising poor rates even higher for their fellow landlords. According to Trollope, the government's best intervention into this situation is the Encumbered Estates Bill, passed in 1849 to ease restriction on the sale of deeply mortgaged estates. The bill was designed to rid Ireland of its most in-competent landlords—who were themselves only renters—and attract new buyers of land with more competence and capital. While the Encumbered Estates Bill imagined a much larger scale of land ownership than did Mill's peasant propri-etary, it shared Mill's aim of building peaceful and productive relationships between the state and the proprietors it would create.

Trollope's endorsement of the Unencumbered Estates Act shows the same preoccupation with a definition of the "true Irish" that James Fintan Lalor showed (see chapter 3). And like Lalor before him, Trollope makes true Irishness about the correct form of land ownership. But where Lalor relies on a patriotic affect to convert Anglo-Irish landlords into true owners of the nation, Trollope im-poses the more prosaic requirement that no one can own who also owes; those who sublet their rented land or mortgaged their property should be "pulled down from their position as men of property, and exposed to the world as men of none" ("Trollope's [Six] Letters" 94). Such men can never be loyal to the state, torn as their allegiances are between the welfare of their estates and the demands of those to whom they owe money.

In his first novels, Trollope also might be seen as imagining the gradual elimi-nation of the middleman from the Irish situation. In *The MacDermots of Ballyclo-ran* (1847) and *The Kellys and the O'Kellys* (1848), Trollope chronicled the tensions of an Irish community divided among a tripartite system of rural landowner-ship in Ireland: Anglo-Irish landlords, Catholic peasants, and a Catholic middle class who, as Laura Berol demonstrates, are alternately victimized (Thady in *MacDermots*) and villainized (Barry Lynch in *Kellys*), without a clear place in the social structure. By the time he returns to the Irish question in his Palliser series, Trollope offers a simpler tale of Irishmen—Phineas Finn and Laurence Fitzgib-bon most prominently—who take their place beside British men in Parliament. But far from retelling the elimination of the middleman imagined in his earlier novels, these plots place a new emphasis on the importance mediated relation-ships have for the fundamental composition of the state, as well as for the expe-rience of property-owning throughout the United Kingdom.

Conspicuously absent from these later novels is the Irish land. Phineas Finn, the main Irish character in the Palliser series, is the son of an Irish doctor, the heir to no landed property at all. His landless condition may be motivated by Trollope's market-friendly desire to sidestep the politicized and confusing is-sues of Irish ownership during the decades when they were most in the public eye. But given how his novels narrate the experience of property in British land,

Trollope's omission of Irish land from his novels seems a response to the sea change in the meaning of landed property in general. No longer the foundational model of the property relationship, land ownership at midcentury, as I argue in chapter 3, began to look like a threat, a too-material and too-secure attachment that very well might sap its owner of agency. This sea change causes Trollope to change tactics from the Irish novels when he moved on to the Palliser series. Instead of having Irish ownership of land symbolize the relationship that will ultimately reconcile the Irish to the British state, Trollope devises another sort of ownership entirely, a shared arrangement I call vicarious ownership. This experience, far from the legally defined leases and sublets that remove a landlord from his property, defies legal definition altogether. Instead, it is an arrangement in which one party undertakes legal ownership while another party, the vicarious owner, enjoys the property in the legal owner's place. It is this ownerly arrangement Trollope imagines not just to structure the status quo of landed property in the British Isles but also to draw owners and nonowners together in intensely symbiotic unions. These symbiotic unions, in turn, model how the state might be experienced throughout the United Kingdom in an era in which the meaning of property was rapidly changing.

Vicarious Ownership after Midcentury

Trollope's extensive dependence on arrangements of vicarious ownership in his Palliser novels highlights a midcentury shift away from thinking about property in terms of a shared family arrangement across generations, but that shift does not entirely arrive at purely alienated, atomized, individual property, as Lauren Goodlad's comprehensive assessment of ownership across a large swath of Trollope's work would have it. In "Trollopian 'Foreign Policy'" she argues that the author's Barsetshire series imagines Englishness as a form of "heirloom property" in which "particular ethical and cultural worth" accumulates "in excess of abstract economic value, and in so doing, binds rather than atomizes" (443). Goodlad asserts that this is a conceit Trollope cannot maintain in the travel writing he carries out at the same time. In those works, he surveys the settler colonies of Australia and New Zealand, as well as North America, as zones defined by owners whose property is purely economic, disembedded from any attachment to culture or history. Thus, in Goodlad's scheme, by the time he settles down to write the Palliser series, Trollope can think of property only in terms of "a substanceless flow of capital and commodities." The result is an England confronting its own "breached sovereignty" when it contemplates the realities of a globalized economy (448).

The story I unearth in this chapter is slightly different. While Goodlad is right to discern a shift away from a model of heirloom property as a dominant model for thinking about membership in a nation, the Palliser novels, I argue, offer a model of ownership-as-membership that avoids complete atomization. At the same time, this model is not necessarily geared toward holding off the horror of endless alienation; in Trollope's universe, a too-sound attachment to property might threaten to breach an owner's sovereignty just as much as would a "flow of capital and commodities." Therefore, Trollope's six volumes of plots tracking the courtships, scandals, bankruptcies, and inheritances of a group of characters all intimately connected with Parliament imagine that an abiding attachment to property and an abiding attachment to the state both involve mediation, something that keeps the bond from dominating the person who experiences it. In its focus on Parliament the Palliser series explores the problem of how the Irish and the British-identified subject who is Jewish also cathect to the state. Trollope's answer seeks in family bonds—most importantly marital bonds—a model for the palpable experience of British citizenship. In a situation where the husband owns and the wife enjoys, Trollope finds a logic that might allot to all citizens an enjoyment of the state, even as most of them remained barred from active participation in its political institutions. Trollope's model does more than just explain the anomalous position of Ireland in the United Kingdom—although with its recourse to the marriage metaphor to justify the union of Britain and Ireland, it definitely does that. Additionally, Ireland's inclusion in the United Kingdom comes to prove that the model of vicarious enjoyment works. Ireland takes on the status of the archetypal enjoyer of property it can never quite own.

This position differs from being heir to a property passed down through the centuries, whose ownership confers identity. Indeed, by the time Trollope begins his Palliser series of novels, the Victorian novel had positioned such a model of heirloom ownership as the opposite of enjoying one's property. The tradition of entailed estates, which generates so much plotworthy misery among offspring, proves that the enjoyment of property in the legal sense often precludes property's enjoyment in the affective sense, perpetually deferring such an experience to future generations. In Trollope's novels, the number of profligate sons, both aristocratic and middle-class, reluctantly exiled by their fathers (in the Palliser series this includes George Vavasor, Lord Chiltern, and Everett Wharton) demonstrates the extent to which inherited wealth requires that no one in any generation really enjoy the family property at all. Victorian novels delight in exposing the mandate to preserve the family property as driven by an illogical and ungenerous tendency toward hoarding. Vigilant safeguarding of property for future generations is revealed as a useless miserliness, as in Mr. Dombey's obsession with the corporate entity of "Dombey and Son," which keeps him from enjoying any affectionate ties to his son. Silas Marner's loss of his gold horde at the moment he gains a human child is perhaps the nineteenth century's most forceful illustration that the careful guarding of property, rather than being necessary for the family's sake, is actually the opposite of family altogether.

As the usefulness of preserving property is called into question, so too is Burke's metaphor of the nation as a familial inheritance. The thingness of the nation, with "its bearings and its ensigns armorial . . . its gallery of portraits; its monumental inscriptions; its records, evidences, and titles" (34) might acquire the same air of futility as the closet where Aunt Glegg stores her fine linen in *The Mill on the Floss* (1860). Guarding her sheets and tablecloths against use, she reserves the household goods for the day of her death, when others might open the closet to discover all she owned but never consumed (34). In the same spirit that leads Eliot's novel to expose the futility of preservation for its own sake, Trollope's Lady Glencora Palliser waxes suspicious of the aristocratic maintenance of estates. Fond of midnight rambles among the ruins of the ancient priory on the grounds of the family estate, she is frustrated by her husband's refusal to see the romantic value of the crumbling walls. In fact, she can only lure her husband to accompany her walks by telling him that the refectory wall needs repairing. "If anything is out of order he has it put to rights at once," she complains. "There would have been no ruins if all the Pallisers had been like him" (*Can You* 1:283). In attending to the preservation of his property, Palliser shows himself unable to enjoy it, and in her romantic appreciation of the ruins, Glencora shows enjoyment to require a certain amount of destruction. Between these two competing impulses, Trollope works out a delicate division of labor that he sees as creating unity, imagining the somewhat destructive enjoyment of the wife to be the necessary complement to her husband's more conservative ownership. In the Palliser series, this balance replaces Burke's model of how property in an estate should work and, by analogy, how the larger structure of government should be enjoyed.

Trollope's understanding of consumption as a component of ownership stems from the nuclear family's relatively modern identity as a unit of consumption. Yet the fact that he works out such an idea through the vehicle of the incontestably aristocratic Palliser alliance is not simply the author's flawed projection of his own middle-class values onto his characters. Preserving property simply for preservation's sake had become less and less tenable even for the great ancestral halls of England. While such properties had been open to middle-class visitors since before the eighteenth century—proof that portrait galleries, armorial ensigns, and titles really *were*, to some extent, national property—the representations of that access changed markedly over the century. Illustrated books that sought to acquaint a mass audience with these national estates, such as Joseph Nash's *Mansions of England in the Olden Times* (1839) and William Howitt's *Rural Life in England* (1838) and *Visits to Remarkable Places* (1840), emphasized the communal history of such properties, offering pictures of bygone days when an entire village would gather in a great hall to celebrate Yuletide or flock to a manorial lawn for Maypole dances. Their depictions highlighted the estates as synonymous with the community able to gather there.

Yet as urbanization and transportation technology made great houses more attractive and more accessible day-trip destinations for more people and classes, there arose a popular notion that such access should continue to be granted not because the properties were the common buildings of an organic community that would always endure but because they functioned as instructive monuments to England's history for those who might otherwise be less aware of the glory of Englishness than were the monuments' aristocratic owners. In this way, the property existed not as a justification in itself, a thing that, like the nation, must be preserved for itself, but as a symbol that could only be appreciated and enjoyed by those who did not properly possess it. By the 1880s, landlords of great estates argued that their ownership was not to their own benefit. "Is there a man so abandoned, so idiotic, so utterly lost to the first glimmerings of self-interest that he would deliberately be saddled with one of these gigantic structures?" Arthur Balfour asked in response to proposed taxes on estates. An owner's only attachment to such homes, he argued, stemmed from the fact that "it is the home which he and his family have lived in perhaps for generations" (qtd in Mandler 162). By contrast, the commoners who clamored for continued access to the houses, collections, and gardens of the aristocracy believed that the objects exercised an improving power on visitors, a pedagogical influence to which the aristocracy was naturally impervious. The assumption on both sides was that the very different relationships to the very same object could potentially draw together owner and enjoyer.

The second half of the nineteenth century spawned many thinkers who imagined a similar vicarious arrangement to draw people into a relationship with the state. In his volume on *The English Constitution* (1867), Walter Bagehot asserts that constitutional monarchy works because the ceremonial element of the monarchy provides a theatrical show of rule for those too unsophisticated to understand the mundane intricacies of a parliament that really rules. "The poorer and more ignorant classes . . . really believe that the Queen governs," he explains, urging his readers to consult with their kitchen maids for evidence (25). For Bagehot, the English constitution provides the best of all possible political arrangements, not because he really has much relation to its more ceremonial parts at all, but because he is able to believe that there is someone else out there, someone much different from him, who is enjoying it for him. Bagehot's attitude toward the ceremonial parts of the nation, which he, as educated citizen with full political rights, must maintain in order that disenfranchised kitchen maids might enjoy them, is intellectually akin to the idea that the aristocracy must keep its great estates in order that the lower classes might enjoy them. Belief and property both are assumed to operate through a certain degree of displaced enjoyment.

Trollope's novels naturalize this arrangement, emphasizing displaced enjoyment as the fundamental requirement of unity—both in marriage and in the multinational British state. For Trollope the desire for someone who will enjoy property in the owner's place is the central motivation for unity in almost every one of the minutely detailed marriage plots that drive the six Palliser novels. By merging the marital with the literal politics of Parliament, these plots make visible Trollope's assumption that the British state itself works on a model of vicarious enjoyment. Trollope understands the legal sense of enjoyment—a term denoting the active experience of one's right to one's property—to depend on enjoyment in the emotional sense. By repeatedly telling the tale of courtships that culminate in one party's vicarious enjoyment of what their beloved owns, Trollope imagines society as wholly dependent on structures of ownership at a moment when franchise reform makes them increasingly irrelevant. With a cast of recurring characters whose lives revolve around the seasonal changes and political tides of Westminster, the novels link the characters' desire for a vicarious experience of property with the readers' desire for a vicarious experience of Parliament. As I sketch out this connection, I first look at the psychological texture of the successful—not to be confused with the virtuous—owner in the Palliser novels. I then examine how that psychological structure is sustained by an impulse toward vicarious enjoyment. While such displacement is modeled on the uneven property distribution of the English common law marriage—in which the wife is the enjoyer of the property her husband legally owns—Trollope also describes it as a fundamental condition of parliamentary government. Finally, I close with a consideration of how, as the movement toward married women's property laws makes a vicarious structure of exclusive property less possible, Trollope also comes to understand Ireland—often portrayed as the wifely nation within the United Kingdom— as providing a way to preserve the vicarious enjoyment model of the British state.

Absent-minded Ownership, Absent-minded Englishness

The jewel in the crown of the Palliser series, at least for literary critics interested in exploring the contradictions of Victorian property, is *The Eustace Diamonds* (1873). Its plot revolves around the very bad and very false Lizzie Eustace, who insists that the diamonds given her by her late husband are her own personal property, rather than a part of the estate belonging to his family. In the legal wrangling that follows, Trollope catalogs types of ownership—portable property, which can be transferred at will; paraphernalia, belonging to a woman's rank, not her person; the heirloom, which functions only as a symbol of the family and not property at all. The intricacies of these different types of ownership take even lawyers by surprise, but Lizzie's insistence on understanding the diamonds as straightforward, absolute, exclusive, alienable property is read as "false, dishonest, heartless, cruel, irreligious, ungrateful, mean, ignorant, greedy, and vile" (*Eustace Diamonds* 1:311). The coupling of this condemnation with her determination to understand her property in its most atomistic, market-friendly sense has been read—and rightly—as one more symptom of the Victorians' profound anxiety about new and ever more pervasive forms of alienable property in a world whose stability is imagined to be ensured by the endurance of great estates and the aristocracy they sustain. Critics such as Patrick Brantlinger (*The Reading Lesson*), Paul Delaney, Juliet McMaster, and Andrew Miller have argued that *The Eustace Diamonds* articulates with unusual explicitness the general Victorian sentiment that landed property indicates a sort of virtue in its owner that portable, alienable property can never impart, and frequently disrupts. But while these critics attend to the ethical register of different types of property, they say very little about how ownership itself is experienced. In Victorian cultural criticism, as in the Victorian novel, the grand elaborations of pressing need, threatened bankruptcy, ruined fortunes, profligate spending, and a world convoluted by the deceptions of a credit economy dominate the world of owned objects, creating an intricate frame around the blank that is actual ownership. In *The Eustace Diamonds* the plot's interest derives from the twists through which Lizzie's ownership of the diamonds is challenged, first by her late husband's family, then by the thieves who make off with the safe in which the diamonds travel, and finally when the diamonds themselves—which have not, as Lizzie fails to mention, been stolen along with the safe—are stolen from her personal jewelry box. The developments that ultimately take the diamonds out of Lizzie's grasping hands succeed in completely drawing attention away from what Lizzie *does* manage to keep, despite the best efforts of her late husband's family in *The Eustace Diamonds* and her homicidal, bigamous second husband in the next Palliser novel, *Phineas Redux* (1874). A sizable estate in Scotland remains hers, and she continues to draw £4000 a year, building up a bank balance that makes her an attractive—and finally invulnerable—financial ally for the speculating Ferdinand Lopez in *The Prime Minister* (1876).

At her lowest point, accused of perjury for lying about the first burglary and sorely fearing that she might be put in jail, Lizzie comforts herself with the idea that "They could not take away her income or her castle" (2:286). Oddly, this seems because, rather than in spite, of the fact that the permanence of her income and real estate remains the stuff of imprecise and contradictory rumors. Lizzie's ownership of the diamonds becomes more subject to public opinion the more she insists that they are hers alone. The plot then seems to affirm public opinion, taking Lizzie's diamonds from her just when the gossiping denizens reach a consensus that the diamonds were, after all, not Lizzie's property. But no such consensus is ever reached about the rest of her husband's legacy, whose terms remain opaque. "When she knew how it was all arranged—as far as she did know it—she was aware that she was a rich woman." But this awareness is one of dim assurance, not technical mastery: "[F]or so clever a woman, Lizzie was infinitely ignorant as to the possession and value of money and land and income. . . . As for the Scotch property,—she thought that it was her own, for ever, because there could not now be a second son,—and yet was not quite sure whether it would be her own at all if she had no son. Concerning the sum of money left to her, she did not know whether it was to come out of the Scotch property, or be given to her separately,—and whether it was to come annually or to come only once" (1:10–11).

This inability to know the property is exactly what seems to work to her advantage. Her lack of knowledge allows her to declare several relationships to the property without ever exactly lying. She claims first that she owns it outright, then that she was made to buy even the furniture in it from her husband's family, and then that she is in debt already. Resting just beyond narration, the property cannot be taken by anyone. Contrary to Mr. Dove's expert legal opinion that "property so fictitious as diamonds" is "subject to the risk of [. . .] annihilation" (2:146) while "the land at any rate can be traced" (2:258), the novel follows its eponymous diamonds on their road to a permanent home: "first to Hamburgh, and then to Vienna" and finally to "the bosom of a certain enormously rich Russian princess" from whose grasp "it was found impossible to recover them" (2:353). The fate of Lizzie's Scotch property, by contrast, is never traced out with such clarity, and in fact it disappears altogether from the horizon in the next two novels, rendered secure by Lizzie's distracted incomprehension of it.

In this preoccupied failure to grasp the particulars of ownership, Lizzie Eustace is joined by a character at the opposite end of Trollope's moral spectrum. The enormously wealthy, conscientious, and upright Plantagenet Palliser, Duke of Omnium—and by the fifth book of the series, Prime Minister of the Realm—shares with the compulsively lying social climber an inability to understand fully the nature of what he owns. Palliser's wealth, which before he becomes Duke of Omnium is of such a size that "he could throw thousands away if he wished it," swells into a "colossal wealth" when he marries his wife, Lady Glencora (*Can You* 1:242). When the old duke passes, Palliser inherits the Omnium fortune, which we are told, outsizes even the queen's fortune. While Palliser considers the happiest days of his life to be those he spends as Chancellor of the Exchequer, working abstruse calculations on the decimalization of currency, where it concerns his own family finances, "Money mattered nothing. Their income was enormous" (*Prime Minister* 53). Yet, with a caution much like the one that inspires Lizzie's visions of her impoverished condition, he still warns his wife against too much expenditure: "I think there should be a limit. No man is ever rich enough to squander" (90). And while Lizzie cannot grasp the legalities of her property, Palliser cannot even grasp the physicality of his estate. He arrives at the great Omnium estate castle of Gatherum determined to "walk about his own grounds," only to stand reflecting on the unfamiliarity of it all; he "could not remember that he had ever but once before placed himself on that spot" (160). In his distant relationship to Gatherum, Palliser emulates his political mentor, the Duke of St. Bungay, who demonstrates his own ownerly powers by being "a great buyer of pictures, which, perhaps, he did not understand, and a great collector of books which certainly he never read" (*Can You* 1:251).

This logic of distant proprietorship seeps into Trollope's narration of England as something toward which we might feel possessive, but only loosely so, in a fashion that keeps England from being too overwhelming or determining of a possession. The Palliser novels offer a striking contrast to the ironic catalog of Irish landscape and habits that mark Maria Edgeworth's national tales or the earnest ethnographies of the industrial north in Elizabeth Gaskell's condition-of-England novels. Both of these earlier novelists proliferate details in their anxiety to dispel the strangeness of their subject to England's core.[2] Instead, Trollope's narrator goes out of his way to explain that he is covering a terrain so familiar to the reader as to warrant no descriptive attention whatsoever. Among the intimates that the narrator hails not as "we Englishmen" but as the more inclusive and vicarious "we, who know the feeling of Englishmen," the physical mass of Westminster, the center of all British political plots, slips out of our field of vision and into unelaborated invisibility (*Prime Minister* 294). "Our great national hall" is to Trollope a mere matter of "that more than royal staircase" and "those passages," which require no great narrative attention because they can go without saying (43, 44). If we are as unfamiliar with them as Palliser is with Gatherum, or as the Duke of St. Bungay is with the contents of his own library, it is proof of the security of our heritage. Trollope's offhand manner of dealing with them affirms their status as symbols of, in Brantlinger's words, "the ultimate possession of the public, the unified, taken-for-granted nation-state with its almost equally taken-for-granted empire" (*Fictions* 171). Trollope speaks as an Englishman from the very center of Englishness by assuming that what is English is an experience so assured and familiar that it is always being carelessly reencountered rather than encountered for the first time.

Trollope's reliance on commonplaces and truths universally acknowledged— what William A. Cohen calls Trollope's "aphoristic rhetoric"—reinforces the sense that the reader has already come across the very structures of thinking in the novel, and need not attend to closely to them (252). Laurie Langbauer agrees that Trollope's "expression of the proverbial is always citational," always dependent on some prior utterance of the same truth (99). In this sense, Trollope's repetitive use of characters is equally citational. In the series that bears their name, the Pallisers appear only halfway through the first volume, as distant relations of the heroine, Alice Vavasor. Even this relationship is described as having already come to an end, after the betrothed Glencora fails to get Alice to help her elope with a former lover. Glencora only makes an actual appearance in the novel after the story of her engagement and marriage to Palliser has been told twice, first through the eyes of her spurned lover Burgo Fitzgerald and next through the eyes of Alice. Trollope already casually refers to its outcome, even before we meet the primary players, as one in which "sagacious heads were victorious, as we know" (*Can You* 1:190). And we might very well know, anyway, since the coerced courtship of Palliser and Glencora also was narrated briefly in another volume, *The Small House at Allington* (1861–64), written immediately before Trollope began the Palliser series. Trollope's serial use of his characters, who are central to some books and only incidental to others, allows the reader to encounter them as a life we already know, even if we are reading only one of the books in the series, out of order. As Phineas Finn sails back to London after a five-year absence in Dublin, he reflects on his old friends, while the narrator briefly catalogs the cast he is sure the reader has already met: "Has it not been written in a former book how this Lady Laura had been unhappy in her marriage, having wedded herself to a man whom she had never loved?" (*Phineas Redux* 1:14).

Fictional characters and public realities are knit together in a narratorial treatment that assumes both to be already well known by the reader; both become a thing to which the reader has a careless proprietary relationship. The opening line of *Phineas Redux*, for instance, manages its reintroduction of the titular character as an allusion to a public event that might be historical or fictional: "The circumstances of the general election of 18— will be well remembered by those who take an interest in the political matters of the country" (1:1). And while the narrator is confident that "those who take an interest in the political matters of this country" have full command of those circumstances, he goes ahead and recaps them for his reader. While Langbauer observes that Trollope's citational habits create a sense of his novels' intertextual relation to a social totality, it is a totality that the narrator never seems to expect, or even desire, that his readers fully grasp. The narrator treats as matter of course this necessity of reminding readers about what is known. Indeed, the logic of his narration reveals that "we, who know the feeling of Englishmen" probably have to be reminded of them frequently because the security of our membership in that "we" involves a certain degree of forgetting—a taking-for-granted of English surroundings that can slide into downright oblivion. The nineteenth-century reader Trollope addresses is revealed to be greatly in need of reminders about what is known about a bewilderingly tangled, not entirely comprehensible, political history that is—for that very reason—irrevocably theirs. For Trollope, this is not the same thing as the slothful ennui of the rich, whose indolence leaves them unable to become impressed by anything they own. Instead, the oblivion in Trollope's novels is the proper mindset of those who are so secure in what is theirs that they can only understand it as a sort of background noise occasionally called to their attention by the presence of someone else, slightly different from them.

Thus, "we who know the feelings of Englishmen" are more reliable than mere Englishmen themselves in making English oblivion apparent. The presence of a stranger frequently provides an occasion for Trollope to call attention to his English reader's sense of Englishness. This emerges in his style of the familiar reencounter with English landscape. "It is quite unnecessary to describe Tenway Junction, as everybody knows it," the narrator explains, before taking the trouble to detail how that well-known spot might appear to the visiting stranger (*Prime Minister* 519). Likewise, during the first change of government in *Phineas Finn* (1869), the narrator reassures his readers of their own grasp of British government: "We who are conversant with our own methods of politics see nothing odd in this, because we are used to it; but surely in the eyes of strangers our practice must be very singular" (121). These strangers' eyes prompt an explication of the purely ceremonial rivalries and speeches that mark the fall of a government, implying an alien's interest in the pageant, so that the reader might properly enjoy the ironic intrigues behind it.

The Problem with Self-Possession

The thoughtlessness intrinsic in Trollope's model of owning is at odds with a narrative of nineteenth-century liberalism in which—in C. B. MacPherson's familiar formulation—the individual is increasingly seen "as essentially the proprietor of his own person or capacities, owing nothing to society for them. . . . The relation of ownership, having become for more and more men the critically important relation determining their actual freedom and actual prospect of realizing their full potentialities, was read back into the nature of

the individual. The individual, it was thought, is free inasmuch as he is proprietor of his person and capacities" (3). MacPherson's notion makes sense in a
market economy, where proprietorship of one's person must entail an ability to
contract freely, consciously calculating how best to use the limited resources of
the self. This idea of self-ownership, however, bears little resemblance to Palliser's experience of himself as owner of his property and his abilities:

> There was such an absence about him of all self-consciousness, he was so little
> given to think of his own personal demeanour and outward trappings—that he
> never brought himself to question the manners of others to him. . . . He could
> put up with apparent rudeness without seeing it. . . . And with it all he had an
> assurance in his own position—a knowledge of the strength derived from his
> intellect, his industry, his rank, and his wealth—which made him altogether fear-
> less of others. When the little dog snarls, the big dog does not connect the snarl
> with himself, simply fancying that the little dog must be uncomfortable. Mr.
> Bonteen snarled a good deal, and the new Lord Privy Seal [Palliser] thought that
> the new president of the Board of Trade [Bonteen] was not comfortable within
> himself. (*Phineas Redux* 2:22)

In this passage—as in the character of Plantagenet Palliser himself—
Trollope valorizes something other than a self-possession grounded on models
of laissez-faire economics. Like the ideal man of property, upon whom the republican ideal of government is based, Palliser is above outside influences, dependent on no one but himself for what he possesses. But what exempts him
from the calculating entanglements of petty politics is also what makes him a
miserable politician. Palliser consistently fails to understand what other people
are feeling or to communicate what might motivate his own actions. As the archetype of the secure property owner, Palliser is also always the last to hear a
rumor or recognize others' motives, hardly traits to ensure success in the intrigues and shifting coalitions of a parliamentary government, even one that
fetishizes the self-forgetful man of independent means.

As a character, however, Palliser never exactly comes to stand for a purely
aristocratic relationship to property any more than he comes to embody new
market-driven understandings of ownership. While Trollope's narrator celebrates
Palliser as "the truest nobleman in all of England," the contours of Palliser's entire
life are shaped by his tendency toward a middle-class work ethic, an absorption
in his work. Eschewing the aristocratic activities of gambling, hunting, and flirting, his failures and successes, both personal and political, often stem from the

same origin: his preference for the steady grind of parliamentary work over the less clearly defined occupations of the upper class. Glencora comments that he would have been much happier if he had been required to have a profession. Palliser counts among the most miserable days of his life the day that his uncle dies and Palliser is compelled to take his place in the House of Lords, leaving behind the more minutely active chambers of the House of Commons.

Palliser's indeterminate status, as an avowedly aristocratic man whose aristocracy allows him to indulge in his compulsively middle-class habits, marks out Trollope's middle course between the republican civic ideal of a man able to work for his country because he is always assured of keeping his property and the market ideal of an individual who must vigilantly treat the self like property, keenly attuned to the possibility of even selfhood being ripped away. In his portrait of Palliser, Trollope compromises between an ownership of self-forgetfulness, in which one is comfortably oblivious to what one owns, and an ownership of self-alienation in which one is anxiously unsure that one can claim property even in oneself. Instead, he assigns the aristocrat a model of ownership in which keeping what one owns always means keeping it for others. But this keeping is far from heirloom preservation. In the pithy words of Lord Chiltern, Master of the Brake Hounds, "A man's property is his own in one sense, but it isn't his own in another" (*Phineas Redux* 1:122). As a "master" responsible for "keeping" the hounds belonging to another man's estate, Chiltern is an expert on the arcane ceremonies of property that keep it from ever being a simple matter of absolute ownership. Engaged for most of *Phineas Redux* in a battle with the Omnium estate over its failure to foster foxes for fox hunting, Chiltern is aligned with a system of property that, instead of allowing an owner to do as he wishes, requires him to keep the property for the pleasure of others. Madame Goesler, in her role as continental observer, comments that Chiltern's struggles only prove that "in this country . . . the owner of a property does not seem at all to have any exclusive right to it." Chiltern, however, contends that the Duke of Omnium is "bound to find foxes for the Brake hunt," even though he takes no part in the hunt himself, and the animals and the hunt do harm to his tenants' crops and livestock; "It is almost a part of his title deeds" (1:136–37).

Chiltern's determination to force the nation's largest estate to contribute to the enjoyment of English sporting types, even if such support proves harmful to the estate itself, has its counterpart in the same book. Representing the Omnium estate after the death of the old duke, Palliser engages in a battle to force Madame Goesler to enjoy her legacy from the duke. She, on the other hand, obstinately refuses the jewels and money left to her by the old duke, just as she once refused the man's marriage proposal, objecting that it would open her up to accusations of mercenary motives in her friendships. Palliser is as incensed by Goesler's rejection of the legacy as Chiltern is at the old duke's failure to keep foxes for other men to kill. Palliser proclaims that Goesler's refusal threatens the entire social fabric, arguing that "the real owner of substantial wealth [Madame Goesler] could not be allowed to disembarrass himself [*sic*] of his responsibilities or strip himself of his privileges by a few generous but idle words." However, the inalienable responsibilities and inalienable privileges of property cancel each other out in his logic. He reasons that she cannot refuse the legacy because "the things were her property, and though she might, of course, chuck them into the street, they would be no less hers" (1:264). Absurd as it is, Palliser's formulation gets at the heart of the matter: The property that underwrites an "independent" life is, of course, the thing from which one can never be independent.

Trollope applies this paradox not just to those with landed property but even to characters who can be said to hold absolute property in themselves. When Trollope's characters find themselves most at liberty, they also find themselves at the brink of suicidal despair. Palliser's annoyance at being made to keep foxes is benign compared to the horror that fills characters who are suddenly struck with an acute sense of their exclusive and unlimited self-possession. Lucy Morris, understanding herself to be abandoned by her wayward fiancé, experiences her despair as "the wearisome possession of herself. . . . How bitter to her was that possession of herself, as she felt that there was nothing to be done with the thing so possessed!" (*Eustace Diamonds* 2:189). This sensation transcends the specifically female position of needing to be affiliated to a man for basic financial security. Phineas Finn, newly widowed from the wife for whom he left politics and returned to his native Ireland, finds the suddenly widened scope of possibilities for his life horrifying in identical terms. He muses, "It is very well for a man to boast that he is lord of himself, and that having no ties he may do as he pleases with that possession. But it is a possession of which unfortunately, he cannot rid himself when he finds that there is nothing advantageous to be done with it" (*Phineas Redux* 1:9). Finn recovers from his angst when he is suddenly able to alight on the thought "Did he not owe himself to his country?" and resolves on a life of politics to relieve himself from too intense a sense of his own freedom (1:9). Lucy, in the end, is also relieved from her sense of self-determination by Frank Greystock's revived fidelity to his promise of marriage.

The Property of the Wife

This sense of relief in owing oneself to one's country, or being able to devote one's talents to one's spouse, is not identical to the masochistic fantasy of complete loss of volition, a desire to be treated as a piece of property. Phineas Finn and Lucy Morris both understand the advantages of being claimed by another. Neither Lucy nor Phineas desires to slave for husband or country; neither is willing to completely sacrifice ideals in order to create a desired relationship. Instead, both display a sense that they themselves are not able to properly enjoy the property they have in their own person; they require another person to undertake the task for them. Such a task can most easily be undertaken from a wifely position. Blackstone's codification of the Common Law corroborates an understanding of the wife, not precisely as a piece of property, but as the promise of its enjoyment. Blackstone is careful to distinguish the English wife's status from that of ancient Roman wife, declared to be the absolute property of the *patria potestas*. In discussing the compensations a court might reward to a husband for wrongs done to the wife, Blackstone notes that these are given to the husband to compensate not for damaged property in the wife but for "the injuries that may be offered to the enjoyment as well as to the rights of property" (1:138). In failing to be identical to property herself, the wife instead occupies the vague zone of "the enjoyment as well as the rights of property."

What distinguishes Trollope's treatment of women and marriage in the Palliser series is the extent to which it calls for attention to a wife's strong legal associations with the legal enjoyment of property. This odd middle space is rarely acknowledged by explicitly feminist rhetoric, which tends to emphasize wives' status as identical to property. Written a few decades after Blackstone makes his distinction, Mary Wollstonecraft's *A Vindication of the Rights of Woman* (1792) launched an attack on "the slavery of marriage" (155) that is foundational for modern feminism. Indeed, during the late eighteenth- and early nineteenth-century movement for the abolition of British slavery, female abolitionists publicized women's shared position with the slaves for whose freedom they campaigned.[3] Yet, as Karen Sanchez-Eppler points out in her work on American female abolitionists, such identification often wanders into appropriation, in which the plight of the slave is altogether replaced by the situation of the white female to whom he or she is compared. Thus, nineteenth-century feminism often formulates women's position as being exactly slavery, only more so. William Thompson's *Appeal of One Half of the Human Race, Women, against the Pretentions of the Other Half, Men* (1825) suggests that even slaves have advantages over the legal condition of married women. J. S. Mill continues this tradition in *On The Subjection of Women* (1869), admitting, "I am far from pretending that wives are in general no better treated than slaves" only to add, "but no slave is a slave to the same lengths, and in so full a sense of the word, as a wife is" (504).

The argument that wives are more like property than even slaves relies on the same proprietary logic that accords a stronger hold to traditional titles than to legal ones. Caroline Norton claims to find "in the slave law of Kentucky, an exact parallel of the law of England for its married women" (19), because neither wife nor slave can enter into a legal contract. She compares her husband's seizure of her literary earnings to a slaveholder's insistence that no slave can purchase his own freedom. She explains, "a married woman is, by the code of England, (as Sam Norris is by the code of Kentucky) *non-existant* in law" (20, emphasis in original). While Norton is unquestionably correct that the slave Sam Norris did not exist as a person under slave law, his body was made into a legally articulable piece of property by a highly elaborated system of sales, titles, and his bureaucratic quantification as three-fifths of a person for census purposes. Her own position as wife remains much less clear.

That inalienable property in the wife eludes a strict articulation that might guarantee but also limit the husband's enjoyment of her is the paradox Jeff Nunokawa draws out in *The Afterlife of Property* (1994). For Nunokawa, even the womanly form of inalienable property is too definite, and thus too vulnerable, to sustain its permanence. The Victorian novel provides for the absolute security of property, he argues, in plots where the only safe property is that already released from its "mortal coils" and elevated to its afterlife "as a fragment of literary fantasy that men can keep to themselves, and as a narrative whose always anticipated conclusion never comes" (14). Nunokawa's sense that a wife might only be a symbolic marker of a disappeared possibility of inalienable ownership comes close to Blackstone's own sense that the wife is the promise of enjoyment, not actually the property to be enjoyed at all.

Those who parse the wifely position assume it to involve a misery befitting outright slavery, even if it is not precisely enslavement. Mary Poovey distinguishes "between [male] property owners, on the one hand, and [female] representatives of property on the other" (*Uneven* 75) in an attempt to reach a more nuanced description of women's relationship to the category of property. While Poovey calls women "the paradigmatic case of human property" after the abolition of British slavery in 1833, she is more focused on women's function as a substitute for property, the conjugal accessory that marked middle-class men as possessing the same virtues and qualities as property owners. While she does not cite Thorstein Veblen's *Theory of a Leisure Class* (1899), her assumptions about wives' "metonymic relation to property" shares with Veblen's scheme a sense that the wife exists as a guarantor of her husband's status. Poovey attributes to the middle-class wife the adoption of a self-sacrificing ethic that will advertise the husband's aristocratic rise above the pettiness of the competitive market. Veblen likewise sees the dress and conspicuous leisure of the middle-class wife as an attempt "at a second remove" to emulate the grand performance of leisure undertaken by the master class and their dependents (84). But while true aristocracy, for Veblen, requires wives to exist simply as extensions of their husbands' already highly visible performance of nonproductive consumption, the case of the middle class is less straightforward, requiring an arrangement of "vicarious consumption," in which a man "appli[es] himself to work with the utmost assiduity, in order that his wife may in due form render for him that degree of vicarious leisure which the common sense of the time demands" (83, 81). Both Veblen and Poovey expect that this wifely enjoyment of the husband's property—which Poovey's Victorian wife fashions into a domestic haven from the divisive forces of the market and which Veblen's Victorian wife quite often displays in "the high heel, the skirt, the impracticable bonnet, the corset, and the general disregard of the wearer's comfort which is an obvious feature of all civilized women's apparel" (181)—will require from the wife a degree of misery, a failure to emotionally enjoy in order to legally perform the husband's enjoyment.

In contrast to these rationalizations of spectacular wifely suffering, Trollope's vision of marriage insists, quite literally, on the wife's genuine affective enjoyment. As he works out the equation in his novel, the wife does not simply promise to the husband the sorts of rewards that might have, in an earlier, more aristocratic age, come with property. Instead, the wife undertakes to enjoy the property in order to ensure that the man is indeed its owner. The first novel of the Palliser series, *Can You Forgive Her?* (1864), centers around heroines struggling toward marriages that might be arrangements of vicarious enjoyment. Alice Vavasor, the vacillating heroine for whom forgiveness is begged in the title, begins to regret her engagement to her flawless fiancé, John Grey, upon the arrival of his letter describing the changes he has undertaken on his own property, Nethercoats, in anticipation of their marriage. Her creeping sense that she cannot possibly enjoy a life in his secluded home in the rural districts of Cambridgeshire leads her to break off the engagement, although she fully admits to still loving Grey. The trials that follow teach Alice that she can, after all, derive true pleasure from her erstwhile fiancé's property. Grey secretly uses his money to pay the expenses that Alice incurs when she draws on her own income to pay for the electioneering expenses of her cousin, George Vavasor. In fact, Alice promises to marry George because she wishes to be a political wife. Upon her reconciliation with Grey, Alice's prospects for enjoying his property brighten considerably when he resolves to spend some of it on trying to get into parliament. One of the last scenes of the novel offers a glimpse of the reformed Alice, primed for a lifetime of marital enjoyment: the stern and unsentimental heroine now weeps for joy over the Sèvres china she has just received for a wedding gift.

Alice's emergence into enjoyment of property upon marriage mirrors the simultaneous crisis in the Palliser marriage. Glencora's near-adulterous flirtation with Burgo Fitzgerald in the early days of her own marriage is less reprehensible for being a potential violation of the Palliser bloodline than it is for being a complete failure of the division of marital labor into owner and enjoyer. Palliser, in his role as contented and obtusely blind owner, never experiences any jealousy over the fact that his pretty and gregarious young wife had, immediately before their marriage, been in love with another man. Dismissing it as "all over now," he even advises Glencora to attend a house party where Fitzgerald will be present. Palliser's unperturbed and unreserved forgiveness of his wife's confession that she still loves Fitzgerald matches Grey's unreproaching generosity in remaining faithful to Alice's best interests even after she becomes engaged to another man. Both men's responses suggest that a woman's wandering eye is not so far outside the scope of her wifely duties as to make her an unsuitable mate. Instead, the clear division of marital roles in regard to property—the clear separation of owner and enjoyer—lies at the heart of every marital reconciliation. Like Alice, who must be lured back from the seductions of spending her own money on George Vavasor's election expenses, Glencora must also be cured of her nostalgia for what her enormous fortune might have done to help the debauched and perpetually indebted Burgo Fitzgerald. Such a cure is effected in Europe, where Palliser has taken his wife for a morally and maritally restorative holiday after she confesses to him her persisting love for Fitzgerald. At a casino in Baden-Baden, they happen upon her erstwhile lover, and she pleads with Palliser, with no sense of self-consciousness, to use his money to help the clearly desperate gambler: "Do something for him;—do, do. Unless I know that something is done, I shall die" (2:368). Palliser understands the plea not as a threat to his marriage but as proof that he has achieved the marital unity he has been trying for: Glencora now can be reassured that in their relationship "[t]here was no expenditure that he would not willingly incur for her, nothing costly that he would grudge."[4] The revelation comes on the heels of Glencora's conception of the much-awaited heir to the Omnium fortune, the seal of success on the couple's marriage, which, rather than raising uncomfortable questions about her previous behavior with Fitzgerald, instead dispels it altogether.

While Alice and Glencora illustrate the imperative for wives to enjoy, the series as a whole makes clear that, as vicarious enjoyer, the wife cannot be the direct owner of the property she enjoys. The marriage of vulgar speculator Ferdinand Lopez flounders when he fails to understand the importance of maintaining this distinction. In an encounter that marks the first sign of the failure both of his marriage and his wealth, Lopez tries to obtain money by asking his wife to write "her own letter" to her father—a letter he dictates—in which she asks for a share of "her fortune." She hesitates at even writing the possessive pronoun in connection to the money: "'But I have no fortune,' she said. He insisted however, explaining to her that she was entitled to use those words" (*Prime Minister* 220). By contrast, married to the consummate English gentleman, Glencora always scrupulously observes the rule of direct ownership's incompatibility with the enjoyment of property. As the wealthiest heiress in the British Isles, far richer than even her husband, Glencora retains legal right to her property through the legal machinations of settlement. But because she only understands that she is attached to this money "after some fashion, of which she was profoundly ignorant," the money is subject to the polite fiction that it is under Palliser's control. During their marriage "she had never said a word to him about her money; unless it were to ask that something out of the common course might be spent on some, generally absurd, object" (53). The pleasure of the absurd object is ensured by her petition to her husband, so that she might enjoy it as an actual owner could not.

The novels offer cautionary tales of what happens when marriage fails to adhere to the narrative of the wife as appointed, vicarious enjoyer. In *Phineas Finn*, Lord Robert Kennedy, the fabulously wealthy, "sole owner" of a manufacturing affair he has inherited from his father, at first shows himself aware of his duty as owner to remain carelessly aloof from his property, which he "certainly did nothing toward maintaining" (82). Yet when he first shepherds Lady Laura Standish around his estate, he reveals a guilty temptation to become utterly absorbed in it: "When I come up here and feel that in the midst of this little bit of a crowded island I have all this to myself,—all this with which no other man's wealth can interfere, I grow proud of my own until I grow thoroughly ashamed of myself" (159). And after marrying Lady Laura, his shame fails to counterbalance his tendency toward what the narrator calls "that great desire to enjoy his full rights, so strong in the mind of weak, ambitious men" (488). When his strict domestic regimen drives Lady Laura to leave him, Kennedy succumbs to an absorption in his own property that is clearly a form of insanity. He becomes "desirous . . . of starving all living things about the place,—cattle, sheep, and horses, so that the value of their food might be saved. . . . Even in bed he inquired daily about his money, and knew accurately the sum lying at his banker's; but he could be persuaded to disgorge nothing" (*Phineas Redux* 2:101, 103). Kennedy, in his miserly madness, sees himself as having been deprived of the person who could ensure that his property would be enjoyed. The longer Lady Laura stays away, the more agoraphobic the once highly mobile Kennedy becomes, as if unable to separate himself from the property without a proxy who can experience it for him. Rather than underwriting his agency, Kennedy's property gradually absorbs it, rendering him a slave in his compulsion to keep.

Wives and Parliament

Lady Glencora's reform as enjoying wife is undone when her husband becomes prime minister. His new position suddenly reminds her that she has money that might be called her own, and she resolves for the first time to spend it. Now that he has reached the highest possible office in the nation, she intends to use the money on securing his political position through social means: "The squandering was to be all for his glory,—so that he might retain his position as a Popular Prime Minister" (*Prime Minister* 90). Her decision reflects a gender asymmetry in the vicarious enjoyment of property. In Trollope's books, women find themselves owners of large fortunes as often as men do, and quite frequently, like men, they yearn for a partner who will help them enjoy such fortune. Both the vulgar Lizzie Eustace and the model of discretion Madame Goesler long to be able to give their money to a man, feeling that it would be more enjoyable if they could give it to someone who needed it. But such an exchange can never be the simple reverse of a male impulse toward a woman who will vicariously enjoy his property because, legally, the money would become the man's, converting the woman into the vicarious enjoyer of her own property. Lizzie, Madame Goesler, and Lady Glencora become the vicarious enjoyers of their own property once they marry. But with their gift—or pretended gift, in the case of Glencora— they convert men into vicarious enjoyers of another sort. Lizzie, Goesler, and Glencora (as well as Alice Vavasor, in a slight variation on the theme) all yearn to use their money on men involved in government. Such involvement, in the logic of the Palliser novels, is a vicarious engagement for everyone.

Women's longing for a political marriage, almost universal in the Palliser series, at first appears to represent their own desire to enjoy vicariously an institution to which they can never belong. But this participation's vicariousness is part of what makes it desirable to them. Alongside their restlessness for something more than the staid domesticity of married life is a disdain for the discourse of individual rights that might award them a more legitimately defined place in the political structure. Alice Vavasor, for instance, "was not so far advanced as to think that women should be lawyers and doctors, or to wish that she might have the privilege of the franchise for herself; but she had undoubtedly a hankering after some second-hand political maneuvering. She would have liked, I think, to have been the wife of the leader of a Radical opposition, in the time when such men were put into prison, and to have kept up for him his seditious correspondence while he lay in the tower" (*Can You* 111).

Lady Laura, who marries Kennedy to keep her hand in politics, also feels that the most desirable aspects of politics are not barred from her current position. And she, like Alice, disdains the feminist campaign for individual women's rights that might make her power less vicarious and more direct: "It was her ambition to be brought as near to political action as was possible for a woman without surrendering any of the privileges of feminine inaction. That women should even wish to have votes at parliamentary elections was to her abominable, and the cause of the Rights of Women generally was odious to her; but nevertheless, for herself, she delighted in hoping that she too might be useful,—in thinking that she too was perhaps in some degree, politically powerful" (*Phineas Finn* 127).

The disdain of Laura and Alice for the individual rights of property and the franchise represents not the conservatism of the ideologically brainwashed but a recognition of the forms of power that come with the vicarious experience of politics. The women who assist Phineas Finn in his political career best exemplify this sort of power. Including him in parties and dinners where he is able to meet the political lights of London and campaigning to find the penniless

Irish MP a paid position in government offices, Laura Kennedy, Violet Effing-ham, Madame Goesler, and Lady Glencora all shape Finn's career, showing themselves to have a power he lacks, even as a member of parliament. When Madame Goesler lets on to Phineas Finn that "a conspiracy had been formed" by the women in his social circle "for forcing upon the future Premier the ne-cessity of admitting Phineas Finn into his government," Finn is reluctant to be the recipient of such help (*Phineas Redux* 1:334). He wants to ask the women to cease their efforts, but "the whole subject was one which would have defied him to find words sufficiently discreet for his object" (1:335–36). Their vicarious position makes them unanswerable, out of the reach of defined channels of power.

The power of vicariousness is not always identical to the social discipline that D. A. Miller understands as operating in *The Eustace Diamonds*. Miller argues that the novel sees public opinion alone as having power to keep Lizzie in line, a task at which the police fail, unsure of how to bring their coercion to bear on an upper-class female. While Miller argues that Trollop gradually devalues state-recognized power in favor of more social forms of internalized discipline, the novels reveal that this is a false opposition. Those in political power already occupy a position easily identifiable as wifely—confined only to certain types of action, submissive to a power larger than they are. When Madame Goesler discusses with Finn his political privileges, it becomes apparent that personal agency is not necessarily a political privilege at all. After listening to the list of reforms she would carry out, Finn dryly dismisses her political opinions: "It is so comfortable to have theories that one is not bound to carry out." Her answer is to ask Palliser—at this point a cabinet member—if his masculine office gives him the ability to carry out his political theories. Palliser replies with the honest evasion, "I think I may say that I always am really anxious to carry into practice all those doctrines of policy which I advocate in theory" (1:405). Palliser's under-standing of his service to the country—to be anxious to carry out what one can clearly not carry out by one's own power—is both an accurate encapsulation of his experience in Parliament and a description of the job that the political wives hold, and the aspiring political wives long to hold, in the Palliser novels. It is this resemblance that enables government to provide to Phineas Finn the same con-solations that marriage to Frank Greystock provides to Lucy Morris.

Politics, it turns out, is no different from the social machinery that a conspir-acy of women can work from a distance. Just as Finn finds himself at the mercy of the powerlessness of women, Palliser experiences his term as prime minister as a loss of agency to those over whom he is supposed to take precedence. Trollope notes near the beginning of *The Prime Minister* that "even the sovereign can abdicate, but the Prime Minister of a Constitutional Government is in bonds" (48). Palliser understands from the start that he is selected to be prime minister not because of his abilities but because his reputation will hold together a coalition remarkable for its lack of goals or common feeling. But he is horrified at the inactivity of this purely symbolic function. As the figurehead of a fractious coalition, he realizes "there was, in truth, nothing for him to do. . . . the real work of the Government had been filched from him by his colleagues, and . . . he was stuck up in pretended authority,—a kind of wooden Prime Minister, from whom no real ministration was demanded" (231). In contrast to the earlier days of their marriage, when Glencora's delighted enjoyment of Palliser's property freed him for the ceaseless activity of Exchequer business, Palliser now seems sunk into a type of enforced enjoyment, while Glencora maintains the busy distraction that used to be his domain: "She was always making up the party,—meaning the coalition—doing something to strengthen the buttresses, writing little letters to little people, who, little as they were, might become big by amalgamation" (229).

Her activity, compared to his enforced inactivity, leads Palliser to an awareness of his own necessarily vicarious role in the government. "It might, in fact, be the case that it was his wife, . . . with her dinner parties and receptions, with her crowded saloons, her music, her picnics, and social temptations was Prime Minister rather than he himself. It might be that this had been understood by the coalesced parties;—by everybody, in fact, except himself. It had perhaps been found that in the state of things then existing, a ministry could be best kept together, not by parliamentary capacity, but by social arrangements, such as his Duchess, and his Duchess alone, could carry out. . . . In such a state of things, he of course, as her husband, must be the nominal Prime Minister" (149).

With this revelation, Palliser changes character. In contrast to his former role as the unselfconscious big dog, oblivious to the yappings of smaller dogs around him, Palliser as prime minister becomes thin-skinned, easily offended, and sensitive to what he sees as violations of his private property by favor-seekers and hangers-on who crowd Lady Glencora's entertainments. Understanding himself as vicarious enjoyer—of his wife's separate property, of Parliament itself—Palliser reverts to the same miserable awareness of his dependence that dogged him in his youth, before his marriage to Glencora inspired the old duke to settle an independent sum on his nephew. And Palliser's rather absent-minded neglect of Glencora that first marked his independence turns into his reliance on Glencora for sympathy and affection. As a result, he and Glencora become a rather tender couple. When Palliser grows to feel "that a grievous calamity had befallen him when circumstances compelled him to become the Queen's Prime Minister," he becomes melancholy and begs Glencora, "Do not separate yourself from me. . . . Do not disjoin yourself from me in all these troubles" (277).

Such a plea seems odd, given that his actual problem is that Glencora does not separate herself from him, insisting that she is just as much a part of the government as he is. One of the central crises of the ministry occurs when she promises vulgar social climber Ferdinand Lopez that Palliser will use his influence to ensure Lopez's successful candidacy for Parliament. Lopez uses Glencora's promise, after he loses the election, to pressure Palliser into compensating his election expenses. Word of it spreads to the press, where Palliser is accused of trying to exercise undue influence in elections. Glencora tries to take the blame, pointing out "They couldn't hang you, you know, because I committed a murder," but Palliser insists that he must take the blame for the promise he never gave. "You cannot divide yourself from me; nor, for the value of it all, would I wish that such a division were possible" (369). Called upon to explain the rumors of his misconduct in the House of Commons, Palliser never breathes a word of Glencora, insisting that he was "acting not as Prime Minister, but as an English nobleman, in the management of his own property and privileges" (493). And indeed, his statements are correct, since it is the duty of the English nobleman— a nobleman oddly but thoroughly imbued with a middle-class work ethic—to allow his wife full enjoyment of his property so that he might get on with other things.

The End of Wifely Powers

In the fifteen years during which Trollope wrote his series, the possibility of vicarious enjoyment through marriage was increasingly called into question. Beginning with the Matrimonial Causes Act of 1857, which made divorce available outside the aristocracy, and leading up to the Married Women's Property Acts of 1870 and 1882, public attention was absorbed in debates on whether marriage did in fact create shared interests, whether property owned by the husband was available for the enjoyment of the wife. Feminists circulated stories of wronged wives, usually from the lower classes, abandoned and unsupported by husbands who still might legally claim any property these women might earn or obtain. As Mary Lyndon Shanley points out, marital property laws horrified more than just feminists outraged at women's conjugal disadvantages. Middle-class merchants, Shanley argues, were equally aghast at the prospect of property that could be enjoyed by one party but only legally owned by the other. Such an arrangement frequently led to women running up debt in their husbands' names, for which their husbands then refused to be responsible since their wives could not legally make a contract for the husband's property.[5]

The idea that marriage might erase the economic agency of the husband became a central argument for those crusading to change marital property laws. Feminist Annie Besant adopted this line of argument in her 1878 "Marriage as It Was, as It Should Be": "Many a man's life is now rendered harder than it ought to be, by the waste and extravagance of a wife who can pledge his name and his credit, and even ruin him before he knows his danger" (29). Trollope's characters feel the force of the argument. In a sentiment that mirrors Alice's ambivalence about a marital loss of freedom, her cousin and fiancé George Vavasor explains that marriage is as much a horrifying loss of agency for men as it is for women. He calls marriage a ceremony in which "a man should give permission to a priest to tie him to another human being like a Siamese twin, so that all power of separate and solitary action should be taken from him for ever" (*Can You* 2:311).

But as Palliser's pleas that Glencora not separate herself from him indicate, imagining a coherent social structure still depended in great part on the sense that affiliation required the different relationships to property that men and women experience. In the Married Women's Property Bill of 1882, Parliament showed itself particularly anxious to preserve a difference in gendered relations to property so that it might also preserve the gendered difference in political participation that property ownership implied. While awarding women increased rights to claim their own property in some circumstances while married, Parliament shied away from granting them the same rights that even a single woman would have in regard to her own property. By awarding to married women "protection, not independence," the law still insisted that the wife's experience of property must remain primarily embedded in that of her husband's (Shanley 130). Trollope likewise seems reluctant to acknowledge changes in women's legal status. While in their official capacity his fictional legislators address issues of franchise reform, Church disestablishment, and Irish tenant right,—all issues that were being actively debated at the time—but they never tackle in Parliament the very current issues of married women's property or women's franchise. Instead, the moment Palliser takes public blame for Glencora's rash political promises stands in for debate on any actual legislation concerning women. During this session, the narrator notes that all the galleries are packed, "for it was the only matter they remembered in which a woman's conduct might probably be called in question in the House of Commons" (*Prime Minister* 492). But given the storm of legislative debate over married women's property and even women's franchise at that time, Trollope is willfully omitting decades of political debate in which women's conduct was repeatedly called into question in the House of Commons.[6]

If such an omission indicates that Trollope is as anxious as Palliser that men and women not be divided, his inclusion in the novels of marriages that fail to cohere around the vicarious enjoyment of property also indicates his awareness of its approaching obsolescence. In the catastrophic Kennedy marriage, Trollope links the literal reengineering of marital property arrangements to the erosion of marriage as a metaphor of multinational unity for the British state. Trollope's mindfulness of the trouble with late-Victorian marriage creates dissonance in his use of the marriage analogy of Anglo-Irish Union. While this notion of the marriage of England and Ireland—with Ireland acting as bride—is perhaps one of the most familiar and pervasive metaphors by which both nations thought about their political union, in Trollope's novels—acutely attuned as they are to the conflicting desires and ambitions of both parties yoked together by marriage—the use of such an analogy carries extra weight.[7] Such a moment comes in *Phineas Finn* when Trollope describes Mr. Monk's attitude to Ireland: "But if it was incumbent on England to force upon Ireland the maintenance of the union for her own sake, and for England's sake—because England could not afford independence established so close against her own ribs,—it was at any rate necessary to England's character that the bride thus bound in a compulsory wedlock should be endowed with all the best privileges that a wife can enjoy. Let her not be a kept mistress. Let it be bone of my bone and flesh of my flesh, if we are to live together in the married state" (551).

While the assertion is made without any detectable irony, it possesses unnerving overtones, coming so soon after Lady Laura's revelation to Phineas that her marriage has left her "no escape, no hope, no prospect of relief, no place of consolation" (539). Mary Jean Corbett notes the jarring connotations of the passage, reading the context of the deeply unhappy Kennedy marriage as a straightforward allegory of the afflictions of Anglo-Irish union. Finn's oddly prolonged and violent involvement in the marriage, however, makes its symbolic value more complex than simple allegory. In *Phineas Redux* the marriage analogy becomes explicitly violent when Kennedy, teetering on the edge of madness, rants to Phineas that Laura must return to the house as his wife because she is "bone of my bone, and flesh of my flesh" (1:87). And yet it is Phineas who is the object of Kennedy's tyranny, not Laura. Even before the Kennedy marriage disintegrates, the coercive atmosphere of the house at Loughlinter elicits from Phineas an uneasy sense that his Irishness implicates him in the abusive marriage plot: "What was he, Phineas Finn, an Irishman from Killaloe, living in that great house of Loughlinter as though he were one of the family, striving to kill the hours, and feeling that he was in some way subject to the dominion of his host?" (*Phineas Finn* 326). After he resolves to avoid both spouses, Finn continues to be drafted against his will as go-between for Kennedy and Lady Laura, an odd domestic third to their troubled marriage. His involvement only ends when Kennedy makes an attempt on his life, an act of violence that leads, through a long chain of uniquely Trollopian gossip trails, to Phineas being imprisoned as the prime suspect in the murder of Mr. Bonteen, a man who had previously made much of Finn's involvement with the married Lady Laura.[8]

Finn's unhappy relationship to the Anglo-Irish marriage analogy does not make him an opponent to Union, by any means. As Irish secretary in Palliser's government, he undertakes an active anti–Home Rule campaign, hoping "to prove to his susceptible countrymen that at the present moment no curse could be laid upon them so heavy as that of having to rule themselves apart from England" (*Prime Minister* 92). He pontificates, "I would endeavour to teach them that they can get nothing by Home Rule,—that their taxes would be heavier, their property less secure, their lives less safe, their general position more debased, and their chances of national success more remote than ever" (104). His easy classification of himself as separate from the "them" of Ireland springs from a double division. On the one hand, Finn considers his permanent home to be in England, where he has by this time married a non-Irish and non-British wife, so that, indeed, Home Rule would not endanger *his* taxes, *his* property, or *his* life. On the other hand, Finn assumes the rhetoric of the elected representative, who speaks of those he represents as "they" even though he ostensibly acts as one who shares with "them" an identity and interests. This coincidence of divisions, whereby those most legitimately at the center of the nation might speak exactly as those who occupy another nation, reveals how the character of Phineas Finn displaces the marriage analogy, embodying in one person the sort of vicarious enjoyment otherwise articulated in marital terms. In Finn, Trollope is able to imagine the anomalous position of Ireland to be fundamental to the English nation, not because it can operate as the metaphorical bride of England, the vicarious enjoyer of English property, but because it can produce an individual consciousness whose internalized strangeness makes even his own experience always seem somewhat vicarious. In other words, Finn does not stand for the Irish wife of the English nation; he is in himself both husband and wife, owner and enjoyer, citizen and stranger.

After all, Finn, who progresses from a penniless and unknown member for Loughshane to Irish secretary under Palliser's government, is never the stranger on whom Trollope frequently relies to make apparent the otherwise invisible practices of Englishness. When we are first introduced to him, he has been studying English law in London for three years and is already well established among a parliamentary social set. Yet Finn's Irish background always hovers nearby as an implied alibi for his tendency to be of two minds, often at the same time. The Catholic son of an Irish Catholic doctor and a Protestant mother, and Catholic brother to several Protestant sisters, Finn carries within himself the divide that makes his own experience of the English nation always vicarious, even when he occupies the center. His entrance into the House of Commons is both vicarious and enjoyed at the same time—"He was confused, half elated, half disappointed. . . . He found himself constantly regretting that he was there; and as constantly telling himself that he, hardly yet twenty-five, without a shilling in the world, had achieved an entrance into that assembly which by the consent of all men is the greatest in the world" (*Phineas Finn* 71). Repeatedly, his Irishness is referred to as causing a profound, but often very useful, disconnect that allows him to maintain opposing positions at once: "He felt that he had two identities,—that he was, as it were, two separate persons,—and that he could, without any real faithlessness, be very much in love with Violet Effingham in his position of man of fashion, and member of Parliament in England, and also warmly attached to dear little Mary Flood Jones as an Irishman of Killaloe" (354).

This is a doubleness Trollope lets Phineas get away with, even though it is identical to the sort of duplicity exhibited by the villains of the Palliser series. Like the ultimately exiled characters of George Vavasor, Ferdinand Lopez, and even Joseph Emilius, Finn is a man championed by women but not quite accepted by masculine English society. Finn's success in keeping his Irish origins a thing entirely separate from his London existence means that "[o]f those who knew him intimately, not one in twenty were aware from whence he came, what his parentage, or what his means of living" (253). This is exactly the same position occupied by both Emilius, who acquires a new name, religion, and marital status on his immigration to England, and the English George Vavasor, of whom "[f]ew of his friends knew where he lived . . . The people at his lodgings did not even know that he had relatives and his nearest relatives hardly knew that he had lodgings" (*Can You* 2:121). It is also the grounds on which Mr. Wharton rejects Ferdinand Lopez as a possible son-in-law (*Prime Minister* 31, 33). Much like the crypto-Judaic social climber, who gains his future father-in-law's grudging acceptance by saving the son of the house from midnight muggers, Phineas also wins the approval of the Standish family by saving son-in-law Kennedy from a late-night garroting. Phineas is rewarded liberally for his bravery. He stands for Loughton fully endorsed by its retiring member, Mr. Standish, thus maintaining his precarious foothold in Westminster and continuing in both his political and romantic triumphs. Lopez, on the other hand, only slides downward after his heroism wins him the hand of Emily Wharton. His financial position plummets, and he loses both the election and the hope of a good reputation in a parliamentary bid that ends in a blackmail scandal. After the collapse of his plans to emigrate and a proposal of elopement humiliatingly spurned by Lizzie Eustace, he throws himself under a train.

That the Irish Phineas Finn is copiously rewarded for exhibiting the same attributes—and even engaging in some of the same actions—as the Jewish Ferdinand Lopez suggests a hierarchy of ethnicities, in which the Irishman can be more successful within English society than can the Jew. Such success, rather than implying a closer national kinship between Englishman and Irishman than between Englishman and Jew, actually seems to depend more on the Irishman's failure to completely assimilate. As Julian Wolfreys and Michael Ragussis point out, the successful adoption of English characteristics by Jewish characters always threatens the coherence of English identity. If Englishness can be so easily imitated, its exclusivity to England might be revealed to be entirely fictional; Englishness might not, after all, belong to the nation. Finn's Irishness never threatens such alienation. Instead, his double life is treated as wholly Irish. In Trollope, the Irish advantage is an ability to simulate Englishness, springing from a specifically Irish talent at being two things at once. Trollope unquestionably imagines Lopez's failure to be rooted in his Jewish heritage, but this flaw also results in Lopez's inability to be consistently duplicitous. Instead, Lopez proves unable to keep hidden the interests and ambitions his heritage has (allegedly) inspired in him. He fails at being something other than what he is, a failure he also recognizes as racial. On his honeymoon with Emily, he resolves not to discuss the topic of the money he desperately needs but then finds himself constitutionally unable to keep his resolution: "It is easy for a man to say that he will banish care, so that he may enjoy to the full the delights of the moment. But this is a power which none but a savage possesses—or perhaps an Irishman" (*Prime Minister* 215).

Finn unquestionably is that Irishman. His ability to be both English and Irish in his vacillating behavior culminates in his appointment to the office of secretary for Ireland, where it is his obligation to shuttle between Dublin Castle and Westminster. This shuttling seems in itself to be the thing that garners an outsider a permanent place in Trollope's scheme of the nation. Finn's wife, Madame Goesler, the only Jewish figure to escape the series' otherwise relentless anti-Semitism, also shuttles between London and Vienna, where she attends to the landed property she owns there. The fact that this property is entirely Phineas's according to English law and entirely hers according to European law further secures Phineas's status as both owner and enjoyer simultaneously.[9] It is no accident, then, that Finn feels prompted to speak out on "that terribly unintelligible subject, Irish tenant right" (703), which, in seeking partial property rights in rented land for the Irish tenant, joins in confusing ways the role of owner and enjoyer. In taking a stand against his own party in favor of Irish tenant right, Finn masters the art of vicarious government. He professes a belief in the reform not because he thinks he can get it passed but just to "make them believe that there is something in it" (703). Such a move is not the trick of an outsider about to be pushed to the margins of the text but a standard move of Trollope's titular "Irish member," whose Irish outsider status is paradoxically what makes him a "member" of the British government. Both different and insider at the same time, Finn affirms the anomalous unity that goes into making up the totality of the United Kingdom of Great Britain and Ireland. Pressed up against the ribs of Britain as he is, Finn proves to be the very heart of England, the vicarious enjoyer with his own cabinet office, the outsider whose relish for government can never be dulled by his participation in it, the split self who enables a narration of England as a nation of independent agents still able to experience their own collectivity.

This Irish state of mind is also, for Trollope, the state of mind in which he hopes to leave his readers. In a series of novels in which the consummation of happy plots—and marriages—tends toward Westminster, Trollope gives the reader the experience of the state that lies at the center of the United Kingdom even as he teaches us to understand our enjoyment of such plots as arising out of an envy for what we lack. Every book, in detailing the esoteric intrigues of elections, party politics, reform bills, Church disestablishment, and the decimalization of the twelve-penny shilling, both instructs us that "[i]t is something to have sat in the House of Commons, though it has been but for one session!" (*Can You* 2:43) and puts the shape of that something in our hands. Yet that shape inevitably dissolves into a bitter longing arising from not having at all. Even as he narrates George Vavasor's first seating in Parliament, Trollope directly addresses his readers, asking pointedly, "hast thou never confessed, when standing [at the gates of the House of Commons] that Fate has been unkind to thee in denying thee the one thing that thou hast wanted?" (2:44). Trollope trains his readers in two incommensurable feelings—intimate familiarity with the workings of the British government and a sense of its impossible distance from our grasp. These two poles are the two poles of collectivity established by Bagehot's sense of a nation that depends entirely on two separate populations, whose harmony can be preserved by their complete failure to understand in the same way the state machinery they share. As Trollope contemplates what to him seems like the inexorable progress toward liberal equality among all people, he trains his readers to preserve within themselves the sense of their vicarious stake in the British state, a vicariousness no longer ensured by the political divisions of property but by the divide in the United Kingdom figured by the Irish Sea.

CHAPTER FIVE

At Home in the Public Domain

George Moore's *Drama in Muslin*, George Meredith's *Diana of the Crossways*, and the Intellectual Property of Union

By the 1880s, British thinking about property had largely transitioned from an assumption that property was a right that existed prior to the law to an assumption that property rights were created and defined by law. Commentators on a wide range of issues showed an increasing acceptance of the idea that the state might create, reassign, or even entirely extinguish rights to property, in the name of the public good. In keeping with this development, liberals and radicals interested in land reform increasingly made the argument that property rights in land could only be allotted by the state. Because of the precedent of the Irish land acts and agitation for land reform within Britain, this logic also seeped into discussions of copyright protection for intellectual property. Proponents for limited copyright reasoned that just as the state might have the right to reassign ownership of land for the public good, so too might the state have the right to limit individual property in copyright for the sake of a wider public domain.

This idea of the public domain—a space in which the state intervenes in order to suspend the rules of private property—preoccupies the two authors I examine in this chapter. George Moore's *Drama in Muslin* (1886) and George Meredith's *Diana of the Crossways* (1885) both imagine a space of ideas that can belong to no one individual as a space of salvation for their two heroines. But the two also tell their stories against the backdrop of Irish agitation for land rights. In doing so, I argue, both authors respond to proposals of Home Rule made in the same years. Both Meredith and Moore came out explicitly in support of Home Rule, and their preoccupation with the public domain suggests one way they might imagine even that measure as a sacrifice without the threat of a real loss. After all, when an author gives up property in his or her ideas, the sacrifice is one that leads to a fuller community access, one from which even the author is not barred. Both Moore and Meredith imply that giving up Ireland to Home Rule simply will make Britain like an author out of copyright. Ireland will persist as a part of the intellectual ether of Britain, regardless of its immediate political configuration. By seeing Ireland as always in the British public domain, the authors envision Ireland's connection to Britain as always presided over by the British state, a state that limits individual property rights in order to protect a public domain belonging to everyone.

Land and Copyright

Jordanna Bailkin, in her work on the early-twentieth-century development of the concept of cultural property, notes that the years 1870–1914 marked a radical unsettling of "ideas about the relationship between property and citizenship in Britain" (11). She points out as a symptom of this shake-up the founding of citizens' groups devoted to redefining or reforming land law— the Liberty and Property Defence League (founded in 1882), the Free Land League (founded in 1885), the Land Law Reform League (founded in 1880), the Metropolitan Public Gardens Association (founded in 1882), the Land Nationalization Society (founded in 1880), the English Land Restoration League (founded in 1883).

For Bailkin's purpose, the formation of these groups mark a crucial moment in art history. Their activism toward redefining property rights in land, she argues, contributed to an environment in which one could think of a nation claiming property rights in cultural objects originating within its borders. Lobbying for the preservation of commons, the creation of urban public spaces, the abolition of primogeniture, the creation of a central land registry, or the retrenchment of landlord duties, their land-based activism, as Bailkin suggests, created the preconditions for new conceptual approaches to culture as collective property.

The moment Bailkin identifies is one in which the concept of property was pulled in two directions in the United Kingdom. More strictly defined as entirely individual and freely alienable in English law, property in land under Irish law became more susceptible to dual interests and dual ownership. The United Kingdom had witnessed several legislative interventions that insisted on the absolute and individual nature of property rights. The Married Women's Property Act of 1882 affirmed, even if it did not entirely enforce, the notion that property was at heart an individual, not a family, right. The 1882 Settled Land Act dismantled many of the checks on alienability that had plagued entailed properties in England. Under the terms of the act, the current proprietor, known as the "tenant for life," had full powers to sell the estate or to work other profitable but permanent changes on the land. But these two legislative assertions of the individualized nature of even landed property were balanced by the Irish Land Act of 1881, the act that had generalized to all of Ireland the principle that a tenant had some form of proprietary right to the land he leased. The Crofters Act of 1886 instituted similar terms for tenants in the Highlands of Scotland and was passed with justifications almost identical to those that surrounded the Irish Land Acts.[1]

In the end, the effect of this spate of communal property "restored" in the name of historicism was not safely quarantined to the Celtic zones of the British Isles. The property activist groups whose foundings dotted the 1880s drew on the deep history of English property law to argue for state intervention into English land rights, even when their most immediate demands were for the extension of absolute individual rights to property in land.[2] Arthur Arnold's Free Land League, for instance, was founded to advocate for the abolition of primogeniture and the easier sale of land, but the group also maintained that the state nonetheless had a dormant "joint interest" in the land. Arnold argued that "[t]he Land belongs to the nation, to the state, to the people," a principle proven by the historical fact that English land law recognizes no absolute title to land, all land being held mediately from the crown.[3] John George Shaw-Lefevre's earlier Commons Preservation Society (1865) drew on historicist approaches in their successful bid to keep Epping Forest, 3,000 acres of wooded land near London, from being enclosed by private owners. Ultimately, the society won their case by proving not only that inalienable usage rights had been held immemorially by the commoners living adjacent to the forest but also that, since all forest lands belonged formally to the crown, enclosure of the forest was an infringement on what was really royal property.[4]

This agitation for redistributed property rights in land had the surprising effect of settling controversies in intellectual property law. Paul Saint-Amour argues that it is in the nineteenth century that "copyright law and its model of individual creation transcended the status of an argument and became consecrated and codified as a dominant discourse" (14). The idea that an author had property in literary work that was absolute, but good only for a limited amount of time, had become simply common sense to a broad swath of the public. In this section, I briefly examine some of the discussions about copyright that Saint-Amour has already mined in his deft analysis of the hegemonic status of authorial property in the last third of the century. I retread this ground to examine how simultaneous legislation in land law affected assumptions about the author as proprietor. What I find is that the author is unquestionably assumed to be owner of literary property but that authors themselves, frequently drawing on what they saw as precedents in land law, are much more willing to concede that such a right, far from being a natural and absolute right prior to all social agreement, is entirely dependent on legislative construction. This willingness to see authorship as constructed by the state leads to a more vivid imagination of what is also constructed by the state as *not* private property: the public domain of ideas. In an age of agitation for footpath access for the lower classes and commons restoration for the agricultural laborer, the public domain had available conceptual models on which it could be based other than the free marketplace of ideas by which it was characterized during the height of free-trade agitation in the 1840s. In the 1880s, the public domain could also be imagined as a commons, a space immemorially available, preserved from the propertizing regimes of the free market by a state whose mandate was to look after the public good and act as trustee for its communal inheritance.

During the course of the century that Saint-Amour terms the "adolescence" of intellectual property, the idea of copyright underwent two major interrogations. The first proceeded from 1837 to 1842, when, under noisy protest from free-trade advocates, the copyright length was extended to forty-two years, or seven years after the author's death, whichever was longer. The second occurred from 1876 to 1878, when, prompted by the fact that international copyright law made British-authored books cheaper in the United States, India, and Canada, a parliamentary commission was established to look into whether copyright was even the most appropriate and enforceable form for rewarding authorial labor.[5] Both episodes framed the dispute as an argument about the comparative value of two goods: the public good to be derived from cheap and easily reproduced literature versus the expedience and/or moral obligation to reward an author for his or her labor. Both the first and second copyright disputes ended in an affirmation of the author's right to enjoy property in his (in parliamentary debates the author was, despite all evidence to the contrary, exclusively male) creation, for at least a limited amount of time. Both disputes essentially dismissed the suggestion that to legalize an author's right to profit from his work was to rob the public of access to ideas. However, the later controversy over copyright differed crucially from the early 1840s debate. First, the later debate more readily integrated the idea that authorial property in literature was entirely a creation of the state. Second, it articulated a more comprehensive picture of the relationship between the author and the public domain.

In the later debates, the notion that an author enjoyed only state-created rights to literary property was more acceptable, especially to those who had already argued, in the debates over landed property, that property in the end is purely an affair of expedience on which the state must deliberate. Commenting on the question of copyright, Matthew Arnold quite freely admits that "there is no question that [an author] can have a right in his productions so far as the law may choose to create one for him," but he also insists that "an author has no natural right to a property in his production." In fact, no one, whether author or mere citizen has "a natural right to anything whatever" even to what "he may produce or acquire" ("Copyright" 322). He concedes that humans show an instinct for property, and that society has a tendency to respect this instinct where it is possible and promotes the public good. But he dismisses the arguments of those who want to settle whether literary property is or is not "property in itself." Arnold admonishes them that "property is the creation of law" only (323).

Arnold's convictions are not far removed from his verdicts on land, both English and Irish. Arguing for changes in land law in England, he notes, "I cannot . . . perceive that man is really conscious of any abstract natural rights at all. . . . All rights are created by law and are based on expediency. . . . Property is created and maintained by law" (*Equality* 46). He cites both the more abstract John Stuart Mill and the decidedly historicist Maine in asserting that rights of bequest are rather new to modern times and not inalienably a right of any proprietor (47). He follows a similar line of argument in an essay anticipating the Second Irish Land Act. While he disapproves of any proposal that will legalize property arrangements in Ireland not also legalized in Britain, he proves equally hostile to those who oppose changes in Irish land law based on the argument that "property is sacred" (290). Such arguments never seem to apply, he notes, when the English discuss Henry VIII's expropriation of monastic property. So confident is Arnold in his dismissal of any natural basis to property rights that he recommends the wholesale expropriation of irresponsible landlords in Ireland. Like the monks whose "irregularities and vices . . . struck at the root of social order" in Henry VIII's time, the Irish landlords, "with their harshness, vices, and neglect of duties," must similarly be dispossessed, purely for "reason of state" (291).

Even when they were not so extreme in their enthusiasm for landlord expropriation, plenty of voices had spoken out in the 1860s and 1870s on Irish land reform and made familiar the argument that property, rather than being a natural right, was simply an expedient arrangement enforced by the state. The formulation of this argument at first depended on the exceptional nature of land, which, having been made by no one, could not be owned on the basis of an owner's right to the fruits of his labor. The *Westminster Review* review of John Stuart Mill's "England and Ireland" argued that a government can "act as a passive trustee for the landed property of the whole nation" and that individual property in land was only enjoyable for a limited time, held "through the temporary forbearance of the State" ("Modern Notions" 178). A few years earlier, the economist T. E. Cliffe Leslie, championing the legitimacy of a shared tenant right to the landlord's property in Ireland, had argued that landlords were mistaken in believing "that the law has conferred on them the same absolute dominion over the land in which they have estates, as traders have over their goods." Mixing historical with theoretical justifications for his argument against a natural right to property in land, Leslie reminds landlords that "the law of the country has maintained from the Conquest that fundamental distinction between property in land, and all other kinds of property" (221). After running through a brief history of English land law from before the Norman Conquest to the present day, he adds the more abstract argument that "Mr. Mill finds a natural claim on the part of the state for the public to the absolute ownership of land, in the fact that man did not make it" (223). On both these bases he grounds his argument that land "belongs by law to the State" and that "[n]o man is in law the absolute owner of lands. He can only hold an estate in them" (221).

While the arguments themselves were controversial, they had already legitimated one of the central transformations of nineteenth-century Britain: the creation of the rail system. As historian R. W. Kostal notes, the private parliamentary acts necessary to create railway companies necessarily assigned to the company the right to expropriate land that otherwise could not have been transferred or sold by the owner subject to the laws of entail. While owners had to be compensated for the railway's taking of their land, and more often than not railway companies negotiated more than fair prices with the largest landholders in order to win their goodwill, the parliamentary acts that brought railway companies into being allowed them power to force an unwilling landowner to sell his land at price determined by an outside agency. The mass land transfer that followed upon the railway mania in the 1840s, Kostal argued, had no precedent for its scale or its speed. As early as the 1840s, rail trade publications were noting with satisfaction that "[t]he tenure by which all land is held in Great Britain . . . is The Public Good. . . . The proprietors of land in England are only perpetual stewards of the soil for the benefit of the people who dwell there on" (qtd in Kostal 179).

For Kostal, such expressions within the rail trade indicate that in practice, if not in publicly accepted theory, Britain already had in place a state that allotted and took away property rights in the name of the public good. The accumulated experience of rail developers and the rising profile of land reformers combined to make such assumptions familiar enough to be cited by 1876, the year the copyright commission, convened by the House of Commons, began its investigation into the status of copyright. Commentators on the commission found a common ground, in fact, between discussions of authorial property and property in land. J. A. Froude, reviewing the arguments contained in the commission's reports ventriloquizes "men of letters" who argue that the fact of copyright's expiration does not prove that copyright is no property at all. He answers for them that "[i]f the State, out of consideration for the public good, has decided that [copyright] shall be [an author's] only for his lifetime and for a few years beyond, the State has done no more than it has done with the most solid of all properties, *land*." He foretells, "A time may come when all land shall be held under the Crown under an expiring lease. . . . It will not be the less a man's property as long as the State allows it to him. A limited tenure may be as complete while it lasts as a tenure in perpetuity" ("Report" 298).

The journalist and novelist Grant Allen also invokes arguments about limited rights to land in his discussion of copyright, but he uses these arguments to suggest that, since intellectual property admits of the fullest, most absolute rights of ownership, it is actually the model of all other property. "The ownership of land is a mere convention," he argues on the grounds that no one can claim a full title to anything they have not made themselves. For that reason, "property is really and naturally property in proportion as it owes little to the raw material and much to the labour bestowed upon it," with the ultimate model of such property being the "literary and artistic work," which outstrips all other property for its spare dependence on raw material (355). But even in asserting the absolute, perpetual nature of an author's property in his work, a right that law neither creates nor destroys but merely recognizes or violates, Allen nonetheless naturalizes the idea that all objects of property are, to some extent, mixed with "raw material," something the producer has not himself produced. Advocating that only the state has the right to take on the role of landlord, Allen also argues that no one produces anything without taking at least something out of this state-owned zone of commonly held property. Land includes not just soil, he reminds his reader: "Wood, water, coal, iron, metals, beasts, building materials, and all the various objects which we use in every industrial art, are all ultimately derived from 'land'" (353). Given the list, it is difficult to avoid the implication that books, too, ultimately come from the land, to which Allen says the state has the ultimate right.

It is this notion that the state *should* be involved in creating, enforcing, and, even if need be, ending, property rights in land, that eased the contradictions of thinking about copyright as property, but property with a limited lifespan. Thomas Farrer, one of the copyright commissioners who suggested that copyright might be more properly treated as a temporary monopoly, on the order of a patent, misjudges how widespread this idea had become when he argues that the understanding of copyright as property required belief in two mutually exclusive ideas. The first is that an author has "an absolute right" not just to the physical object he produces in his literary labor but also to its form, and that "this right is as unqualified in its nature, extent, and duration as that of any owner of any property whatsoever" (837). This first idea coexists with the contradictory second idea, Farrer argues, that "the author has no right over his idea or over the form of his idea after it has left his own mind or his own closet and has been given to the public" (838). But Farrer's polarization of ideas, in which one either had absolute and total control over an object, and thus could call it property, or only a limited right to it, and thus could claim no property to it at all, was already outdated, ignoring as it did decades of discussion about the limited rights any landowner might claim to his property. Farrer found himself on the losing end of an argument that an author should be rewarded through a royalty system, rather than subjected to the fiction of authorial property.

I do not wish to overstate my argument. The notion of an author who has a natural right to profit from the work, and to control the work's reproduction by virtue of having created it, was very much in operation during discussions of copyright in 1876 through 1878, as it still is today.[6] However, alongside those notions, the 1876–78 copyright debates featured many statements accommodating the idea that copyright amounted to a limited, state-created right in authorial property, rather than a natural right. And these statements more often than not referred to the partial ownership of land, allotted by the state, as the precedent for thinking of such rights as property. "We forbid entails beyond certain limits, we prevent the accumulation of property after death, we take away a man's land whether he wishes to sell it or not, if the land is required for public purposes," Edward Dicey says by way of preamble to his more expansive argument that "there is no abstract principle or standard by which you can determine what degree of protection should be granted to property in general." Thus, the discussion about copyright is simply a question "of degree, not of principle" (127, 130).

This willingness to make intellectual property a question "of degree, not of principle," also enabled an approach to thinking about the author's relationship to the public domain that was not simply one of competing interests, in which an author's work either belonged exclusively to him by virtue of it being entirely his creation or belonged exclusively to the public domain because the nature of the world of ideas admitted of no individual property at all. Instead, there were more moderate versions of authorship that departed from a model of self-generated originality. Froude willingly dispenses with the ideal of the entirely autonomous author: "When all is said, an author's work is but partially his own. His ideas and sentiments he has in common with his age. His facts are generally collected by the labour of others. How much of any book is the author's own it is impossible to say" (300). The value of an original piece of literature, he argues, was not in its having been irreducibly original but in articulating the ideas that "lie undefined in all men's minds." Froude explains, "The man of genius sees clearly what others half perceive at moments and lose again. He seizes upon it and fixes it in a shape visible to all, and the rest of us ever after are put in practical possession of the treasures of our own minds" (337). In Froude's vision, the work of the author is pulled from the public domain, "seized" for a moment, and then released again.

When the narrative of authorial property's release into the public domain was assumed to be a narrative of an absolute and natural right given up, its sacrificial valence was unmistakable. An author gives up his creation for the good of the community, sometimes even at the founding moment of the community.

Trevor Ross points out that the late-eighteenth-century decision to limit the time during which copyright could be enforced was also the decision that formalized an idea of a reading public who could claim a national literature as their heritage. The personage of "the common reader," he notes, first emerges in literature that calls for the defeat of perpetual copyright (16). In the most extreme formulations of the public domain as a nationally available commons, opponents of copyright argued that only literature written for no reward at all would be of a high enough quality to be truly beneficial to the British public. Only a sacrificial disavowal of remuneration on the part of the author could create a worthy national literature.

But by the 1870s, once the notion of the state's involvement with property had become a familiar, if not entirely uncontroversial, way to think about property in land, the concept of the public domain was less susceptible to sacrificial terms. Instead of the author being called upon to give up everything for the public good, an author under limited copyright might trust the state to weigh his interests in balance with the public's. In suggestions that the state might take on the role of landlord for the entire United Kingdom, guarding the land from complete susceptibility to free-market alienation, lay a model for the state to act as a trustee that guaranteed communal property's accessibility and required sacrifice from no one. After all, as the oft-cited argument went, did the state not fairly compensate landed proprietors for the land it commandeered for railways, rather than requiring a full sacrifice? After the passage of both Irish Land Acts, the state had become the entity that could allot rights to both tenant and landlord, and thus the entity that could mediate the competing needs of public domain and individual author. The state imagined to have the right to confiscate land from the (properly compensated) proprietor was the state that could be imagined as doing the same, in the most public-minded way, for the literary author.

The state, more solidly imagined as arbiter of authorial property rights, then, could be the entity that guarded against a too-total sacrifice on the part of any author. That is the logic put forth by both the novels I examine in this chapter. Telling the story of two fictional authors—not insignificantly, women authors—whose literary accomplishments are portrayed not as works of self-generated genius but as straightforward takings from a public domain, both novels narrate the authors as avoiding the life of sacrifice that their situations seem to demand. Both novels, explicitly concerned with the injustice women suffer in a patriarchal society, imagine the public domain of ideas as a safe space for women, one not entirely equivalent to the free-market economy in which a too-public woman might be mistaken as prostituting herself in the form of her literary works. Instead, these books present their two female authors as taking from a common fund of ideas, protected by the state, rather than depleting their own selves in the act of writing.

Both Meredith and Moore freight their plots of antisacrifice with the politics of Ireland in an era of Home Rule agitation and British-sponsored Home Rule bills. Certainly if Moore and Meredith were motivated to imagine women saved from a life of sacrifice, they had even more motive to imagine the Irish as saved from a similar life. The nationalist movement in Ireland took shape under a sacrificial logic in which nationalist martyrs would commit themselves to privation, prison, and even death in order to found an independent Ireland. By crafting plots of antisacrificial logic against an Irish backdrop, Meredith and Moore flatten out a rhetoric of nationalist martyrdom. Instead, they present Ireland as both producer and consumer of a pool of common ideas that Britain and Ireland share, a pool of which Ireland will always remain a part, regardless of Home Rule. Despite the pro–Home Rule stance of both authors, the books imagine the persistence of Union in structuring the public domain. The copyright debates of the decade before the proposal of the first Home Rule bill underscored one thing with clarity: that Ireland was, if nothing else, a sharer in Britain's copyright regulations and thus part of the British public domain. This was not the case with Canada or India, where cheap editions of British texts from America flooded the market. American disregard for British copyright constituted different publics in Canada and India, whose access to literature differed widely from the reading public in the British Isles. But in Ireland, as in Britain, the same rules of copyright held throughout the nineteenth century, constituting the entire United Kingdom as one public domain. Meredith's and Moore's novels might be thought of as imaginatively seeking to keep Ireland there.

Drama in Muslin: Writing from the Public Domain

While George Moore was not a prominent commenter on copyright, he was, even at the beginning of his career, very savvy about the ambivalent propertization that copyright afforded an author. The exclusive property of copyright, he knew, could be property for more than just the author. Newly returned to the United Kingdom from almost a decade in bohemian Paris, Moore in the early

1880s vowed to be "Zola's ricochet in England," a champion both of Émile Zola's naturalist style and a translator of his actual work.[7] The mutual copyright treaties among European nations allowed Moore to claim his own proprietary interest in Zola's work, as the exclusive translator of it in Britain. Moore insinuated himself into Zola's life with the proposal to represent his literary interests in England, a proposal that also advanced Moore's literary interests. Returning from France, where he had discussed business matters with Zola, Moore published "A Visit to M. Zola" in the *St James Gazette* (82).

But Moore, in his run-ins with Mudie's Circulating Library, was also on the receiving end of the ways that nonowners could block proprietary rights. His emulation of Zola's naturalist style in his first novel, *A Modern Lover* (1883), earned him a reputation for indecency that met with a chilly reception at Mudie's, the largest purchaser of triple-decker novels in the United Kingdom. Mudie's often bought out entire first runs of novels for their system of national lending libraries. A sizable purchase of one's novel by Mudie's often insured its long-term success. Readers who encountered the original at the lending library were often buyers of later cheap one-volume editions of the novel. Rather than exercising a monopoly on production, Mudie's exercised a monopoly on consumption (a monopsony, in economic terms). Without Mudie's patronage, a novel had very few other channels for sales.[8]

Outraged that Mudie's had decided to buy only fifty copies of his first novel, because of—according to Moore—complaints about the book they had fielded from "two ladies in the country," Moore launched an attack against the lending library. He published his second novel *A Mummer's Wife* (1884) only in a cheap one-volume edition, hoping to bypass lending library patronage altogether. He let loose an invective against Mudie's in the form of an article, "A New Censorship of Literature," in the *Pall Mall Gazette*. In it he praises recent articles on the reform of English fiction written by Walter Besant and Henry James, but he foretells that such advice can never be taken while Mudie's controls all literature with their "absolute dictatorship," a combined practice of censorship and undue influence over publishing practices. The piece simultaneously attacks Mudie's for impeding Moore's authorial autonomy and announces Moore's recuperation of the same—he reports that sales of his newly released novel in one volume has been met with wild success. He then turns upside down the hierarchy Grant Allen suggested, in which the author of imaginative literature is most owner of his own work because he is least indebted to anyone for its raw material. Instead, Moore suggests that the current state of publishing yields the most freedom to authors who take freely from the public domain of ideas. With his commitment to one-volume publishing, Moore predicts, "I shall now, therefore, for the future enjoy the liberty of speech granted to the journalist, the historian, and the biographer, rights unfortunately in the present day denied to the novelist" (2).

The sort of property copyright was for George Moore—susceptible to others' claims of interest in it, in danger of control by consumers, only controllable if the owner compromises in the amount of profit he will realize from it—was not entirely different from the sort of property that land was for him, as an Anglo-Irish landlord in the middle of the Land War. The Moore estate was in County Mayo, ground zero for Land War agitation, and its tenants combined in a refusal to pay all rent. After a decade as an expatriate in France, Moore returned to Ireland in 1879 when the agent who looked after the estate resigned, announcing that any collection of rent was impossible. In his memoirs Moore records his reaction as one of outrage at having been robbed, layered with an ironic recognition of tenant rights to the resources on which he lived. How dare they, he asked, "refuse to starve that I may not be deprived of my demi-tasse at Totroni's?" (qtd in Frazier 65).

At the time he was composing his third novel, *A Drama in Muslin* (1885), land and copyright were not entirely separate in Moore's mind. The term "nursemaid" is one he uses to condemn both Mudie's, the infantilizing self-appointed moral guardian of the British reading public, and the Land League, the corrupt instigators of community violence.[9] Both organizations exercised a monopolistic pressure that allowed them to fix prices (on novels purchased from publishers, on rent) and attenuate the legal owner's full access to profit in his own property. But if both Mudie's and the Land League are in some ways barriers to Moore's experience of full ownership, the implicit solution he proffers in *Drama* is not the restoration or enforcement of absolute individual property but rather an engagement with forms of creation that are always somewhat communal, always dependent on a pool of property never properly belonging to any one person. By celebrating such forms of creation against the backdrop of the Land Wars, Moore also offers his readers a vision of government, whether the official government at Westminster or the informal state created by the Land League, as always constituted by its impulse to relieve owners of the unbearable burdens of enforcing individual rights to private property.

The saving powers of the public domain are crucial to his heroine, Alice Barton. A morally serious but iconoclastic young woman, recently returned from convent school to her family home, an Anglo-Irish estate in West Ireland, at the height of the Land War, Alice feels out of place among her female friends who are primarily concerned with clothes, balls, and landing a husband. She can anticipate only a useless life for herself, as a member of an upper class superfluous to its country and as a woman destined only for a marriage market bereft of men. Unsurprisingly for a late Victorian fictional heroine, Alice finds that professional writing offers her a way out of the destiny she anticipates for herself as "a poor plain girl whom no one would ever think of marrying" (203).

What *is* surprising is that Alice's vocation succeeds precisely to the extent that it fails to follow the model of author as romantic genius. The book opens with a graduation performance of a play she has written herself. The work takes its cue from its schoolgirl audience, telling the tale of a prince who takes a beggarwoman for his bride; it also takes its plot from Alfred Lord Tennyson's ballad "The Beggar Maid" (1842), which itself was taken from Thomas Percy's *Reliques of Ancient Poetry* (1765), a work that gained its reputation by presenting its poetry as part of a literary heritage so long in circulation that it already belonged to its audience, even before they consumed it. This is the sort of promiscuous borrowing from both audience identity and prior literature for which the novel rewards Alice. Instead of being reformed into a more original and mature writerly identity as she begins to write for public consumption, she meets with success by taking her own work from all available sources. Her first attempt at marketable literature, "The Diary of a Plain Girl—Notes and Sensations," simply records her observations of Dublin during the social season there. The novel's narrator praises Alice's literary efforts for their distance from originality: "She saw life from a normal and sensible standpoint, and her merit lay not in the peculiarity or the keenness of her vision, but in the clearness and the common sense she infused into the writing" (233).

The narrator's praise for Alice's clear-eyed writing, the fact that "the artistic question troubled her little," is in no way a contemptuous portrayal of feminine writing as always insufficiently original. To the contrary, her mentor, the English journalist and novelist Mr. Harding, models a writing practice that is far from imaginative creation. He explains to her that he has come to Dublin for the purpose of writing a series of articles on the current state of Ireland. He plans to "take a series of representative characters—the landlord, the grazier, the tenant farmer, the moonlighter, the parson, the priest—and tell their history, their manner of life, and their aims and ambitions" (196). After he has farmed them out in individual sketches to periodicals, he plans to publish them in book form.

His model of writing—taken from reality, adapted for the market, and explicitly constructed around "representative" figures—offers very little room for the imaginative exercise of the authorial mind. Indeed, his talents in the novel are portrayed not as an eye for the singular but rather a talent for understanding the general, the type. He first catches Alice's attention by telling her, rather than asking her, that she is staying at the Dublin hotel in order to attend the Lord Lieutenant's Drawing Room, an annual event akin to the British presentation at court. When she asks how he knows, he claims a knowledge of generalities. It is, he says, the "the natural course of events: a young lady leaves school, she spends four or five months at home, and then she is taken to the Lord Lieutenant's drawing room" (147).

So invested is Harding in types and representative figures that he barely seems to exist as an individual. Despite the weeks they spend together in Dublin, Alice realizes that she never knew "the real man," and the reader is left unsure as to whether there is a real man to be known (188). Instead, he is described as a "literary shopboy" who "flaunted samples of everything he had in stock" for Alice, a man who "paraded his ideas and his sneers as the lay figures [ie, dummies used for modeling] did the mail armour on the castle stairway" (154, 188). For Harding there is no intrinsic connection between internal powers of creation and any of the ideas he purveys, either in writing or in conversation. Taking her cue from him, Alice peddles her own experience not as peculiarly her own but coming merely from a plain girl whose specific identity is irrelevant.

Moore drafts both Alice and Harding into a literary practice that he himself puts into action in his novel, presenting his novel as in no way original. The ripped-from-the-headlines quality of his novel is just one of the many strategies that Moore uses to distance his story from original creation. By the time Moore wrote *Drama in Muslin* it was quite common practice in the historical novel to peg fictional events to real dates and events in the historical world. Moore, however, did so with a journalistic immediacy, dating his plots to quite recent developments in the four years before his book's publication. As if to distance any event from authorial creation and associate it more firmly with mere reporting of public events, Moore often positions a copy of the *Freeman's Journal* in a character's lap or on a breakfast table in order to introduce any political discussion of the Irish situation. He is equally meticulous about giving exact dates to events, subordinating his own plotting to the historical plot of the Land Wars in Ireland. Talk of a potential Coercion Act, which would suspend civil rights in Ireland, of the impending Land Act, of the Phoenix Park murders, of the brief lull in the Land War at the end of 1883 all punctuate the marital misadventures of his female characters. At the same time, his descriptions often feature the prefatory tick "you see," which implies his writing is no more than a repetition of the reader's own sensory experience: "You see a huge shouldered mother, a lean-faced crone, and a squatting tailor . . . ; you see a couple of girls, maids of all work, who smile and call to the dripping coachmen," he reports of the scene just outside Dublin Castle on the night of Alice's debut, adding a couple of pages later, "By your side a weak girl is being driven along by a couple of police officers" (170, 174).

This presentation of authorship as mere reporting of what is already perceived, simply borrowing from events that are part of the public record, can be traced to Moore's interest in a naturalist literary style that treats individuals as products of their environment. His Darwin-inflected insistence on types and representative figures drains the characters of particularity and as a consequence implies that no authorial originality went into creating them. Rather than being an unusual heroine, Alice is, the narrator insists, "a representative woman of 1885"; she and her friend Cecelia, despite all appearances of anomaly, are "curiously representative . . . of this last quarter of the nineteenth century" (228, 196). As a representative woman, the product of no autonomous creation, Alice claims no autonomy even for her own subjectivity. As she sets out to write her first piece for publication, she explains to her friend Cecelia that "conscience is no more than indirect laws—the essence of the laws transmitted by heredity." Far from claiming originality for her thinking, Alice merely sees it as having been produced by her situation. The narrator chimes in to reinforce Alice's lack of volition in her own authorship, indeed a lack of volition in all authorship: "The aesthetic and philosophic aspirations of an epoch—ideas which we believe to have been the invention of individuals are but the intellectual atmosphere of that epoch breathed in greater or less quantities by all" (228).

Alice and Harding, then, might be exemplary vessels for "the intellectual atmosphere of the epoch" by virtue of their recognition that they truly cannot call anything their own. Alice is acutely aware of the lack of charms she has to trade on the marriage market. Harding introduces himself as a writer without a claim to anything Irish at all that might give him particular business in Ireland. "As I do not possess a foot of land," he explains to Alice, "my claim to collect rent would rest on even a slighter basis than that of the landlords." This dispossession has its advantages since, as Harding reports, the result is that "I really feel safer in Ireland than elsewhere." He then adds, with knowing provocation, "Besides I am interested in agrarian outrage and the non-payment of rent" (148). Harding's "interests" allow him to inhabit a position of dispossession similar to that occupied by the impoverished Irish peasants. In Moore's view of Ireland, journalist, unmarried Anglo-Irish women, and the peasants of the Irish Land War are all joined in a mutual lack of property.

State Intervention and the End of Purity

One of the hallmarks of this novel of the Irish marriage market in the time of the Land War is Moore's ambivalent allegorizing of his young female characters as both like the oppressed Irish peasants and like the helpless Anglo-Irish. At first his allegory seems to be that the girls he describes are emblematic of the general thoughtlessness and helplessness of the Anglo-Irish. Describing a Sunday on which the Land League holds a mass meeting and the young women plan a ball, the narrator offers a rather damning double picture in which "the peasants tramped away to the meeting where they would lay claim to the land that they tilled; the young ladies would soon return to their fine house to consider the skirts they would wear at the ball" (72). When offering free, indirect discourse on Anglo-Irish reaction to the Land War, the narrator seems to conflate the viewpoint of the women and the entire class: "An entire race, a whole caste, saw themselves driven out of their soft, warm couches of idleness, and forced in to the struggle for life. The prospect appalled them . . . What could they do with their empty brains? What could they do with their feeble hands?" (95).

But the allegory also swings the other way. In explaining his choice to focus on the story of young women's search for husbands in the midst of the Land War, the narrator explains, "The history of a nation as often lies hidden in social wrongs and domestic griefs as in the story of revolution, . . . and who would say which is of the most vital importance—the thunder of the people against the oppression of the Castle, or the unnatural sterility, the cruel idleness of mind and body of the muslin martyrs?"—"muslin martyrs" being the author's favorite term for his female characters (203). These "martyrs," like the nationalist martyrs who fight the Land War, seem at times to have extraordinary powers to bring down aristocrats. When the penniless Violet, after a merciless campaign waged by both her and her mother, charms a debt-saddled marquis into a proposal of marriage, he wanders the streets of Dublin for hours afterward, stunned that he has passed up the chance to marry a wealthy woman whose money might help save his family estate. His capitulation to the charms of one of these "muslin martyrs" evokes in him a sense of the impending collapse of Ireland's current social order. Passing O'Connell's statue, he reflects that "this was the man who had done the work; it was he who had withdrawn the key-stone of the edifice, soon to fall and crush all beneath its ruins." Walking by the Bank of Ireland and Trinity College, he muses that "all this would go too. . . . There was a taint of assassination and doom in the air" (218). Ireland's aristocratic infrastructure seems equally vulnerable to nationalist agitation and to "the great feminine tide" beneath which, the narrator reports, "there is an under-current of hatred and revolt" (195).

That Moore's muslin martyrs are both as helpless and useless as the Anglo-Irish, and powerful and rebellious enough to bring down the entire social order, is part of their position in an environment that shapes its inhabitants. They take on characteristics of the groups around them. Moore's treatment of Ireland during the Land War suggests that this environment in particular generates a pointed awareness of the impossibility of tracing individual origins. The same holds true for individual property. Discouraging her daughter Olive's penniless suitor, Mrs. Barton explains that she simply cannot come to a financial settlement that would enable the marriage: "Irish money can no longer be counted upon. . . . We do not know what is or is not our own" (126). The condition is as true intellectually as it is financially. The narrator, surveying Dublin as a provincial outpost of empire, notes its failure to engage in any culture that stands for original creation: "Is there a girl or young man in Dublin who has read a play of Shakespeare, a novel of Balzac, a poem of Shelley?" he asks. "Gossip and waltz tunes are all that they know." Dublin is the heart of the public domain, subject only to repetition, not origin: "We are in a land of echoes and shadows . . . shadows and echoes, and nothing more" (158).

Despite this moment that implies the superiority of the romantic author and his readers, the novel is structured in such a way to imply that original action will save no one. Crafting a life out of echoes and shadows becomes the secret to survival. Alice's friendship with Dr. Reed, a "commonplace man," offers her a way out of her useless life in the west of Ireland (91). Instead of the journalistic novels of Harding, Dr. Reed has authored a medical textbook, a work based entirely in information and observation, not originality. His confession of having done so is what piques Alice's interest in him. In a plot development that recapitulates countless plots of the marginalized woman made central by her true heart and her skills in nursing, Alice and Reed's romance flourishes as they both nurse her sister Olive back to health. The narrator concedes that the end of his novel is no original ending at all. He describes their deepening affection as a literal recapitulation of Victorian novels already written and well read: "in talking of the rights and wrongs of Rochester's love for Jane, and Maggie Tulliver's for Stephen, the lovers revealed to each other their present state of soul" (296).

Alice and Dr. Reed's ability to create a life for themselves out of the public domain bears a resemblance to the shared property arrangements that the Anglo-Irish in the novel hope will save them. Throughout the novel, Anglo-Irish cries for government intervention form a relentless background chorus. Visitors to the Barton house comment on the danger of riding out in public as they leave: "I don't know what we shall do if the Government don't put down the land league; we shall all be shot in our beds at night" (29). Dinner parties occasion similar reflections, "I do not think we shall soon have bread, much less flowers, to place on our tables, if the Government do not step in and put down the revolution that is going on in this country" (42). But for the bulk of Moore's novel, such wishes go disappointed. Despite the very real interventions the British government made during the Land War—civil rights were suspended so that agitators could be jailed without charge; Land League leaders and Irish members of Parliament alike were imprisoned; the army was sent out to harvest crops that peasants refused to bring in—Moore presents the characters' wish for a government that will protect their private property as one of yearning unmet. Instead, what the novel frames as relieving the Land War is the passage of the Irish Land Act of 1882, the government's suspension of entirely individual private property. "The landlords cried the Land Act was ruin, but only to conceal their joy," the narrator reports, "For they knew that if the Government fixed their rents, the Government would have to enforce the payments of those rents" (264). The novel narrates the cessation of the Land War as a sudden freedom from the burdens of enforcing private property rights, an implicit freedom from the burdens of private property altogether, that the Anglo-Irish of the novel see as keeping them safe.

In the Second Irish Land Act, the government enforcement of a space where property rights were not exclusive relied on the same powers the state claimed in creating a public domain—both in land and in ideas. But Moore's novel takes state powers one step further. Moore frames the British state presence in Ireland as also intervening to make sure that marriageable women are not the exclusive private property of their families. Moore describes the ceremonial presentation of young marriageable women at the drawing room at Dublin Castle to the lord lieutenant as a figurative deflowering, "a lingering survival of the terrible Droit de Seigneur." Once presented to the lord lieutenant and "having received a kiss on either cheek, the debutants are free to seek their bridal beds in Patrick's Hall" (175). The implications of a state rape are disturbing, and Moore plays them up for titillating effect. But his description of the women's presentation at Dublin Castle as sexual is also an indictment of a double standard that requires women to be sexualized—dressed in shoulder-baring gowns, forced to kiss a man they have never met—yet punishes them for their sexuality.

Thus, instead of narrating the drawing room as a loss of volition for the women, Moore suggests that it is the beginning of their own sexual choices. No longer virginally sealed within themselves, the women are freed from a sexual purity the narrator describes as "pale and lonely," "stainless and sterile," a sort of "white death" (100). After their presentation at the castle, Violet charms her way into a marriage proposal from a marquis, May pursues an illicit sexual relationship with a neighbor, and Cecelia opts to enter a convent. Preparations for the drawing room also prompt Alice to admit to herself that she, too, experiences sexual desire.

Purity, like traceable origins and exclusive property, winds up having negative connotations, and Moore's novel imagines ways for even reproduction to be freed from such exclusivity. The public domain Alice engages for her writing winds up funding a sort of public domain in reproduction. Her friend May finds herself unmarried and pregnant by a man who has left for Australia, and Alice discovers that she is able, through what she earns by writing, to help May board in another town and pay for the delivery of the child. The baby, ostensibly deposited in an orphanage, becomes one more product of environment rather than individual creation. Alice's support of the child in the place of the father also rips it out of any familial context of privacy and exclusivity. Alice's meditation on the situation punningly connects letting go of strict rules of sexual morality to letting go of ideas that might underwrite exclusive property. At first feeling judgmental of May's behavior, Alice reminds herself, "There is no absolute right; what is right for one may not be right for all" (263).

A world without absolute right is a world without absolute origin, in which case one's origins are up for grabs. After Harding meets Alice and diagnoses her representative status, he suggests that despite following the identifiable trajectory of every Irish girl newly liberated from school, she is essentially a London suburbanite. He anticipates he will meet her again someday in London because "man's moral temperament leads him sooner or later back to his connatural home," which is not the same as a birthplace. "You are a Kensingtonian. I see nothing of the Irish in you," Harding tells her, predicting that "you will drift to your native place—Kensington. Your tastes will bring you there" (198).

Harding's prophecy comes true at the end of the novel, as Alice and Dr. Reed come together, funded by their earnings, to live in Kensington. Both still writing, they move to a newly populated suburb defined by being none of its inhabitants' place of origin. Even the landscape, the narrator comments, looks "as common as if it had been bought—as everything else is in Ashbourne Crescent [their street]—at the Stores" (325). This commonness is in some ways vulgarity—the narrator acknowledges that this suburb, "in its cheapness and vulgarity," might present itself as just as provincial and unoriginal as Dublin itself. But if this is merely another "land of echoes and shadows," then its very unoriginality is the source of its stability. It is "more than anything else representative . . . of the genius of the Empire," and the narrator concedes that "at present it commands our admiration, for it is, as has been said, more than all else, typical England" (326). The heart of what is unoriginal is also the heart of a global power so secure that the sun never sets on it.

Dr. Reed's and Alice's exodus to the suburbs of London is an exodus from the logic of sacrifice, whose effectiveness depends on the gravity of individual—or even group—loss. For Alice, especially, it is an exit from the marriage market painted in such vividly sacrificial language. And her "representative" suburban home is presented as a haven from sacrifice for more than just Alice. As the book ends, Olive, Alice's younger sister, shows up in tears on Alice's door step, sick of the marriage market and eager for escape. The welcome she receives from Alice stands for an escape not just from the marriage market but from the morass of Ireland as well. "Ireland is worse than ever," Olive complains. "We shall all be ruined, and they say Home Rule is certain" (329). In an environment where Home Rule is inevitable—and it is a conclusion Moore's narrator predicts on many occasions, referring to a spirit of nationalism in Ireland that cannot be put down—the only way to avoid its worst effects is to let go of the idea of individual property, even in oneself, in order to refuse the logic of sacrifice.

Diana of the Crossways: The Geography of the Public Domain

If *Drama in Muslin* presents the logic of the public domain as one that relieves individuals of the pressures of defending their property, then George Meredith's 1885 veiled retelling of Caroline Norton's life story offers similar relief, resurrecting the Edgeworthian logic that one cannot give up what one does not

own. The difference is that Moore makes his final model of the public domain
purely intellectual in nature. Those who escape the Land Wars are the ones
who know how to use the stuff of the public domain for their own profit, without mistaking it for their own property. Meredith, by contrast, makes the literal property of land the model for a public domain that tangles Britishness and
Irishness in one enmeshed cultural terrain. Meredith's heroine, his "woman of
two natures," cycles more rapidly through opinions and guiding principles
than she does through her multiple first and last names, yet her identity remains inalienably "of the Crossways"—the house and ten acres in the Sussex
Downs she has inherited from her father, the "iridescent Irishman" Dan Merion (161). As the absentee owner of her childhood home, Diana sees the Crossways as her native ground, her source of income, and her emotional lodestone.
Yet over the course of the novel she makes two unsuccessful attempts to detach
herself from it. First, when she is planning to flee to the continent from her husband's unfounded but very public accusations of adultery, Diana is persuaded
at the hearth of the Crossways to remain in England, rather than abandon country, reputation, and property to her husband. Second, long after she believes
she has sold the estate for ready cash, she discovers that it has been bought by
her long-suffering, faithful friend, the railway baron Thomas Redworth, who
outfits the house with belongings she also believes she has sold. Her marriage
to Redworth at the close of the novel marks her return to a property that Diana
cannot leave behind.

Once again, the structure of being unable to give up what one does not own
emerges as a way of imagining Britain's permanent relationship to Ireland.
Vaguely set sometime between 1838 and 1846, Meredith's plot follows English-
born but Irish-identified Diana from her hasty and ill-fated first marriage
through two entanglements that, while never strictly adulterous, compromise
her reputation after her marriage. Her flirtatious friendship with the worldly
prime minister Lord Dannisburgh leads her husband to file a suit for criminal
conversation against the man. After the ensuing scandal estranges her from
both her husband and Dannisburgh, Diana next becomes entangled with his
nephew and heir, the more discreet and disciplined Percy Dacier, a rising young
parliamentarian. Separated from her husband and attempting to make her own
way as a writer of novels, Diana arranges her household as a political salon of
sorts for Dacier, orchestrating gatherings and dinners for his political advantage, even as she declines to consummate their relationship by eloping with
him. The arrangement ends abruptly when Diana sells to a newspaper a state

secret Dacier has confided in her, precipitating a political scandal. Bankrupt and alone, Diana is nursed back to health by her childhood friend, Emma Dunstane, and subsequently accepts a marriage proposal from Redworth after her first husband's death. Restored to the Crossways, which Redworth has kept intact for her, Diana prepares at the end of the book to leave for Dublin, where Redworth will assume his new post as Irish secretary, his interest legitimized by his long fidelity to the English-born, Irish heroine.

Yet as much as Lizzie Eustace remains fixed in the minds of critics for what she gives up, not what she keeps, Diana's actions as alienating property owner attract critical attention over and above her inability to sever herself from the property she alienates.[10] Just as *The Eustace Diamonds* garners critical attention for its engagement with movable property, *Diana of the Crossways* gets attention for the questions it poses about intellectual property, in the form of Diana's books, her vivacious wit parlayed into political capital for Dacier, and the political secret she sells for money. Critics treat Diana's decision to sell Dacier's state secret as the central point of interest in the novel, one that dramatizes the possibilities of a post–Third Reform Act world, where intellectual property might be seen as superseding the old world of political power grounded in real property. Tim Dolin sees the novel as Meredith's progressive vision of a world, one that extends political authority to women and colonial subjects based on their possession of the "property of wit" (107). Elaine Hadley sees the explicit liberalism of Meredith's narrative as undermined by a darker logic of the plot (Melodramatic 202–7). While he hails the day when women's rights will be recognized, she argues, his plot imagines a world where women never maintain the same control over property, real or mental, that men do. Both Dolin's and Hadley's readings proceed from the narrator's condemnation, in the opening paragraphs of the novel, of a world that has failed to recognize that women possess Wit, "a quality certifying to sound citizenship as authoritatively as acres of land in fee simple, or coffers of bonds, shares, and stocks" (2). Gender equality, Meredith implies, will inevitably follow from the general recognition of the political power of intellectual property.

But the book is somewhat belated if it is supposed to be a plea for women's political recognition based on their possession of mental property in the absence of claims to material property—or even a manufactured plea that masks a deeper ambivalence about women's rights, as Diane Elam has argued. After all, the Second Married Women's Property Act, passed the year before Meredith began the long composition of *Diana*, ensured that even married women could legally retain control of their own property.[11] And it is the possibility of ever holding property in one's own ideas that the introductory chapter of the book throws into disarray. Opening with the line, "Among the Diaries beginning with the second quarter of our century, there is frequent mention of a lady then becoming famous for her beauty and her wit," the narrator presents himself as mining a series of published diaries and memoirs to unearth a portrait of Diana's true character, which might counter the "multitudes of evil reports" that persist about her scandal-riddled life.

The narrator's methods suggest that wit, when recognized as belonging to someone as clearly as do "acres of land in fee simple, or coffers of bonds, shares, and stocks," simply does not tell the story in the same way it is able to when it is built from the scrap pile of the public domain. The narrator assembles a "naked body of the fact" concerning Diana through a collage of quotations attributed to her, whose compilation he defends as "veraciously historical, honestly transcriptive" (13). Implicit in this method is an agnosticism about authorial originality. Mining nonfiction, the narrator pieces Diana together out of quotes and anecdotes small enough to be part of the public domain. Acknowledging that she is a published novelist and poet in her own right, the narrator nonetheless can only find the true Diana in those ephemeral pieces of wit belonging to no one. It is in those pieces that he also finds the truest expression of his own authorship, which, as it turns out, is no authorship at all, just mere transcription.

This is an aesthetic credo Meredith reinforces in his story of Diana, whose restoration to virtue is not accomplished by a restoration to privacy after her story is made all too public. Instead, Meredith exposes his heroine to situations in which what is hers is saved by its association with the public domain. What she owns, both real and intellectual property, remains so insistently public that it never achieves the status of private property. But of course, what cannot become private property cannot be alienated like private property either, and this is the safety of the public domain Meredith imagines for his heroine. The real property of the Crossways she is able to keep by giving up is literally saved by the public domain, in this case by the Redworth's railway fortune, amassed because of the state's power to expropriate private land for the public good.

The anachronistic control Diana retains over her property spotlights Meredith's preoccupation with property whose ownership is never straightforward. Given the high profile of married, and separated, women's property in the Married Women's Property debates, these anachronisms would have been especially easy to spot in a novel ostensibly set forty or fifty years earlier.[12] That the heroine continues to draw rental income from the Crossways after her separation from her first husband, and that she at least goes through the motions of selling the property of her own volition, would have directly contradicted the laws of her time, which gave married women no legal status apart from their husbands, and thus no property of their own.

Meredith's historical inaccuracies about property seem all the more glaring in a novel clearly modeled on the illustrious career of Caroline Norton.[13] A novelist and luminary of London society in her day, Norton would have been well remembered by Meredith's audience for her dramatic expositions of the legal disabilities under which she suffered as a woman separated from her husband. Norton authored numerous pamphlets arguing for legislative change on questions of maternal infant custody and married women's right to property, pamphlets influential in changing laws concerning both separated women's access to their children and their recourse to divorce and married women's right to claim individual property even after marriage.[14] Meredith's novel baldly contradicts Norton's historical position as a woman unable to control her own property, a position she did much to publicize. Instead, Diana emerges as a Norton figure oddly assured of both property and marital maintenance, asserting of the Crossways that "[t]he place was hers, she said; her own property. Her husband could not interdict a sale."[15] This assertion, despite its legally shaky grounding, turns out to be true where her first husband, Warwick, is concerned. Diana successfully completes a full transfer of the property for cash while he is alive.

In his anachronistic treatment of married women's legal ownership, Meredith crafts a story in which the real-life woman who made her name publicizing her inability to control property turns into a fictional character able to control property effortlessly. And in doing so he also demonstrates the impossibility of any woman's story being her own property. Drawing the story out of the public domain of gossip, Meredith also reengineers it to correspond recognizably with the life of Katherine O'Shea, the married mistress of Charles Parnell, the leader of Ireland's Home Rule party, whose political maneuvering on behalf of Parnell (she helped broker the agreement by which Gladstone finally let leaders of the Land League out of jail in 1885) resembles Diana's own political efforts on behalf of Dacier.[16]

Reengineering the contours of two well-known lives, Meredith's tale offers a reassuring logic of permanent connectedness in a book that obliquely gestures toward the Irish upheaval of the 1880s. Meredith began *Diana* in the years 1883–84 and published the full book in 1885. In that year Gladstone first hinted he was ready to propose a formal Home Rule bill for Ireland, a move Meredith strongly supported and an issue on which he was to style himself an expert in the next decade.[17] And just as Meredith's adaptation of Caroline Norton's life in the 1840s takes on dimensions of Katherine O'Shea's life in the 1880s, his fictional retelling of the turbulent politics of the 1840s adopts overtones from the British-Irish tensions of the 1880s. This historically doubled structure allows Meredith to imagine Home Rule as a development that can never be a loss. Projecting this latter-day hypothetical repeal back onto the repeal of the Corn Laws—a political move also couched in the rhetoric of sacrifice for the good of both Britain and Ireland, and even the world—Meredith implies that Home Rule too is a sacrifice that will not end in loss.[18]

Meredith uses the logic of the intellectual public domain—the domain made up of ideas whose status as private property has been sacrificed for the greater good—to accomplish two things. First, like Moore before him, Meredith sees the public domain as a place that absolves women from the status of property and provides a space where they might be appropriately public without being commodified. Second, whereas Moore imagines that Ireland itself is part of the British public domain, and so, even in being given up, can never be lost, Meredith establishes an association between Ireland and intellectual property rights that extends its analogy to the property most insistently associated with Ireland: real property in the land. The property that can be given up but not lost is Diana's homestead, the Irish property on English ground that is the Crossways, through which Meredith imagines Ireland's persistence in the public domain.

Property, Not Commodity

Paying attention to Meredith's preoccupation with state-enforced zones of non-propertization changes our interpretation of the novel's gender politics. While Meredith's credentials as a sincere and firm supporter of Victorian feminism are impeccable, the ending of *Diana* at first seems to point to that support's troubling limits. Having been punished both for her political aspirations and her own cultivation of a relationship outside of a marriage that was wrecked by her husband, Diana seems only ambivalently rewarded by her final engagement to Redworth. Her marriage hardly makes for a happy ending, Diane Elam argues. Diana "is commodified and exchanged in true capitalist fashion. Warwick possesses her first, but Redworth emerges from the transaction as the final owner of the highly valued commodity" (193). I argue that while the ending—and, indeed, the novel as a whole—never allows the reader to imagine Diana as happily settled, with the wounds of patriarchy entirely erased, it also deals in complex forms of property that disrupt any easy equation of Diana with a commodity.

Plentiful evidence exists for a pessimistic interpretation of Diana's second marriage. When Redworth reveals that he has saved the Crossways and furnished it with all the small possessions she had put up for sale to pay her London debts, Diana reacts more like a woman cornered than a woman rescued. Redworth "appeared to Diana as a fatal power . . . : one of those good men, strong men, who subdue and do not kindle." Because of this power to subdue, she reflects, "[t]he Crossways had been turned into a trap" (379). Once she reconciles herself to the idea of marriage to Redworth, her view of the impending nuptials hardly inspires confidence. She tells her friend Emma, "I am going into slavery to make amends for presumption" (402). Redworth's own reaction to their engagement seems to bear out Diana's dread of enslavement. Venturing to embrace her for the first time, he exclaims, "now you belong to me!" Diana finds him "violently metamorphosed to a stranger, acting on rights she had given him" and herself "bound verily to be thankful for such love" (406, 407).

But in his commitment to the public domain, Meredith mitigates the force of the slavery and entrapment that Diana perceives as lurking in her marriage to Redworth. Since all property in the novel—the Crossways, state secrets, Diana's writing income, the property across which railroad tracks run—seems to undergo a cycle of existing as private property, being sacrificed, and finally becoming transformed into a more permanent and abiding public property, it would not be out of place to read Diana's own propertization in marriage to be a move in the same direction. In a novel whose logic always favors the public domain, Redworth's claim to own Diana cannot last forever.

At the same time, in a novel that favors the logic of the public domain, the line between public and private matters, even if it is a moveable line. Given Meredith's interest in the public domain, we might read Diana's narrative not as one in which a woman seeking publicity is turned into a commodity but as one in which a woman suffers when what belongs to the public is treated as purely private property. Her first flirtation with Lord Dannisburgh is especially troubled in this regard. She strikes up a friendship with the minister in the interest of securing a place for her husband in a government office, or perhaps in Parliament.

Diana and Dannisburgh are brought together by the informal property sharing of patronage, a relationship in which public and private prerogative are the same. The two engage in a model of female participation in the state that also depends on the blurring of public and private, with Diana acting—at least in her own description of the situation—as political counselor to Dannisburgh. Her problems begin when her husband recognizes a public-private divide where she sees none and tries to push her into the mold of entirely privatized property. "He took what I could get for him and then turned and drubbed me for getting it," Diana offers as explanation for her husband's subsequent action against Dannisburgh for adultery (130).

What saves Diana from the disaster of her husband's privatizing urges is also a form of patronage, an informal inclusion in state structures that keep Diana from being entirely private. After her husband's legal proceedings begin, Diana wages a campaign to protect her reputation, carefully cultivating patrons and sympathizers through parties and dinners. These connections, in turn, are enabled by the multiple champions she has who are parliamentary members, able to network with the powerful on her behalf. The strategy pays off in the form of several male supporters whose elite whisper campaigns and ties to publishers secure her a book contract, favorable reviews, and even a pseudonymous identity as exiled European royalty.

The novels Diana publishes repeatedly fantasize a woman's informal attachment to the state. Diana makes a lucrative living telling the story of the not-entirely-private woman. Her first novel, *The Princess Egeria*, ostensibly tells a tale of a woman engaged as adviser to a head of state, as the name "Egeria" implies.[19] Her second novel continues Diana's strategy of taking her material from the parts of her life dominated by the state. *The Young Minister of State* appears modeled on Dacier, a rising member of Parliament with whom she has become involved and who thinks of her as *his* "Egeria" (186). Her next book, *The Cantatrice*, is based explicitly on a parliamentary member's obsession with an opera singer. That the opera singer is not Diana seems to be a part of what blocks the author during its long composition. Her mind continues to compose "long dialogues" for *The Young Minister* instead. When she begins a book based on Redworth, *The Man of Two Minds*, he is well into his own parliamentary career, the ins and outs of which he has openly shared with Diana.

But far from unambiguously commodifying her own life story, Diana attempts to build a life in which she brings herself and her books into the public domain. Diana's earnings fund her attempt to act as political patron herself. As her relationship with Dacier becomes more intense, she uses her earnings to throw politically advantageous dinner parties for him, turning her house into a sort of salon to nurture his career. Diana imagines that her commitment to state affairs creates a public domain of sorts in her own household, one where all information and utterances might be separated from their authors and made available for the good of the state. The narrator describes Diana's social gatherings as an assemblage of information to which no one person could lay claim: "The talk was on high levels and low; . . . now a story; a question opening new routes; sharp sketches of known personages; a paradox shot by laughter as soon as it was uttered; and all so smoothly; not a shadow of the dominant holder-forth or a momentary prospect of dead flats" (297). Beyond her entertaining duties, Diana spends much of her time visiting and socializing in order to gather information that will help her build facts into policy recommendations; "making abstracts," as she calls it, to keep Dacier well informed. At its most thriving, their unconsummated romance is the wellspring of a common fund. Dacier credits her with portraying colleagues of his she's never met with more accuracy than he could. He reports repeating her witticisms to them and getting all the credit. Diana is delighted to be part of this nonpropertized economy, telling him, "I glow with pride to think of speaking anything that you repeat" (280).

But Dacier, like Diana's husband Warwick before him, disrupts this charade of nonpropertized domain, wanting to claim Diana all for his own. In doing so, he also disrupts an economy in which the goods of the state are his to enjoy, not to own. Where Warwick wanted to deny the patronage of the prime minister behind his position, Dacier also succumbs to the temptation of treating a state secret as his own absolute property, something he might trade for his own advantage. Late at night he visits Diana to announce to her that the administration has abruptly changed position and will pass the repeal of the Corn Laws. Before telling her, he teases her with promises about how large the secret is, asking, "What am I to have for telling it?" (304). After imparting his news, he steals a kiss and continues to beg for "a trifle of recompense" in exchange for the news (306). Even as he leaves, he asks her to promise to consummate their relationship at some future date.

The scene is a moment of intense humiliation for Diana, and not just for its revelation of a sexually coercive side to a man she had previously adored. Having told both herself and others that her relationship with Dacier was one conducted "on public grounds," she now is forced to admit to herself that she too is guilty of wanting to stake a private claim to Dacier. "I kept up a costly household for the sole purpose of seeing him and having him near me," she admits to herself in the anguished hours after the encounter (311). She is just as guilty of overprivatizing the affair as he is, who "had brought political news, and treated her as—name the thing!" (311).

Diana's reaction to Dacier's attack seems motivated by revenge, but it also restores publicity to the privacy with which Dacier wanted to treat the state secret. Diana and her maid proceed to newspaper offices that night where Diana sells the secret. The move offers Diana an opportunity for shoring up her own deflated sense of selfhood. She gleefully anticipates the reaction of an editor who had previously told her that her political information was "stale" (310). But her treatment of the secret also demonstrates that Diana has a sharper perception of intellectual property's relationship to the public domain than does Dacier. Knowing that news of the Corn Law repeal will ultimately be general knowledge, she first responds to the secret less as if it were property than an advance copy of the newspaper. "We two are a month ahead of all England," she exclaims to Dacier. When he tries to gain sexual favors for the news he imparts, she insists, "no payments!" (305). Her sale of the secret to a newspaper is less the vending of personal property than the release of information whose propertized life was always limited. Diana reasons with herself, as she rushes to the newspaper office in the middle of the night, that in the end, the piece of information belonged only to the public domain: "This news, great though it was, and throbbing like a heart plucked out of a breathing body, throbbed but for a brief term, a day or two; after which great though it was, immense, it relapsed into a common organ, a possession of the multitude, merely historically curious" (310).

In the end, Diana's reasoning proves right. As far as its effects are felt within the novel, this premature publication of a state secret only matters insofar as it breaks Diana and Dacier apart. While Dacier imagines that the leak will allow a campaign to gather in opposition to repeal, the threat never materializes (322). Public rumors of the ministry's change of policies never change the course of a history that Meredith's reader already knows. Even public reaction to the leak is quickly effaced by news of Dacier's impending marriage to the heiress Constance Asper, which "did away with the political hubbub" (338). Briefly possessed of information she recognizes as tending toward national property, Diana's handling of it has not so much the effect of a sale but of the short-circuiting of its propertization, making it available to all, and thus unavailable

to any one party for the purpose of a trade. Having already cut off the possibility that Dacier could exchange the secret for sexual favors, Diana also ultimately
disrupts her own trade of the secret for money, retroactively rendering it a gift.
When the editor's promised compensation arrives, she has legally become a
widow and inherited all the property that her first husband had withheld from
her during their long separation. No longer needing the money, she burns her
editor's check.

Diana's participation in the literal public sphere of the news occasions the
narrator's reflections on both the positive and negative effects of the public
domain. Dacier abandons Diana almost immediately after realizing what she
has done, and he becomes engaged to a crypto-Catholic heiress whose profession
that "all secrets are holy, but the secrets of State are under a seal next to divine"
renders by contrast Diana's actions the work of a sturdy English Protestantism
free of conspiratorial tendencies (332). Oddly, it is Diana's maid, Danvers, who
registers the most negative implications of Diana's foray into the public release
of information. Waiting for her mistress in the outer offices of the newspaper,
Danvers seems to undergo the experience of a piece of news whose propertized
qualities are in the process of evaporating with the passing of minutes: "She lost,
very strangely to her, the sense of her sex and became an object—a disregarded
object. Things of more importance were about. Her feminine self-esteem was
troubled; all idea of attractiveness expired. Here was manifestly a spot where
women had dropped from the secondary to the cancelled stage of their extraordinary career in a world either blowing them aloft like soap bubbles or quietly
shelving them as supernumeraries" (314). "Disregarded," "expired," and "cancelled," Danvers experiences the sensation both of news out of date and a woman
grown too old. This, then, is the dangerous underside of Diana's affinity for the
unpropertized world of the public domain: a woman's person, too, bears analogy
to the expired property of copyright, grown too old for usefulness and released
into a sphere where it exists entirely unperceived.

Diana's recuperation from the heartbreak of losing Dacier, then, is also the
recuperation of the public domain into a model where property that eludes individual ownership might nonetheless be treated as counting, That model turns
out to be the public domain in the land. The narrator's assessment that Diana's
"fall had brought her renovatingly to earth" resonates in more than one way—
returned to "the land," that metonym for the aristocracy among whom she now
makes her home, Diana also nurses her wounds with a literal attention to the
earth. Where at the beginning of the book Emma accompanied Diana on her

quests through political theory and economy, she now feeds Diana's "craving . . . for positive knowledge" with "shells and stones and weeds . . . botanical and geological books" (364).

Surprisingly, the guiding genius behind this particular course of recovery is Thomas Redworth, her faithful friend the railroad baron. Diana and Emma find that Redworth is actually an accomplished naturalist. They discover that "he knew every bird by its flight and its pipe, habits, tricks, . . . and his remarks on the sensitive life of trees and herbs were a spell to his thirsty hearers" (365). They even discover that the railway baron "had printed, for private circulation, when at Harrow School, a little book, a record of his observations in nature" (365). Redworth excuses himself on the grounds that his work had been only a compilation of available facts and that he had put nothing of himself into it. He had not fallen into the propertizing mania of romantic authorship: "he had not published opinions" (365).

His very slow courtship of Diana seems to partake of the same character of avoiding his own opinion. Redworth's success comes to seem more probable as his reflections on the role of the state come to bear the marks of Diana's ideas rather than his own. Pondering the problem of adulterated beer, he finds himself led on a line of thought not his own: "Capital, whereat Diana Warwick aimed her superbest sneer, has its instant duties. She theorized on the side of poverty, and might do so: he had no right to be theorizing on the side of riches" (385). The man who will clasp Diana in his arms call her "my own" already lives in a condition in which "he thought within her thoughts, or his own were at her disposal" (407, 386). He also deliberately delays the marriage until it can be more than just a private affair. Recalling that Diana once spoke contemptuously of being a mere "Mrs.," he waits until he has been appointed chief secretary of Ireland to propose to her. He offers her not just a home but a public function, one that unites England and Ireland.

The Property of Blended Spaces

In this section I examine Meredith's figurative tendencies more closely in order to explore the formal technique by which he undermines the allegory of Union with which his plot flirts even as he creates a plot of land that bears the burdens of this exploded allegory. We might think of Meredith as importing the entire logic of the Irish national tale, with its unifying marriage plot, onto British soil. Rather than setting his novel on a plot of land in Ireland, the property ownership of which requires British and Irish to marry, Meredith imagines Irish land to always already be located at the heart of England.

Meredith's knots of extended and occasionally unparsable metaphor were seen as a hallmark of his technique, one that made him both admirable and unreadable. In the *Atheneum*, W. E. Henley offers high praise for the newly published *Diana*, only to admit a fundamental problem encountering Meredith's "metaphors in four dimensions (as it were), whose conquest appears to demand the instant and active exercise of all the five senses at once, and which even then emerges from the fight unvanquished" (qtd in Williams 260). Virginia Woolf was less kind to her father's Victorian friend, commenting several decades later that Meredith "wishes to crush the truth out in a series of metaphors or a string of epigrams with as little resort to dull fact as may be. Then, indeed, the effort is prodigious, and the confusion often chaotic" (qtd in Williams 274). Even twentieth-century critics have similarly condemned Meredith's stylistics as an unfortunate tendency that hides his real value—see, for instance, Judith Wilt's comment on his "perpetual, dazzling, in a sense desperate dependence upon metaphor" (77–78).

Elizabeth Bradburn, however, has suggested that these Meredithean moments are worth noting for their modeling of complex cognitive processes. His metaphoric language creates a "blended space" from several "input spaces"—figurative language, plot elements, thematic messages. These elements sit upon one another, creating distortions and new convergences of meaning. This overlay, the conceptual equivalent of the picture produced by an entire stack of transparencies placed at once on an overhead projector, always exceeds easy correspondence among elements; for instance, the metaphoric layer of meaning cannot be easily mapped onto the plot since the clear outlines of the elements become distorted by this association. The process of blending makes it impossible to tell where one begins and the other ends. The effect, Bradburn reports, is the exposure of "latent contradictions and coherences between previously separated elements" (881). Such contradictions and coherences can be partial and impressionistic, creating meanings that blend into a densely overloaded environment in which no one element can be safely distinguished as the figurative illustration for another element's more fundamental meaning.

Meredith's prose might described as heightening all the partial and incomplete aspects of metaphoric thinking, constantly exposing the limits of neat analogical readings. Meredith's is a style bent on exposing the unlimited potential for boundary failure that lurks behind every metaphor, causing different levels of a metaphor to bleed into one another, or causing multiple metaphors that coexist in a text to distort and disrupt one another. The passage Bradburn uses to illustrate Meredith's creation of blended spaces, a passage in which the heroine, Diana, confronts her deteriorating financial situation, might be seen as exemplary in this regard.

> [Diana] examined her accounts. The Debit and Credit sides presented much of the appearance of male and female in our jog-trot civilization. They matched middling well; with rather too marked a tendency to strain the leash and run frolic on the part of friend Debit (the wanton male), which deepened the blush in comparison. Her father had noticed the same funny thing in his effort to balance his tugging accounts: "Now then for a look at Man and Wife," except that he made Debit stand for the portly frisky female, Credit the decorous and contracted other half, a prim gentleman of a constitutionally lean habit of body, remonstrating with her. "You seem to forget that we are married, my dear, and must walk in step or bundle into the Bench" Dan Merion used to say. (219)

In this example, the passage starts out with a simple metaphor—Debit and Credit are married like male and female. Yet this simplicity is almost immediately complicated by an abrupt shift from a figure of speech that links financial and marital elements to a conceit that focuses on the elements that become linked under the domain of financial (Debit and Credit) and those linked under the domain of the marital (husband and wife). Meredith's proliferation of metaphorical elements reveals the reversible nature of the metaphor: Is Debit to Credit as husband is to wife? Or as wife is to husband? And of course the growing crowd of elements calls into question the idea of correspondence between parts. Debit and Credit battle one another, rather than cooperating to create the financial domain. Far from being eternally yoked in the marital domain, husband and wife emerge as figures on the verge of divorce.

The wars that complicate his metaphors also unsettle the relationship between the symbolic content of Meredith's conceits and the mimetic content of the plot. As the passage continues, it invokes the immediate storyline concerning Diana's attempts to support herself after becoming estranged from her boorish first husband: "Diana had not so much to rebuke in Mr. Debit; or not at the first reckoning. But his ways were curious. She grew distrustful of him . . . His answer to her reproaches pleaded the necessitousness of his purchases and expenditure: a capital plea; and Mrs. Credit was requested by him, in a courteous manner, to drive her pen the faster, so that she might wax to a corresponding size and satisfy the world's idea of fitness in couples. She would have costly furniture, because it pleased her taste; and a French cook for a like reason, in justice to her guest; and trained servants" (219).

Such language at first seems to point toward an allegorical correspondence between symbol and plot. Certainly Diana *had* grown distrustful of her husband, as the unsuitability of his "ways" grew clearer to her, and these discoveries led her, as the "Mrs." of the pair, to "drive her pen the faster." Yet here the resemblance between plot and metaphor falters. No amount of pen-driving can reconcile Diana and Warwick to "the world's idea of fitness in couples"—indeed, her pen is the tool that allows her to keep herself, in a financial and physical sense, far away from her husband. Still, correspondence between plot and metaphor never entirely disappears. The abrupt resumption of the actual story line ("she would have costly furniture") is not marked by any clear announcement of a return to mimesis. The uncertain referent of the "she" who "would have costly furniture" in the last sentence (and in the sentence before, the uncertain referent of the "her" to which the pen belongs) leaves Diana and Mrs. Credit linked, acting as the same person, a pair whose connection supplants that of husband and wife altogether.

Meredith leans heavily on these partial references to create a political backdrop in his book that, while ostensibly about the moment of the repeal of the Corn Laws, seems to more explicitly reference the current moment of Irish land agitation. The main event that shapes Diana's political involvement is the 1846 repeal of the Corn Laws. The permanent removal of tariffs on wheat imported into England would have been remembered in Meredith's time as significant landmark in the English evolution from the ascendancy of a land-based ruling class to a more broadly conceived political authority. Passed after a long campaign for repeal led by the Anti–Corn Law League, a political action group spearheaded primarily by manufacturing interests in the north of England, the act marked a moment in which England consented to depend on foreign lands for the raw produce of agriculture in order to focus on the manufacturing economy that would make it the "workshop of the world."[20] Seen as the act that ushered a golden age of free trade into Victorian England, the repeal of the Corn Laws was also remembered for the dramatic political conversion that brought it about. Prime Minister Robert Peel, who had taken office promising to uphold the Tory party line committed to keeping the laws in place, eventually changed his position, splintering his party and effectively ending his political career.

In keeping with his preference for half references and partial metaphors, Meredith's vocabulary for narrating repeal shies away from invoking the event too specifically. Characters talk about "the prospects of the League" and predict that "the country will beat the landlords" (285, 286). Even the moment in which the prime minister's change of position is revealed, a moment that forms the climax of Meredith's novel, shies away from specifically naming what it is that so impresses the characters. Dacier tells Diana the news, never mentioning the Corn Laws by name, instead insisting that she guess the news. Diana breathlessly asks, "The proposal is—? No more compromises!" to which he assents "Total!" (305). The actual content of the decision is never explicitly described. This vocabulary of "total repeal" that "the league" demands in opposition to the "landlords" describes the position of the industry leaders who led the Anti–Corn Law League in the 1830s and 1840s. However, it also impressionistically invokes the contemporary Irish land wars and Land League agitation against Irish landlords in the 1880s. Even in the England of anti–Corn Law activism, "total repeal" would have referred both to the demands of the Anti–Corn Law League and to Daniel O'Connell's high-profile campaign for an end to Union, launched by his declaration of 1843 as the "year of repeal." Meredith slyly grants O'Connell the possibility of that repeal, too, in failing to name the exact repeal foretold by Dacier's state secret, and exact year in which it occurs.[21] Home Rule becomes, through these partial allusions, an already-canonical event in nineteenth-century British history.

The techniques that allow Meredith to incorporate the Home Rule that has not happened yet into British history are also those that allow him to incorporate Irish land into the heart of England. He does this through the real property central to his book, Diana's childhood home of the Crossways, a physical plot of land whose figurative work in the novel is never done. Enfolding union and blockage, England and Ireland, alienability and inalienability, the Crossways exceeds its mere materiality even within the plot, meaning for Diana, "Dada in his best day and all my youngest dreams" (54). As the place to which she flees "by instinct" when in trouble, the Crossways is Diana's refuge. But then, as the narrator is careful to point out, where Diana is concerned, "metaphors were her refuge" (109, 231). And no other metaphor receives the star billing or sustained attention devoted to the Crossways, a single spot named not for itself but for the multiple directions it points. To say that the Crossways—the physical territory that is Diana's own—functions like a crossways—joining opposing routes—is to make a statement fundamentally Meredithean, in which the assertion that a thing functions like itself is only to multiply meanings, not to contain them.

The signifier "crossways" enters Meredith's text as both proper and common noun. Meredith's prose alternates between using the Crossways as a proper noun, which signals one irreproducible place, and bringing into play an idiomatic use of "crossways" as a common noun, which signals both the widened scope of movement made possible by the technology of crossroads and the paralysis brought on by the clash of opposing ways. When Redworth remembers his early fatal hesitation in proposing to Diana, the Crossways carries connotations of blockage and movement for him. He remembers her departure for her childhood home as the emblem of his indecision, the last moment he sees Diana unengaged; "Her destiny of the Crossways tied a knot, barred a gate, and pointed to a new direction of the road" (49). In spite of Diana's affectionate regard for the Crossways, its negative connotations also spill into her vocabulary. The common noun "crossways" becomes for her a signifier of paralysis rather than possibility. Recalling her ill-fated marriage, she remarks, "We walked a dozen steps in stupefied union, and hit upon crossways" (131). Describing her dependence on Redworth long after her marriage to Warwick has disintegrated, she notes, "I am always at crossways, and he rescues me" (259).

By failing to substitute for the estate called by the name "the Crossways," the signifier "crossways" loudly calls attention to its Meredithean ability to stir up allusions to plot structure without resolving into an easy metaphor for it. Redworth has indeed rescued Diana in a scene set at the Crossways, when he talks her out of fleeing to Europe and convinces her to stay and defend her reputation against her husband's public accusations of adultery. Yet this rescue from snares she calls "crossways" is hardly a rescue from the Crossways; staying near the property and retaining control over it are her rewards for staying in England. Likewise, Diana's report of her marriage foundering when the couple "hit upon crossways" works against the literal grain of the story. After all, Diana's affection for Augustus Warwick, the nephew of her tenants at the Crossways, first springs from his proximity to the home she holds so dear. His promise that the couple can spend part of each year in her childhood home seems part of the terms of her agreement to marry him. And the first hint of their marital trouble comes not from the Crossways but from when Warwick wants to leave the estate for London.

This property of contradictory meanings, the property that also cannot be given up, operates both as figure of union—two roads meeting—and as figure for blockage and opposition—two ways irreducibly opposed. Inevitably, the Union of Great Britain and Ireland adds yet another overlay to this property, making the political union one that simultaneously contains England and Ireland, marriage and divorce. Diana's identity within the novel as "a woman of two natures" seems a native trait acquired from the English home of the Crossways where she came by her Irish identity. Located in the Sussex Downs, the home is invariably named as Diana's inheritance from her father, the "iridescently Irish" Dan Merion, whose national identity secures Diana's identity as "honest Irish" even though she is born and raised in his house in southeast England. Diana occupies a double position familiar to almost all of English realism's Irish characters: "In England she was Irish. . . . Abroad, . . . though not less Irish, a daughter of Britain" (139). Yet unlike so many other Irish characters in the fiction of the nineteenth century, Diana's doubleness is not so much a product of her birthplace in Ireland but rather arises from her attachment to the estate of her father, an estate whose English location seems permeated with an animating Irishness.

Meredith grounds Diana's Irishness in the physical spaces of the Crossways. The book makes mention of the bloodlines through which Diana claims her Irishness—a half-English mother, and a father whose only distinguishing characteristic seems to be an Irishness of such prominence that his paternity "would make her Irish all over" regardless of the mother (25). Yet Diana views the actual grounds of the estate as the spot from which her Irishness is generated. Taking her first steps out into society as a separated woman, Diana wins a place at dinner parties through her animated delivery of Irish anecdotes, the production of which seems to have happened first on her paternal estate; "The old dinner and supper tables at the Crossways furnished her with an abundant store" (124). While others discuss her Irishness as a portable trait, visible in her body and manner as "proofs of descent from the blood of Dan Merion—a wildish blood" (31), Diana herself relies on the Crossways to connect her to the memory of her father's Irishness. The house operates as a museum of Dan Merion's spirit, the place where Diana keeps "souvenirs of her father, his cane, and his writing-desk, and a precious miniature of him hanging above it" (54, 75). Her best friend, Emma Dunstane, describes her attachment to the house as a specifically Irish attachment: "Tony is one of the women who burn to give last kisses to things that they love. And she has her little treasures hoarded there. She was born there. Her father died there. She is three parts Irish—superstitious in affection" (75).

Making a property in England the source of Diana's quality of Irishness becomes a perverse way for Meredith to ensure both the external, material source of her Irishness and its inalienability. Irish nationalism in the nineteenth century positioned itself as an identity predicated on dispossession of real property. Dan Merion's property in England implies just such a dispossessed identity; what else would such an assuredly Irish man be doing in England if not fleeing the consequences of dispossession in his own country? Diana, as the female inheritor of his estate, can step into this logic of dispossession, never quite owning the estate and yet never quite being a claimant in the original act of dispossession either. Unable to precisely articulate her relationship to the Irish, Diana is only able to say vaguely of the Irish people that "I have them in my heart, though I have not been among them for long at a time" (204).

Meredith claimed such Irishness for his own. Because his mother's maiden name had been "McNamara," Meredith considered himself half-Irish, although no apparent family connections to Ireland remained.[22] He considered himself in natural sympathy with the Irish because of his own Welsh descent.[23] Yet he does not allow Diana a merely racial connection to the Irish people, a portable identity composed entirely of bloodlines. Instead her Irishness remains about the land. For Meredith this "Irish" estate is a reassuring figure, a space of literal Irish land that England cannot give up, even after Ireland goes its own way. But it is also reassuring for the same reason that so many of the writers in my study found the figurative power of Irish land so attractive in the nineteenth century. The Crossways is a piece of land so animated by an Irish cultural identity that even its location cannot dictate its conformity to state interference. Somewhere in England, Meredith assures us, there is a plot of land that will remain forever Ireland. And it is that plot of land that keeps the English free.

Afterword

In *The Prime Minister*, Sir Alured, the present baronet of "a handsome old family . . . whose forefathers had been baronets since baronets were first created" (113), solemnly instructs his nephew and heir, Everett Wharton, on protocol for allotting property to tenants: "'I do like the farms to go from father to son, Everett. It's the way that everything should go. Of course, there's no right. . . . No, nothing of that kind. God in his mercy forbid that a landlord in England should ever be robbed after that fashion.' Sir Alured, when he was uttering this prayer, was thinking of what he had heard of an Irish land bill, the details of which, however, had been altogether incomprehensible to him" (598).

The more Trollope reveals about Alured, the less coherent the nature of his alarm is. His objection to the First Irish Land Act, to which he refers, cannot rest on his disdain for community tradition, which the act purported to uphold. Alured has already shown himself to be a fierce devotee to tradition. Although his estate had been destined for a profligate nephew whom he abhors, Alured doggedly declines his power to choose a more suitable heir, preferring to leave his estate in the hands of a wastrel rather than violate the time-honored patterns of inheritance. When that heir providentially dies, Alured's instructions that Everett follow established relations between landlord and tenant reveal that Alured sees his proprietorship of the estate as shaped by a system of established practices he cannot disrupt. His insistence on handing down farms from father to son as "the way everything should go" seems to contradict his equally vehement imperative that "the way everything should go" not be interpreted as "a right."

Alured's semantic hairsplitting on the matter is emblematic of a larger tendency in Victorian thinking about property. No matter how often advanced liberals like John Stuart Mill or Matthew Arnold might protest that the state had a perfect right to dictate the distribution and uses of landed property, no matter how thoroughly the establishment of railways in Britain had proven that the state used such power quite extensively, the Victorians still preferred to imagine land as a zone in which the state could not interfere with redefinitions and redistributions of rights. But, as Alured also demonstrates, Victorians also preferred to think of property in land not as a zone of complete liberty for the owner but rather as a source of compulsion. Serious about understanding privileged subjects as constrained by responsibilities, not simply buoyed up by freedom from want, and equally serious in their antistatist sentiments, Victorians tended to think of responsibility and obligation as something endowed upon an owner by his own property rather than imposed by the state.

Alured offers one glimpse of the pleasures that come from being compelled to do something by one's own property. But as this book shows, writing concerned with Irish land ownership teems with such examples—Edgeworth's landowners, gleefully unable to leave the property to which they are connected; Mill's peasant proprietors, energetically animated to cultivate their lands; Young Ireland's patriots, revolutionarily justified by a tie to the land they can never forswear; Trollope's wives, obligated to enjoy estates to which they have no title. All of these figures understand themselves as compelled to do something, not by the state that grants them rights, but by property that attaches to them in ways more profound than the state could ever accomplish with mere legislation. The pleasures of being compelled into action by one's property in land are thrown into unusually sharp relief by the Irish, or those enmeshed in the nineteenth century's long British-Irish entanglement.

Sir Alured notwithstanding, the pleasures of landed property's compulsions were not as immediately available in a purely English context. As the nineteenth century wore on, both Martin Weiner and Krishan Kumar have pointed out, England became increasingly identified with the land, seeing its culture as summed up either by the great country estates or by agricultural village communities. But as Elizabeth Helsinger and John Plotz have both made clear, that identification often depended on the representation of land made in portable objects that were paintings, engravings, or novels. Constable's countryside, Mitford's village commons, Thomas Hardy's Wessex, and of course Jane Austen's estates in the Home Counties came to stand for England, and these representations were of a size to travel easily to the far outposts of empire along with mercantile populations, settlers, imperial administrators, and military personnel. But these objects, in their portability, subjected the English landscape to the problem of how it attached to those who formed an English identity through them. Elaine Freedgood observes that even as Hardy offered his readers an immersion in his fully elaborated fictional English countryside, he also called their attention to "an intensifying alienation between people and their belongings" (154). Such alienation problematizes even readerly identification. In Hardy, Freedgood observes, "the characters within the novel are severed from their own relations to things they own, and the readers of the novel are estranged from the subjects and objects of the novel by this internal alienation" (153). Unable to be entirely sure which objects might make them owning subjects and which objects were to be understood as falling within their ambit in purely accidental ways, owners could hardly be expected to derive a clear sense of duty from their property.

Both Freedgood and Plotz challenge the standard critical notion that the Victorian era was one of relentless commodification, one in which the threat of a piece of property's alienation is the primary way Victorians experienced their things. Freedgood and Plotz demonstrate that the objects in Victorian novels carry cultural meanings that are not entirely disrupted, even by the threat of alienation. But in telling the story of what such objects mean, and *how* they mean in a culture of rising commodification, they necessarily place what it actually means to own on the backburner. In his extensive analysis of *Portable Property*, Plotz's emphasis falls decidedly on portability, not on property.

As Irish land makes its way into British and Irish writing, it offers something that representations of English land do not: a thorough contemplation of what it means to be attached to a piece of property. The concern about what made something property and what made somebody an owner was hardly obsolete to Victorians, especially as they questioned both the political meanings that had long attached to the land and as they contemplated the possible expansion of state powers. The English countryside, shrunk into representations of portable proportions and available for a small bit of the middle class's disposable income, tended to efface such questions. Discussion of the Irish experience of property, by contrast, tended to offer not a vicarious experience of, or identification with, Irish land, but an intricate examination of how law, money, and history had all worked together to create owners and nonowners, as well as those who fell in between the two categories, experiencing proprietary feelings without the benefit of legal title.

The pieces of writing that I have chosen to examine in this book not only offer extended meditations on what it means to be attached to property in land; they also provide oblique commentaries on the positive effects of such contemplation. Read together, they promote the message that sustained contemplation of property—even property not legally one's own—attaches one to it in a way that consolidates one's identity. This identity consolidation, they suggest, happens through attachment's power to cure one of acquisitive urges. Mill's peasant proprietors, Trollope's enjoying wives, even Diana, reattached to the Crossways, all are imagined as relieved of desire for an unlimited expansion of their powers by a relationship that orients them toward the intimate knowledge of and interaction with one piece of property. Desire for property leads to the sort of industry that fuels the world's progress, Trollope observes in his travel book, *North America*, but the verdict of the writing I have examined here is that actually having that property—even in a way not formalized or codified by state power—cures that restlessness.

The Irish context naturalizes such a conclusion. In their protests against the Union, the Irish framed their demands in terms not of expansion but of staying put. What the Irish said they wanted was to be left alone—left alone by the so-called Church of Ireland, left alone by the landlords, and left alone by the Westminster Parliament. By framing the struggle for Irish national independence in terms of a struggle for land, Irish nationalists implied that the desire for land was not a desire for expansion but a desire for self-containment. The international economy that Irish emigrants formed in order both to support the poor in Ireland and to fund the blossoming nationalist movement also suggested that the Irish desire for land was the opposite of imperialism. The Irish went abroad not to conquer the world but simply to obtain the resources they needed to fully claim their homeland.

The reality of the situation was, of course, more complicated than the rhetoric of Irish land hunger admitted. Irish plans for Home Rule foundered because the Irish were reluctant to forego what they saw as their fair share in the British empire, an empire whose military, civil service, and settler population would have been substantially thinner without the Irish. But the rhetoric of a deep Irish attachment to Irish land allowed Ireland to play a role in the British empire that no other nation or zone could play. By maintaining its relationship to Ireland, Britain might recognize itself as a great imperial power, capable of controlling and subordinating a cultural zone that would never be properly assimilated into the dominant British culture. But by maintaining its relationship to Ireland, Britain might also keep to itself a culture it fantasized as entirely anti-imperial. In this British fantasy, the Irish were focused only on those possessions that entirely absorbed their identity, forswearing the acquisitive impulses that had distorted the British identity as its empire spread across the globe. Keeping an Ireland preoccupied with keeping its own land was for Britain the promise that Britain, too, might keep its own identity.

Notes

Introduction

1. *Hansard's Parliamentary Debates*, vol 15, 28 Feb 1833, columns 1327, 1333. E. D. Steele cites this debate in *Irish Land and British Politics* 32.

2. *Hansard's Parliamentary Debates*, vol 15, 28 Feb 1833, column 1338.

3. Scholars interested in "thing theory" have also noticed the poverty of an approach to objects that dwells only on an object's status as a commodity. Bill Brown's *A Sense of Things* might be seen as leading the charge to integrate an understanding of an object's production and exchange into a larger field of cultural meaning that answers questions such as "What desires did objects organize? What fantasies did they provoke?" (12). Elaine Freedgood and John Plotz, whose work I discuss in the conclusion, both have done admirable work in that direction for the field of Victorian literature and culture. Their focus on the symbolic resonance of things, however, leads them away from the questions of how Victorians understood owned material to attach to owners. Claire Pettit's highly original work in *Patent Inventions* focuses on *how* Victorians imagined owners and property to be attached and does so in a way that challenges commodification as the only available model of property. Pettit explores how developments in patents and licensing influenced Victorian authors' conceptions of their intellectual property in their own literary creations. I hope to add to that work by focusing on property not intellectual in nature.

4. On this point, see Bigelow, *Fiction, Famine* 61. See also Fraser, *John Bull's Other Homes* 4–5.

5. On the centralization of policing in Ireland, see Saville, *Consolidation of the Capitalist State* esp chapter 5. See also Crossman, *Politics, Law, and Order* esp chapters 1 and 2. On the centralization of the educational system, see Akenson, *The Irish Education Experiment* esp chapter 4.

6. Kathryn Kirkpatrick's introduction to the Oxford Classics edition of *Castle Rackrent* sums up several of the ways scholars have thought about Edgeworth's Irishness and her Anglo-Irishness.

7. See Frazier, *George Moore*.

8. See Jones, *The Amazing Victorian* 211.

9. See Kinzer *England's Disgrace?* 90.

10. Neil McCaw has also edited a useful volume of essays on British perceptions of Irishness in the nineteenth century.

11. See especially "Adulteration and the Nation" and "Violence and the Constitution of the Novel" in *Anomalous States* (1993).

212 Notes to Pages 15–27

12. See Frey, *British State Romanticism*; Goodlad, *Victorian Literature and the Victorian State*; and Morris, *Imagining Inclusive Society*. An overview of the late Foucauldian characterization of governmentality can be derived from his essays "Governmentality," "Omnes et Singulatim," and "The Subject and Power" in *Power*, and from the first three lectures in *The Birth of Biopolitics*.

13. For a full articulation of this idea, see Foucault, "Omnes et Singulatim."

CHAPTER ONE: Disowning to Own

1. Such self-abasement has been variously chalked up to Edgeworth's susceptibility to self-doubt, to the false consciousness of patriarchal exploitation, and to Edgeworth's awareness of the strategic advantages of identifying with the patriarchy. For the first interpretation, see Marilyn Butler's *Maria Edgeworth*. For the second, see Gilbert and Gubar, *Madwoman in the Attic*. For the third, see Kowaleski-Wallace, *Their Fathers' Daughters*.

2. For the extent to which Walter Scott's literary debt to Edgeworth went unacknowledged, see Ferris, *The Achievement of Literary Authority* 106. See also Connolly, "Irish Romanticism" 417.

3. On Edgeworth's habit of treating the landed estate as a microcosm of society at large, see Ferris, "The Irish Novel" 239 and Burgess, "The National Tale" 48.

4. Paine's critiques were especially well-known in Ireland, where cheap editions of *Rights of Man* circulated widely among the United Irishmen who would go on to organize the 1798 rebellion. On the influence of Thomas Paine on the United Irishmen, see McDowell, "Administration and Public Services" 353; see also Dickson, "Paine and Ireland" 135–50.

5. See Ferris, *The Achievement of Literary Authority* 106.

6. For a version of this tradition as it was promulgated among the Defenders, a Catholic secret society in prerebellion Ireland, see Elliott, "The Defenders in Ulster" 223 and Whelan, "United Irishmen" 274.

7. In Latin American national tales, Sommer notes a strategic bid for legitimacy on the part of the creoles, who, "without proper genealogy to root them in the land . . . had at least to establish conjugal, and then paternity rights, making a *generative* rather than *genealogical* claim" (15, emphasis in original). Yet such a strategy obviously does not eliminate the possibility of competing generative claims. Margot Gayle Backus has explored the affective implications of Anglo-Irish claims to inheritance. While she is interested in demonstrating that "the Anglo-Irish child is responsible for upholding an irrational belief in the legitimacy of the family's claim to land and power in Ireland," I am more interested in how the competing claims of inheritance might make legitimacy a less than useful category in post-Union Ireland (87).

8. See also T. O. McLoughlin's comments that *Rackrent* "can be read as a rambling maudlin account of colonial-style living, or as a narrative which through irony becomes an anti-colonial critique of the way the English have subverted Ireland's Catholic gentry" (194). Likewise, Daniel Hack comments that the novel "votes in favor of Union, but makes it inconceivable" (150). Susan Egenolf has noted that "the aim of the novel becomes to replace the monolithic traditional history with a dialogic narrative whose meaning the reader constructs" (55).

9. See Boyce, *Nationalism in Ireland* 113–14.

10. No consensus exists among twentieth- and twenty-first-century Irish historians about the extent to which the British government's widespread procurement of sinecures and blatant bribes for Irish members of Parliament in exchange for votes was business as usual for a government that considered borough seats the private property of the landed proprietor, nor do they agree as to what extent it was bald corruption for a British government already invested in eliminating patronage and jobbery. I mention this controversy only to underscore my point that Union passed in an environment in which it both was and was not a procedure along the lines of a buyout of property in exchange for political sovereignty. Patrick Geoghegan encapsulates this ambivalence in his explanation that "[w]hile it was generally accepted that seats were a form of personal property the [British] ministers were aware that compensating borough proprietors for their abolition would raise unwelcome allegations of corruption against them" (38). James Quinn argues that the British policy of borough compensation was business as usual, and he quotes Cornwallis on being sickened by the policy of bribery he carried out in the service of Union (see esp 104–5).

11. Along these lines, Gilbert and Gubar suggest that this substitution of colonizer's voice for colonized might be a gesture of solidarity between the women and the tenants rendered equally helpless to an unfair patriarchal structure (150). Eagleton similarly muses that Edgeworth's adoption of Thady's voice acknowledges a shared and ambivalent subordination between upper-class woman and house servant (*Heathcliff* 161).

12. Such a tradition begins with Thomas Flanagan's identification of *Castle Rackrent* as the first Irish novel (6–7). See also Cahalan, *The Irish Novel* 1, 7.

13. Critics read in Thady an intrinsic colonial duplicity that makes him both sycophantically stupid and uncannily sly as the family retainer. His exposure of his lords' improvident idiocy demonstrates both his guileless loyalty and his flair for subtle sabotage. For a succinct summary of the debate on Thady's intention, see Corbett, *Allegories of Union* 39–40.

14. David Lloyd contests this interpretation of Irish history as uniquely violent and thus uniquely resistant to novelization, pointing out that the French novel is considered to have reached its apex in the nineteenth century, in the midst of profound upheaval (127–30).

15. Indeed, the Rackrents were at one time a Catholic family, meaning that they arose from either Irish or Old English stock, and yet in the novel they come to stand for Anglo-Irish ascendancy at its worst.

16. See also Marilyn Butler, *Maria Edgeworth* 368–69.

17. Edgeworth presents her father's actions as an exchange "contributing to the melioration of the inhabitants of the country, from which [he] drew [his] subsistence," and she notes the goal's accomplishment: "Altogether, he was fit to live in Ireland and to accomplish his own wish of meliorating the condition of his own people" (*Memoirs* 1, 37).

18. Bhabha argues that colonial discourse hews to a white, Christian, rational identity that is always already compromised by its violent trespass into nonwhite, non-Christian countries. As an example, he cites V. S. Naipaul's mimic men as natives who in their desire to embrace colonial culture emerge as "almost the same but not white" masqueraders, exposing the inauthenticity of colonial authority; the authority is revealed as arbitrary, independent of white Englishness since white Englishness can be learned by those who are neither white nor English (89). According to Bhabha, "The *menace* of

mimicry is its *double* vision which in disclosing the ambivalence of colonial discourse also disrupts its authority" (88, emphasis in original). Bhabha's influential argument that colonial discourse always contains within it the seeds of its own disintegration requires an understanding of colonial discourse as relentlessly, explicitly, and unironically insisting upon its own authority, easily "stricken by an indeterminacy," as if the advantages of ambivalence and irony were apparent only to the colonized (86).

19. In her 1812 Irish tale, *The Absentee*, which I do not discuss, Edgeworth arguably does craft a narrative in which an Irish landlord (or rather, landlord to-be) gains knowledge of Ireland and of estate management through careful study rather than through any sort of event of dispossession. However, that novel shares affinity with Edgeworth's nonfictional and nationally unspecific *Essays on Professional Education* (1809). Her next novel, *Patronage* (1813), set in Britain, shares similar affinities with *Essays* and, before Edgeworth conceded to her father's editing suggestions, had originally featured *The Absentee*'s plot-line as a subplot. *The Absentee*'s Irish setting, then, seems to be more an occasion for Edgeworth to develop a narrative of professional development than to comment specifically on Union.

20. For a broad overview of these developments, see S. J. Connolly, "Union Government" and R. B. McDowell, "Administration and the Public Services."

21. Flanagan bases this pronouncement on Edgeworth's 1834 comment "It is now impossible to draw Ireland as she now is in a book of fiction." Eagleton uses this same comment to explain Edgeworth's failure to produce any more Irish novels, although she makes the comment seventeen years after the publication of *Ormond*, her last Irish novel (176).

22. For Edgeworth's late-life disappointment in the failure of her own tenants to be deferential to landlord rule, see Butler, *Maria Edgeworth* 452–53.

CHAPTER TWO: The Forbearance of the State

1. Mark Tunick (587, 588) rounds up recent criticisms of Mill's imperialist thinking, including his "championing" of despotism, his willingness to "impose the individualist liberal values of his England on the rest of the world," his advocacy of cultural assimilation, and a general undercurrent of racism in his writing.

2. While she is not interested in attributing to Mill the notion that character operated as a form of property in her later work, Hadley also takes the notion as a given of Victorian culture in her later work *Living Liberalism* (see 98, 238).

3. In addition to Carlisle's work, which pays attention to Mill's newspaper writing on Ireland, E. D. Steele's two seminal articles on "J. S. Mill and the Irish Question" are interested primarily in discussing Mill's engagement as part of a larger Irish history. Lynn Zastoupil's "Moral Government: J. S. Mill on Ireland" explores Mill's engagement with Ireland as a part of his more general attitudes toward empire, and especially toward India. Mary Jean Corbett's *Allegories of Union in Irish and English Writing, 1790– 1870* provides a narrative of Mill's engagement with Ireland as a counterpoint to Matthew Arnold's. Bruce Kinzer's *England's Disgrace?* provides the most exhaustive treatment of John Stuart Mill's thinking on Ireland but devotes more attention to how Ireland affected Mill's economic thinking than to how it might have influenced his most canonical political work.

4. See my discussion of this concept in the introduction.

5. Adam Smith's *Wealth of Nations* (1776), David Ricardo's *Principles of Political Economy* (1817), and J. R. McCulloch's *Principles of Political Economy* (1825), all earlier standard texts of classical political economy, focused on questions of profit and value, assuming a Lockean view of property without ever addressing the concept with its own chapter.

6. For an account of the sources feeding Mill's overview of propertied relationships to land, see Dewey, "Rehabilitation of the Peasant Proprietor." See also Kinzer, *England's Disgrace?* chap 3.

7. Mill made this maxim from Young so integral to almost all his arguments about property in land that by 1876 J. A. Froude referred to it as Mill's own particular gospel: "The magic of property, as Mr. Mill long since pointed out, will turn an arid waste into a garden" ("Landed Gentry" 680). So closely does Mill continue to be associated with the idea that one need look no further than Google to find copious misattributions of the slogan to Mill rather than to Young.

8. For an extended reading of the instabilities Mill generates in trying to argue for the existence of an Irish character produced by historical circumstances, see Carlisle, *John Stuart Mill* esp 145–56.

9. See Kinzer, *England's Disgrace?* 86 and Steele, "Reform" esp 423, 431. Lynn Zastoupil rounds up several arguments on the radicalism of "England and Ireland" in "Moral Government."

10. The Irish nationalist rhetoric of a prior history of communal property thrived both before and after Maine's initial work was written. Paul Bew quotes Parnell in 1881 stating that British holdings had been confiscated of the whole of the Irish people since all "held the land in joint ownership with the chieftains" (20). Charles Gavan Duffy, in *The League of North and South* (1886), also repeats as conventional wisdom the idea that "the peasantry had a living claim as the descendants of those who had owned the land in common with the Celtic chiefs and had been wrongfully deprived of their property" (qtd in Steele, *Irish Land* 19). Likewise, the Ballinasloe Tenants' Defence Association declares "The Tanistry laws of Ireland, embodied in the Brehon code, made every member of the sept joint owner of the land during his lifetime" (qtd in Bull 70). The National Land League of Mayo's "Declaration of Principles" included a quote from Mill's "England and Ireland" (Davitt 160).

CHAPTER THREE: Native Property

1. Clare Pettit quotes this to nice effect in *Patent Inventions* 22. She is among the critics who see this paradox as alarming the Victorians. However, she suggests that some Victorians looked to the model of patent licensing for a much more flexible, less contradictory way to think about intellectual property.

2. For one account of this ideal of property ownership, see Klein, "Property and Politeness." See also Fulford, *Landscape, Liberty, and Authority*, and Pocock, *Virtue, Commerce, and History* esp chapter 3.

3. See Simpson esp chapter 5 for an account of the long history of this tendency in English legal thought. For an account of Blackstone's specific tendency to reify property rights, see Kennedy esp 317–46. See also Gordon esp 100–101. Mark Rose offers a discussion of how the reification of property shapes the copyright debates in *Authors and*

Owners esp 90–92. For a discussion of how Blackstone's sense of the thingness of property translated into a popular preoccupation with the visible boundaries of land, see E. P. Thompson, *Customs in Common* esp 97–184.

4. On Blackstone's marriage of liberal theories of property with the deep history of English law, see Boorstin, *Mysterious Science of Law.*

5. Qtd in Underkuffler 131. Underkuffler also cites Charles Reich's article "The New Property" for his assertion that "[p]roperty draws a circle around the activities of each private individual. . . . Within that circle, the owner has a greater degree of freedom than without. Outside, he must justify or explain his actions, and show his authority. Within, he is master, and the state must explain and justify any interference" (n 31).

6. Drawing on the moral philosophy of the time, scholars of eighteenth-century literature have since the 1990s made a case for the existence of a commercial pattern of personhood that was more about circulation than any stable experience of property or personhood. See Gallagher, *Nobody's Story;* Lynch, *The Economy of Character;* and Pinch, *Strange Fits of Passion.*

7. Here I am telling the story of one moment in which the idea of property as the vessel of a communal heritage emerged, for specific historical reasons, as a plausible way to think about ownership. I do not mean to imply that the Romantic era in England saw the first and only shift of this sort in thinking about property, nor do I mean to imply that only the Victorians were troubled by conflicting narratives of property. Wolfram Schmidgen's rich *Eighteenth-Century Fiction and the Law of Property,* for instance, makes the case for an eighteenth-century tradition of property proceeding from "a communal imagination that closely aligns persons and things" (1). This would mean that even during the eighteenth-century in which Republican landownership was celebrated as allowing for a unique form of individual independence, a counter-tradition existed that did not so sharply distinguish controlling owner from the inanimate material that was his property.

8. See Easby, "Myth of Merrie England," and Mandler, *Fall and Rise of the Stately Home.*

9. Elizabeth Helsinger suggests that both Clare's and Constable's representations suggested ways out of an atomizing vision of possessive individualism. See *Rural Scenes and National Representations* esp chapters 1 and 4.

10. These visions were quite specifically English, and no equivalent representations of the Scottish land circulated as a reminder of a landed tradition that might be considered not just Scottish but British. However, Scotland's increasing profile as a tourist destination for the English—and ultimately the summer home of the royal family—did establish it in the popular mind as land that was available for the enjoyment of a British subject at large. That Scottish tourism was associated with hunting made it the literal site of customary communal property, given game's status as exceptional property, both exclusive to the aristocracy but available to them regardless on whose estate the quarry might be found. See Colley, *Britons* 158–72.

11. See Poovey, *Uneven Developments* esp chapter 4.

12. No laws made the entail of an estate compulsory. The laws enforcing primogeniture only made it compulsory in the case of an owner dying without a will. There were almost no cases of major landholders dying intestate.

13. This notion of property was not labeled as a "bundle of rights" when it emerged. U.S. legal scholar Wesley Hohfield is credited with creating the paradigm through his

legal work separating out the meanings of rights, privileges, powers, and immunities, which he argued could be paired with their opposites—duties, disabilities, and liabilities. Subsequent theorists on property law sometimes applied Hohfield's vocabulary when they broke down the idea of property into separate attributes, such as the right to exchange or the right to occupy. Other theorists used his framework to argue that "property" as a concept had no intrinsic qualities that made it separate from any set of rights created by contract. The debate over whether property marks out specific types of rights or whether it is now simply an anachronistic category that should be subsumed under contract law continues among legal scholars. A. M. Honore's essay "Ownership" is considered the classical defense of property's stable attributes: he enumerates eleven key ingredients that are featured in the overwhelming majority of cases of ownership. In a similar vein, Thomas Merrill and Henry E. Smith argue that property always denotes rights that can be said to be good against all the world—not just particular people. Arianna Pretto-Sakmann assembles a strikingly Blackstonian argument that even the modern law of property applies only to "rights in corporeal things enlarged to include those few ideational things capable of spatial identification" (vii). Kevin Gray argues that while no real set of attributes unifies property law, it is nonetheless useful to identify what falls under the category of "property" in order to be able to identify what is not propertizable under the law. On the other side of the debate, Thomas Grey's article "The Disintegration of Property" is considered the canonical assertion that property as a category is essentially anachronistic and meaningless. For an account of Hohfield's role in developing the idea of property as a bundle of rights, see Vandevelde, "The New Property of the Nineteenth Century," and Heller, "Boundaries of Private Property."

14. John Plotz (xv) also notes that these items' status lie somewhere between fungible commodity and irreducibly unique artifact.

15. See Robbins, *Upward Mobility* esp 75–84. Robbins offers an earlier version of this same argument in "How to Be a Benefactor."

16. Qtd in Jones, "Rethinking Chartism" 109; see also 110, 126–35. On the Chartists' dependence on both constitutional and natural rights arguments, see Epstein, "The Constitutional Idiom." See also Finn, *After Chartism* esp 61–104.

17. See Perkin, "Land Reform and Class Conflict." See also Readman, *Land and Nation.*

18. Qtd in Tierney 371. For the broad background on O'Connell's utilitarian nationalism, see also McGraw and Whelan, "Daniel O'Connell."

19. It is one of the ironic features of this rhetoric of recovering old communal customary rights that the Ulster Custom, a practice cultivated among a group of Scottish-descended Presbyterians, was effortlessly grafted on to talk of ancient Irish septs and their communal property.

20. Parliament's passage of the First Land Act marked an abrupt departure from almost a century of legislation designed to bring Irish land practices more into line with those in England—and which ultimately resulted in making land in Ireland more freely alienable than it was in Britain. In the 1840s the Devon commission, designed to inquire into the condition of Irish estates, dismissed Ulster Custom out of hand as an anomalous infringement on property rights that should be abolished. The commission's recommendations resulted in the Unencumbered Estates Act of 1849, which aimed to break up the aristocratic monopoly by freeing impoverished landlords from a shared ownership across time. The act voided Irish entail, allowing estates to be liquidated to

repay debts and ostensibly to be transferred to more responsible landlords. It was followed in 1860 by the Cardwell Act and Deasy's Act, both of which were explicitly formulated to stave off shared synchronous ownership. The Cardwell Act emphasized the landlord's ultimate control over the property, providing compensation on a tenant's improvements only if the landlord had initially given consent for such improvement. Deasy's Act reaffirmed the landlord's absolute power over the land, emphasizing the purely contractual nature of his relationship to the tenant, by strengthening his power to eject for nonpayment. Cumulatively, the effect of legislation up until the First Land Act had been to make land more easily transferred than English estates. In England, absolute individual property in land finally won out over hereditary dictates in the 1882 Settled Land Acts. For an account of the Irish legislation, see Bull, *Land, Politics, and Nationalism* 44–46 and appendix, or Clark, *Social Origins of the Irish Land War* 175–77.

21. Significantly, Gladstone consulted with no Irish leaders, not even Irish members of parliament, in deciding on the content of either Land Act.

22. See Maine, *Lectures on the Early History of Institutions* (1874).

23. I do not mean to suggest that if we discard Maine's explanatory framework, we need to dismiss any notion that tradition informed an Irish sense of land ownership. I am persuaded by historian Philip Bull's more moderate position that there were indeed two competing views: the British view, committed to a rather static laissez-faire economics, and the Irish approach, "less anchored in historical structures" than nationalist rhetoric suggested "and more a product of reactions and responses to the impositions of landlord and government expectations." Bull suggests that traditional forms of Irish property did indeed inform rural practices but that such influences were only one among many strands making up the "interplay of traditional practice, historical perception, myth, and the impact of contemporary and social forces" that shaped the Irish understanding of their relationship to property (10).

CHAPTER FOUR: The Wife of State

1. *Castle Richmond* 345. Most scholars' interest in the novel has been to demonstrate the extent to which its mimetic content unsettles this pronouncement. See, for instance, Morash, *Writing the Irish Famine* 40–50; Corbett, *Allegories* 137–47; Nardin, "*Castle Richmond*" 88–89; and Matthews-Kane, "Love's Labour Lost."

2. Trollope's tactics also depart from the ornate period details of Walter Scott and, to a lesser extent, Benjamin Disraeli's odd mix of national and international ethnography.

3. On British women abolitionists, see Ferguson, "British Women Writers."

4. *Can You* 2:362. Of course, the narrator qualifies this description of Palliser's generous sentiment toward Glencora in the next sentence, explaining, "But when she asked for a favour, he was always afraid of an imprudence. Very possibly she might want to drink beer in an open garden" (2:362–63). Such a qualification suggests Palliser's trepidation that what Glencora might actually enjoy has nothing at all to do with his property.

5. See also Griffin, "Class, Gender, and Liberalism" 80. For an account of the sorts of lawsuits to which women's inability to contract subjected husbands, see Finn, "Women, Consumption, and Coverture."

6. Such occasions include the 1857 Matrimonial Causes Act, which made divorce available without an act of Parliament; John Stuart Mill's 1866 presentation of the Women's Suffrage Bill to Parliament; the 1869 Municipal Corporations Act, which allowed single, property-owning women to vote in local elections; the First Married Women's Property Act (1870), the Amendment to Married Women's Property Act (1874); and the Married Women's Property Act (1882). All these controversies involved prolonged discussion about how exactly women would or would not conduct themselves if accorded new political privileges.

7. For a discussion of the gendered aspects of the Union-as-marriage analogy, see Corbett, *Allegories of Union.* On the trope in Trollope's Palliser novels particularly, see also Dougherty, "An Angel in the House," and Frank, "Trial Separations."

8. Phineas Finn's imprisonment provides another example of Trollope's vision of government as a vicarious experience that can be just as confining as wifehood. The problem of how Finn will support himself while he is in Parliament is solved by his imprisonment. Hoping that a paid government position will solve his financial straits, he no longer has to worry about his living expenses once he is incarcerated—either option leaves him bound and dependent on the state.

9. Annie Besant points out in her 1879 pamphlet on marriage reform that "[i]n Austria . . . wives retain their rights over their own property" (29).

CHAPTER FIVE: At Home in the Public Domain

1. On the historicist underpinnings of the final Crofters legislation, see Dewey, "Celtic Agrarian Legislation." See also Shaw, "Land, People, and Nation."

2. Bailkin rounds up this list of groups in *The Culture of Property,* 11. Paul Redman's *Land and Nation in England* does an excellent job providing the intertwined histories of these groups, whose particular moment in the history of thinking about property made them an unpredictable blend of historicism and abstract principle, free market liberalism, socialism, and "pure squire Conservatism" (11).

3. A. Arnold 189, 185. See also G. S. Woods's entry on Arthur Arnold in the *Oxford Dictionary of National Biography.*

4. Shaw-Lefevre esp 187, 230. Shaw-Lefevre registers his impatience with historicist thinking on 224–25.

5. For an overview of the 1842 Copyright Act, see Vanden Bossche, "The Value of Literature." For an overview of the 1876–78 commission, see Saint-Amour, *The Copywrights* esp chapter 2. Brad Sherman and Lionel Bentley's *The Making of Modern Intellectual Property Law* also provides a valuable overview of how the developments in copyright dovetail with developments in patent law during the nineteenth century.

6. Alongside Grant Allen, the author Charles Reade was a vociferous defender of the natural right of an author to perpetual property in his creation. See Dicey, "The Copyright Question" esp 126, 133.

7. Frazier 115. For Moore's relationship to Zola's work, see esp chapters 3 and 4.

8. W. H. Smith was also a lending library of significant size. They purchased only twenty-five copies of *A Modern Lover.* Moore's outrage, however, was aimed almost exclusively at Mudie's, the bigger library.

9. His labeling of Mudie's as "nursemaid" happens in his pamphlet "Literature at Nurse?" published months before *A Drama in Muslin* began to appear in serial form. Moore categorizes the Land League as "political parasites" sustained by "nursemaids in America" in *Parnell and His Island* (56), which he wrote immediately after *Drama in Muslin*.

10. See Dolin, *Mistress of the House*; see also Marcus "*Clio* in *Calliope*."

11. See Elam, "We Pray to Be Defended." Meredith began writing the novel as a serial in 1883, publishing it in its full form only in 1885. The preceding fifteen years had seen the passage of the Married Women's Property Act of 1870, which allowed wives to retain property in earnings, investments, and willed legacies under 200 pounds. The 1882 Married Women's Property Act allowed women to contract for their own property, although not, significantly, for their own persons. See Shanley esp 105–29. The Third Reform Act, which passed in 1884, ensured that anyone who held land worth over 10 pounds or rented a household for 10 pounds a year could vote. This still left some of of the male population disenfranchised. Since the Municipal Corporations Act of 1869 had given propertied women the right to vote in local elections, this means that women might even exercise some of the privileges of property that a large portion of the male population did not have.

12. Critics both contemporary and Victorian wax irritable over this discrepancy in Meredith's novel. An unsigned review in the June 1, 1885, edition of the *Times* notes that Meredith's treatment of Diana's control over the Crossways gives the novel a "distinctly modern" tone even though it is supposed to be set fifty years in the past. Gillian Beer accuses Meredith of being carelessly anachronistic with his treatment of property in the novel (145).

13. He mentioned to several people during the course of the novel's composition that it was based on Caroline Norton, a resemblance contemporary critics picked up on. In later editions of the book in the 1890s, however, at the behest of friends of the late Norton, who objected to the perpetuation of the rumor that she was responsible for leaking Prime Minister Peel's decision to repeal the Corn Laws to the press, Meredith inserted a disclaimer at the opening of the book disavowing the resemblance: "A lady of high distinction for wit and beauty, the daughter of an illustrious Irish House, came under the shadow of a calumny. It has latterly been examined and exposed as baseless. The story of Diana of the Crossways is to be read as fiction."

14. Chapter 3 of Mary Poovey's *Uneven Developments* documents the contradictory tactics used by Norton in calling attention to the injustice of the divorce laws at the time. Elaine Hadley uses Norton as an extended example of the melodramatic tactics that the marginalized used to gain a hearing in Victorian England (*Melodramatic Tactics* esp 140–77).

15. *Diana* 285. The mechanism that would make this possible—the establishment of the property in trust for Diana, under the laws of equity—was almost never used for a property of the small size that the Crossways seems to be.

16. Meredith met Katherine O'Shea while he worked reading aloud for her aunt, Mrs. Wood. As a good friend of several leading liberal MPs, he would have been familiar with the affair, although it was not widely public knowledge. See Marcus, "*Clio* in *Calliope*" 22, and Dolin, *Mistress of the House* 122 n 4.

17. See Stone, *George Meredith's Politics* 109–10.

18. One of Prime Minister Robert Peel's justifications for finally repealing the Corn Laws in 1846 was that it would allow for the cheap importation of food into an Ireland already feeling the first effects of the potato crop failure. See Hilton on the sacrificial rhetoric that structured anti–Corn Law arguments.

19. Egeria, in Roman mythology, was the nymph or goddess who acted as adviser to Numa Pompilius, one of the first Roman kings.

20. While Cain and Hopkin argue that manufacturing power never gained the political power attributed to it in nineteenth-century England, Howe and Hilton still make a convincing case that the rise of industry was the story the nineteenth century told itself about the transformation of its own economy.

21. The addition of this vocabulary seems quite calculated on Meredith's part. Comparing the serialization of the tale in the 1883 *Fortnightly Review* to the significantly revised 1885 novel version, Meredith bibliographer Michael Collie observes that the late revisions "reduce the importance of the topical allusions to the repeal of the Corn Laws" (54). J. S. Stone speculates the revisions were made to enhance the book's modern appeal: "Corn Law Repeal was practically a forgotten issue in 1885, whereas Irish agitations were very much a current political problem" (100). But it would be inaccurate to describe the novel as reducing allusions to the Corn Laws in order to foreground Ireland. In adapting his serial into a novel, Meredith makes considerably more references to both repeal of the Corn Laws and Ireland, references that often appear together. In the novel, Diana studies economic questions surrounding the Corn Laws in chapter 4, an undertaking never mentioned in the serial. Diana and Dacier discuss both the Corn Laws and Ireland in the novel long before repeal comes into view. In the couple's first conversation alone together at Lugano, the novel details political content to their conversation while the serial includes only a personal exchange (chapter 14 in the serial, chapter 15 in the novel). Chapter 22 in the novel contains an encounter between the pair that never takes place in the serial, an encounter where the twin specters of Irish distress and Corn Law agitation are invoked. Chapter 21 in the novel (which contains much of the material from Chapter 17 in the serial version) contains details of Diana's advice to both Redworth and Dacier on the subject of Ireland that were not included in the serial.

22. For Meredith's belief in his Celtic roots, see Jones, *The Amazing Victorian* 211.

23. So far as biographers can determine, Meredith visited Wales only once in his lifetime. See Stevenson, *The Ordeal of George Meredith* 281, and Jones, *The Amazing Victorian* 211.

Works Cited

Akenson, Donald. *The Irish Education Experiment: The National System of Education in the Nineteenth Century*. London: Routledge and Kegan Paul. 1970.

Allen, Grant. "Landowning and Copyright." *Fraser's Magazine* 609 (Sep 1880): 343–56.

[Amos, Sheldon]. "The Irish Land Question." *Westminster Review* (American ed) 93 (Jan–Apr 1870): 42–55.

Armitage, W. H. G. "The Chartist Land Colonies, 1846–1848." *Agricultural History* 32, no 2 (Apr 1958): 87–96.

Arnold, Arthur. *Free Land*. London: C. Kegan Paul, 1880.

Arnold, Matthew. "Copyright." *The Fortnightly Review* 27, no 159 (Mar 1880): 319–34.

———. "Equality." In *Mixed Essays, Irish Essays*, 37–72.

———. "Incompatibles." In *Mixed Essays, Irish Essays*, 273–333.

———. *Mixed Essays, Irish Essays, and Others*. New York: Macmillan, 1883.

Backus, Margot Gayle. *The Gothic Family Romance: Heterosexuality, Child Sacrifice, and the Anglo-Irish Colonial Order*. Durham, NC: Duke UP, 1999.

Bagehot, Walter. *The English Constitution*. 1867. In *Bagehot: The English Constitution*, ed Paul Smith. Cambridge Texts in the History of Political Thought. Cambridge: Cambridge UP, 2001.

Bailkin, Jordanna. *The Culture of Property: The Crisis of Liberalism in Modern Britain*. Chicago: U of Chicago Press, 2004.

Beer, Gillian. *Meredith: A Change of Masks: A Study of the Novels*. London: Athlone Press, 1970.

Bentham, Jeremy. *Theory of Legislation; Translated from the French of Etienne Dumont by R. Hildreth*. Boston: Weeks, Jordan, 1840.

Berol, Laura. "The Anglo-Irish Threat in Thackeray's and Trollope's Writings of the 1840s." *Victorian Literature and Culture* (2003): 103–16.

Besant, Annie. "Marriage, As It Was, As It Is, and As It Should Be: A Plea for Reform." 2nd ed. 1882. In *A Selection of the Social and Political Pamphlets of Annie Besant*, ed John Saville. New York: Augustus M. Kelley, 1970.

Bew, Paul. *Land and the National Question in Ireland, 1858–1881*. Atlantic Highlands, NJ: Humanities Press, 1979.

Bhabha, Homi. *The Location of Culture*. New York: Routledge, 1994.

Biagini, Eugenio. *Liberty, Retrenchment and Reform: Popular Liberalism in the Age of Gladstone 1860–80*. Cambridge: Cambridge UP, 1992.

———, ed. *Citizenship and Community: Liberals, Radicals, and Collective Identities in the British Isles, 1865–1931*. Cambridge: Cambridge UP, 1996.

Bigelow, Gordon. *Fiction, Famine, and the Rise of Economics in Victorian Britain and Ireland*. Cambridge: Cambridge UP, 2003.

Blackstone, William. *Commentaries on the Laws of England*. Vol 1, *Of the Rights of Persons*. Chicago: U of Chicago Press. 1979.

———. *Commentaries on the Laws of England*. Vol 2, *Of the Rights of Things*. Chicago: U of Chicago Press, 1979.

Bolton, G. G. *The Passing of the Act of Union: A Study in Parliamentary Politics*. Oxford: Oxford UP, 1966.

Boorstin, Daniel. *The Mysterious Science of Law*. Boston: Beacon, 1941.

Boyce, D. George. *Nationalism in Ireland*. 2nd ed. London: Routledge, 1991.

———. "Weary Patriots: Ireland and the Making of Unionism." In *Defenders of the Union: A Survey of British and Irish Unionism since 1801*, ed D. George Boyce and Alan O'Day, 15–38. New York: Routledge, 2001.

Bradburn, Elizabeth. "The Metaphorical Space of Meredith's *Diana of the Crossways*." *Studies in English Literature, 1500–1900* 43, no 4 (2003): 877–95.

Brantlinger, Patrick. *Fictions of State: Culture and Credit in Britain, 1694–1994*. Ithaca, NY: Cornell UP, 1996.

———. *The Reading Lesson: The Threat of Mass Literacy in Nineteenth-Century British Fiction*. Bloomington: Indiana UP, 1998.

Brewer, John, and Susan Staves, eds. *Early Modern Conceptions of Property*. London: Routledge, 1996.

Brontë, Charlotte. *Jane Eyre*. 1847. New York: Oxford UP, 1980.

Brown, Bill. *A Sense of Things: The Object Matter of American Literature*. Chicago: U of Chicago Press, 2003.

Bull, Phillip. *Land, Politics, and Nationalism: A Study of the Irish Land Question*. New York: St. Martin's, 1996.

Burgess, Miranda. "The National Tale and Allied Genres, 1770s–1840s." In *The Cambridge Companion to the Novel*, ed John Wilson Foster, 35–59. Cambridge: Cambridge UP, 2006.

Burke, Edmund. *Reflections on the Revolution in France*. Oxford: Oxford UP, 1993.

Butler, Marilyn. "Edgeworth, the United Irishmen, and 'More Intelligent Treason.'" In *An Uncomfortable Authority*, ed Heidi Kaufman and Christopher Fauske, 33–61. Newark: U of Delaware Press, 2004.

———. Introduction to *Castle Rackrent; Ennui*, by Maria Edgeworth. London: Penguin, 1992.

———. *Maria Edgeworth: A Literary Biography*. Oxford: Clarendon, 1972.

Butt, Isaac. *Land Tenure In Ireland: A Plea for the Celtic Race*. Dublin: John F. Fowler, 1866.

Cahalan, James M. *The Irish Novel: A Critical History*. Boston: Twayne, 1988.

Cain, P. J., and A. G. Hopkins. "Gentlemanly Capitalism and British Expansion Overseas: I. The Old Colonial System, 1688–1850." *The Economic History Review*, ns, 39 no 4 (Nov 1986): 501–25.

———. "Gentlemanly Capitalism and British Expansion Overseas. II: New Imperialism, 1850–1945." *The Economic History Review*, ns, 40, no 1 (Feb 1987): 1–26.

Campbell, George. *Irish Land*. London: Trubner, 1869.

Carlisle, Janice. *John Stuart Mill and the Writing of Character*. Athens: U of Georgia Press, 1991.

Carlyle, Thomas. *Chartism*. London: James Fraser, 1840.

———. *Past and Present*. Edited by Richard Altick. New York: New York UP, 1965.

Chase, Malcolm. "'Wholesome Object Lessons': The Chartist Land Plan in Retrospect." *English Historical Review* 118, no 475 (Feb 2003): 59–85.

Clark, Samuel. *Social Origins of the Irish Land War*. Princeton, NJ: Princeton UP, 1979.

Cleary, Joseph. *Outrageous Fortune: Capital and Culture in Modern Ireland*. Dublin: Field Day Publications, 2006.

Cleary, Joseph, and Claire Connolly, eds. *The Cambridge Companion to Modern Irish Culture*. Cambridge: Cambridge UP, 2005.

Cohen, William A. "Trollope's Trollop." *Novel* 28, no 3 (Spring 1995): 235–56.

Coleridge, Samuel Taylor. "The Idea of the Constitution: On the Constitution of the Church and State, According to the Idea of Each." 1829. In *Coleridge's Writings on Politics and Society*, ed John Morrow, 1:154–217. Princeton, NJ: Princeton UP, 1994.

Colley, Linda. *Britons: Forging the Nation, 1707–1837*. New Haven, CT: Yale UP, 2009.

Collie, Michael. *George Meredith: A Bibliography*. Toronto: U of Toronto Press, 1974.

Connolly, Claire. "Irish Romanticism, 1800–1829." *The Cambridge History of Irish Literature*, ed Margaret Kelleher and Philip O'Leary, 1:407–48. Cambridge: Cambridge UP, 2006.

Connolly, S. J. "Union Government, 1812–1823." In Vaughn, *Ireland under the Union*, 48–73.

Corbett, Mary Jean. *Allegories of Union in Irish and English Writing, 1790–1870*. Cambridge: Cambridge UP, 2000.

Crossman, Virginia. *Politics, Law, and Order in Nineteenth-Century Ireland*. New York: St. Martin's, 1996.

Davis, Thomas Osborne. "Commercial History." In *Thomas Davis: Essays and Poems*, 133–36. Dublin: M. H. Gill and Son, 1945.

———. "A New Nation: Proposal for an Agricultural Association between the Landowners and Occupiers. To the Landowners of Ireland." *The Nation*, Apr 19, 1847, 38.

———. "Our National Language." In *Essays and Poems*, 103.

———. "Udalism and Feudalism." In *Essays and Poems*, 137–55.

Davitt, Michael. *The Fall of Feudalism in Ireland, or The Story of the Land League Revolution*. New York: Harper and Brothers, 1904.

Deane, Seamus. *Strange Country: Modernity and Nationhood in Irish Writing since 1790*. Oxford: Clarendon, 1997.

Delaney, Paul. "Land, Money, and the Jews in the Later Trollope." *Studies in English Literature* 32 (1992): 765–87.

Dewey, Clive. "Celtic Agrarian Legislation and the Celtic Revival: Historicist Implications of Gladstone's Irish and Scottish Land Acts 1870–1886." *Past and Present* 64 (1974): 30–70.

———. "The Rehabilitation of the Peasant Proprietor in Nineteenth-Century Economic Thought." *History of Political Economy* 6 (1974): 17–47.

Dicey, Edward. "The Copyright Question." *Fortnightly Review* 19, no 109 (Jan 1876): 126–40.

Dickens, Charles. *Great Expectations*. 1861. New York: Penguin, 1985.

Dickson, David. "Paine and Ireland." In Dickson, Keough, and Whelan, *The United Irishmen*, 135–50.

Dickson, David, Dáire Keough, and Kevin Whelan, eds. *The United Irishmen: Republicanism, Radicalism, and Rebellion*. Dublin: Lilliput, 1993.

Dolin, Tim. *Mistress of the House: Women of Property in the Victorian Novel.* Aldershot, UK: Ashgate, 1997.

Dougherty, Jane Elizabeth. "An Angel in the House: The Act of Union and Anthony Trollope's Irish Hero." *Victorian Literature and Culture* 32, no 1 (2004): 133–45.

Duffy, Charles Gavan. *Young Ireland: A Fragment of Irish History, 1840–1850.* 1881. New York: Da Capo, 1973.

Duncan, Ian. *Scott's Shadow: The Novel in Romantic Edinburgh.* Princeton, NJ: Princeton UP, 2007.

Dunne, Tom. "'A Gentleman's Estate Should Be a Moral School': Edgeworthstown in Fact and Fiction, 1760–1840." In *Longford: Essays in County History,* ed Raymond Gillespie and Gerard Moran, 95–121. Dublin: Lilliput, 1991.

———. "Maria Edgeworth and the Colonial Mind." The 26th O'Donnell lecture, delivered at University College Cork, June 27, 1984.

Eagleton, Terry. *Heathcliff and the Great Hunger: Studies in Irish Culture.* London: Verso, 1995.

Easby, Rebecca Jeffrey. "The Myth of Merrie England in Victorian Painting." In *History and Community: Essays In Victorian Medievalism,* ed Florence Boos, 59–80. New York: Garland, 1992.

Edgeworth, Maria. *Castle Rackrent.* In *The Novels and Selected Works of Maria Edgeworth,* ed Jane Desmarais, Timothy McLoughlin, and Marilyn Butler, vol 1. London: Pickering and Chatto, 1999.

———. *Ennui.* In *Novels and Selected Works,* vol 1.

———. *Memoirs of Richard Lovell Edgeworth.* Vol 2. Shannon: Irish UP, 1969.

———. *Ormond.* Edited by Claire Connolly. London: Penguin, 2000.

———. "Simple Susan." *The Parent's Assistant or Stories for Children.* London: Macmillan, 1903.

Egenolf, Susan. *The Art of Political Fiction in Hamilton, Edgeworth, and Owenson.* Farnham, UK: Ashgate, 2009.

Elam, Diane. "'We Pray to Be Defended from Her Cleverness': Conjugating Romance in George Meredith's *Diana of the Crossways.*" *Genre: Forms of Discourse and Culture* 21, no 1 (Summer 1988): 179–201.

Eliot, George. *The Mill on the Floss.* 1860. London: Penguin Popular Classics, 1994.

Elliott, Marianne. "The Defenders in Ulster." In Dickson, Keough, and Whelan, *The United Irishmen,* 222–33.

Engels, Friedrich. *The Condition of the Working Class in England.* 1845. New York: Oxford UP, 1993.

"The English Parliament and the Irish Land." *Westminster Review* (American ed), Apr 1870, 198–207.

Epstein, James A. "The Constitutional Idiom: Radical Reasoning, Rhetoric, and Action in Early Nineteenth-Century England." *Journal of Social History* 23, no 3 (Spring 1990): 553–74.

Farrer, T. H. "The Principle of Copyright." *Fortnightly Review* 24, no 144 (Dec 1878): 836–51.

Feaver, George. *From Status to Contract: A Biography of Sir Henry Maine, 1822–1888.* London: Longmans, 1969.

Ferguson, Moira. "British Women Writers and an Emerging Abolitionist Discourse." *The Eighteenth Century* 33, no 1 (1992): 3–23.

Ferris, Ina. *The Achievement of Literary Authority: Gender, History, and the Waverley Novels*. Ithaca, NY: Cornell UP, 1991.

———. "The Irish Novel 1800–1829." *The Cambridge Companion to Fiction in the Romantic Period*, ed Richard Maxwell and Katie Trumpener, 235–49. New York: Cambridge UP, 2008.

———. "Narrating Cultural Encounter: Lady Morgan and the Irish National Tale." *Nineteenth Century Literature* 51, no 3 (1996): 287–303.

———. *The Romantic National Tale and the Question of Ireland*. Cambridge: Cambridge UP, 2002.

Finn, Margot. *After Chartism: Class and Nation in English Radical Politics 1848–1874*. Cambridge: Cambridge UP, 1993.

———. "Women, Consumption, and Coverture in England, c. 1760–1860." *Historical Journal* 39, no 3 (1996): 703–22.

Flanagan, Thomas. *The Irish Novelists, 1800–1850*. New York: Columbia UP, 1959.

Foster, John. *The Speech of the Right Honourable John Foster, Speaker of the House of Commons of Ireland, Delivered in Committee on Monday the 17th Day of February 1800*. Dublin: J. Debrett, 1800.

Foucault, Michel. *The Birth of Biopolitics: Lectures at the Collège de France, 1978–79*. Edited by Michel Sennellart. Translated by Graham Burchell. New York: Palgrave Mac-Millan, 2008.

———. "Governmentality." In *The Foucault Effect: Studies in Governmentality*, ed Graham Burchell and Peter Miller, 87–104. Chicago: U of Chicago Press, 1991.

———. *Power*. Edited by James D. Faubion. Translated by Robert Hurley et al. New York: New Press, 1994.

Frank, Catherine O. "Trial Separations: Divorce, Disestablishment, and Home Rule in *Phineas Finn*." College Literature 35, no 3 (Summer 2008): 30–56.

Fraser, Murray. *John Bull's Other Homes: State Housing and British Policy in Ireland, 1883–1922*. Liverpool: Liverpool UP, 1996.

Frazier, Adrian. *George Moore, 1852–1933*. New Haven, CT: Yale UP, 2000.

Freedgood, Elaine. *The Ideas in Things: Fugitive Meanings in Victorian Novels*. Chicago: U of Chicago Press, 2004.

Frey, Anne. *British State Romanticism: Authorship, Agency, and Bureaucratic Nationalism*. Stanford, CA: Stanford UP, 2010.

Froude, J. A. "On the Uses of a Landed Gentry." *Fraser's Magazine* 14, no 84 (Dec 1876): 671–85.

———. "Report of the Copyright Commission. Presented to Both Houses of Parliament. London: 1878." *Edinburgh Review* 148, no 304 (Oct 1878): 295–343.

Fulford, Tim. *Landscape, Liberty, and Authority: Poetry, Criticism, and Politics from Thomson to Wordsworth*. Cambridge: Cambridge UP, 1996.

Gallagher, Catherine. *Nobody's Story: The Vanishing Acts of Women Writers in the Marketplace, 1670–1820*. Berkeley: U of California Press, 1994.

Geoghegan, Patrick. "The Making of the Union." In *Acts of Union: The Causes, Contexts, and Consequences of the Act of Union*, ed Dáire Keogh and Kevin Whelan, 34–45. Dublin: Four Courts Press, 2001.

Gibbons, Luke. *Edmund Burke and Ireland: Aesthetics, Politics, and the Colonial Sublime.* Cambridge: Cambridge UP, 2003.

Gilbert, Sandra, and Susan Gubar. *The Madwoman in the Attic: The Woman Writer and the Nineteenth-Century Literary Imagination.* New Haven, CT: Yale UP, 1979.

Glendinning, Victoria. *Anthony Trollope.* New York: Knopf, 1993.

Goodlad, Lauren. "'Character Worth Speaking Of': Individuality, John Stuart Mill, and the Critique of Liberalism." *Victorians Institute Journal* 36 (2008): 7–46.

———. "Trollopian 'Foreign Policy': Rootedness and Cosmopolitanism in the Mid-Victorian Global Imaginary." *PMLA* 124, no 2 (2009): 437–54.

———. *The Victorian State and Victorian Literature.* Baltimore: Johns Hopkins UP, 2003.

Gordon, Robert W. "Paradoxical Property." In Brewer and Staves, *Early Modern Conceptions of Property,* 95–110.

Gottlieb, Evan. *Feeling British: Sympathy and National Identity in Scottish and English Writing, 1707–1832.* Lewisburg, PA: Bucknell UP, 2007.

Gray, Kevin. "Property in Thin Air." *The Cambridge Law Journal* 50, no 2 (Jul 1991): 252–307.

Grey, Thomas C. "The Disintegration of Property." In Wellman, *Property Rights and Duties of Redistribution,* 69–82.

Griffin, Ben. "Class, Gender, and Liberalism in Parliament, 1868–1882: The Case of the Married Women's Property Acts." *The Historical Journal* 46, no 1 (Mar 2003): 59–87.

Hack, Daniel. "Inter-Nationalism: *Castle Rackrent* and Anglo-Irish Union." *Novel: A Forum on Fiction* 29, no 2 (1996): 145–64.

Hadley, Elaine. *Living Liberalism: Practical Citizenship in Mid-Victorian Britain.* Chicago: U of Chicago Press, 2010.

———. *Melodramatic Tactics: Theatricalized Dissent in the English Marketplace, 1800–1885.* Stanford, CA: Stanford UP, 1995.

———. "The Past Is a Foreign Country: The Neo-Conservative Romance with Victorian Liberalism." *Yale Journal of Criticism* 10, no 1 (1997): 7–38.

Hansard's Parliamentary Debates. Vol 15. 1833.

Healy, T. M. *Why There Is an Irish Land Question and an Irish Land League.* 2nd ed. Dublin: R. M. Webb and Son, 1881.

Heller, Michael A. "Boundaries of Private Property." *Yale Law Journal* 108, no 6 (Apr 1999): 1163–1223.

Helsinger, Elizabeth. *Rural Scenes and National Representations.* Princeton, NJ: Princeton UP, 1997.

Hilton, Boyd. *The Age of Atonement: The Influence of Evangelicalism on Social and Economic Thought, 1795–1865.* Oxford: Clarendon, 1988.

Honore, A. M. "Ownership." In Wellman, *Property Rights and Duties of Redistribution,* 26–135.

Howe, Anthony. *Free Trade and Liberal England, 1846–1946.* Oxford: Clarendon, 1997.

Howkins, Alun. "From Diggers to Dongas: The Land in English Radicalism, 1649–2000." *History Workshop Journal* 54 (2002): 1–23.

"Irish Land." *The Saturday Review* 28 (Aug 21, 1869): 271–77.

"The Irish Land Question." *Fortnightly Review* 1 (1865): 385–401.

Jackson, Alvin. "The Survival of the Union." In Cleary and Connolly, *Cambridge Companion to Modern Irish Culture*, 25–41.

Jones, Gareth Stedman. "Rethinking Chartism." In *Languages of Class: Studies in English Working Class History 1832–1982*, 90–178. Cambridge: Cambridge UP, 1983.

Jones, Mervyn. *The Amazing Victorian: A Life of George Meredith*. London: Constable, 1999.

Kaufman, Heidi, and Chris Fauske. *An Uncomfortable Authority: Maria Edgeworth and Her Contexts*. Newark: U of Delaware Press, 2004.

Kennedy, Duncan. "The Structure of Blackstone's Commentaries." *Buffalo Law Review* 28 (1978–79): 205.

Kiberd, Declan. *Irish Classics*. Cambridge, MA: Harvard UP, 2001.

Kinzer, Bruce L. *England's Disgrace? J. S. Mill and the Irish Question*. Toronto: U of Toronto Press, 2001.

Kirkpatrick, Kathryn J. Introduction to *Castle Rackrent*, by Maria Edgeworth [1801], vii–xxxvi. Oxford: Oxford UP, 1995.

Klein, Lawrence E. "Property and Politeness in the Early 18th C. Whig Moralists: The Case of *The Spectator*." In Brewer and Staves, *Early Modern Conceptions of Property*, 221–33.

Kostal, R. W. *Law and English Railway Capitalism, 1825–1875*. Oxford: Clarendon, 1994.

Kowaleski-Wallace, Elizabeth. *Their Father's Daughters: Hannah More, Maria Edgeworth, and Patriarchal Complicity*. New York: Oxford UP, 1991.

Kumar, Krishan. *The Making of English National Identity*. Cambridge: Cambridge UP, 2003.

Laird, Heather. *Subversive Law in Ireland, 1879–1920: From Unwritten Law to Dail Courts*. Dublin: Four Courts, 2005.

Lalor, James Fintan. *Collected Writings*. New York: Woodstock Books, 1997.

———. "Letter to the Irish Felon." 1848. In *Collected Writings*, 52–66.

———. "To the Editor of the Irish Felon." 1848. In *Collected Writings*, 52–66.

———. "To the Irish Confederate and Repeal Clubs." Originally published in *The Irish Felon*, Jul 1848 [written in last week of Jan 1847]. Reprinted in *Readings from Fintan Lalor*. Belfast: Republican Press Centre, 1975.

Langbauer, Laurie. *Novels of Everyday Life: The Series in English Fiction, 1850–1930*. Ithaca, NY: Cornell UP, 1999.

Leslie, T. E. Cliffe. "Political Economy and the Tenure of Land." *Fortnightly Review* 5 (1866): 220–28.

Lloyd, David. *Anomalous States: Irish Writing and the Post-colonial Moment*. Dublin: Lilliput, 1993.

Locke, John. *Two Treatises of Government*. 1690. Edited by Peter Laslett. Cambridge: Cambridge UP, 1988.

Lockhart, J. G. *Memoirs of the Life of Sir Walter Scott*. Vol 10. Edinburgh: Adam and Charles Black, 1882.

Lynch, Deidre Shauna. *The Economy Of Character: Novels, Market Culture, and the Business of Inner Meaning*. Chicago: U of Chicago Press, 1998.

MacDonagh, Oliver. *States of Mind: A Study of Anglo-Irish Conflict, 1780–1980*. London: George Allen and Unwin, 1983.

MacPherson, C. B. *The Political Theory of Possessive Individualism: Hobbes to Locke*. London: Oxford UP, 1962.

Maine, Henry Sumner. *Ancient Law: Its Connection with the Early History of Society and Its Relation to Modern Ideas.* 1861. Boston: Beacon, 1963.

———. *Lectures on the Early History of Institutions.* 4th ed. 1885. Holmes Beach, FL: Gaunt, 1998.

———. *Village-Communities in the East and West.* 1871. New York: Henry Holt, 1880.

Mandler, Peter. *The Fall and Rise of the Stately Home.* New Haven, CT: Yale UP, 1997.

Marcus, Jane. "'*Clio* in *Calliope*': History and Myth in Meredith's *Diana of the Crossways.*" *Bulletin of the New York Public Library* 79 (1976): 167–92.

Marx, Karl. *Capital.* Vol 1. Translated by S. Moore and A. Aveling. New York: International Publishers, 1974.

Matthews-Kane, Bridget. "Love's Labour Lost: Romantic Allegory in Trollope's *Castle Richmond.*" *Victorian Literature and Culture* 32, no 1 (2004): 117–31.

McCaw, Neil. *Writing Irishness in Nineteenth-Century British Culture.* Aldershot, UK: Ashgate, 2004.

McDonough, Terrence, ed. *Was Ireland a Colony?: Economics, Politics and Culture in Nineteenth-Century Ireland.* Portland: Irish Academic Press Dublin, 2005.

McDowell, R. B. "Administration and the Public Services, 1800–1870." In Vaughn, *Ireland under the Union,* 538–61.

McGraw, Sean, and Kevin Whelan. "Daniel O'Connell in Comparative Perspective, 1800–1850." *Eire/Ireland* 1–2 (2005): 60–89.

McKenna, Theobald. *A Memoire on Some Questions Respecting the Projected Union of Great Britain and Ireland.* Dublin: John Rice, 1799.

McLoughlin, T. O. *Contesting Ireland: Irish Voices against England in the Eighteenth Century.* Dublin: Four Courts, 1999.

McMaster, Juliet. "Trollope's Country Estates." In *Trollope Centenary Essays,* ed John Halperin, 70–85. New York: St. Martin's, 1982.

Mehta, Uday Singh. *Liberalism and Empire: A Study in Nineteenth-Century British Liberal Thought.* Chicago: U of Chicago Press, 1999.

Meredith, George. *Diana of the Crossways.* New York: W. W. Norton, 1973.

Merrill, Thomas W., and Henry E. Smith. "What Happened to Property in Law and Economics?" *Yale Law Journal* 111 (2001): 357–98.

Mill, John Stuart. *Autobiography.* 1874. Edited by Jack Stillinger. Boston: Houghton Mifflin, 1969.

———. "The Condition of Ireland." In *Newspaper Writings, January 1835–June 1847,* vol 24 of *Collected Works of John Stuart Mill,* ed Ann Robson and John Robson, 879–1034. Toronto: U of Toronto Press, 1986.

———. *Considerations on Representative Government.* In *On Liberty and Other Essays,* 203–467.

———. *England and Ireland.* London: Longmans, Green, Reader, and Dyer, 1869.

———. "Maine on Village Communities." 1871. In *Writings on India,* vol 30 of *Collected Works of John Stuart Mill,* ed Ann Robson and John Robson, 215–28. Toronto: U of Toronto Press, 1990.

———. *On Liberty.* In *On Liberty and Other Essays,* 1–128.

———. *On Liberty and Other Essays.* Edited by John Gray. Oxford: Oxford UP, 1991.

———. *On the Subjection of Women.* 1869. In *On Liberty and Other Essays,* 470–582.

————. *Principles of Political Economy with Some of Their Applications to Social Philosophy.* Vols 2–3 of *Collected Works of John Stuart Mill,* ed Ann Robson and John Robson. Toronto: U of Toronto Press, 1977.

————. "The Right of Property in Land." In *Newspaper Writings, December 1847–July 1873,* vol 25 of *Collected Works of John Stuart Mill,* ed Ann Robson and John Robson, 1235–43. Toronto: U of Toronto Press, 1986.

Miller, Andrew H. *Novels behind Glass: Commodity, Culture, and Victorian Narrative.* Cambridge: Cambridge UP, 1995.

Miller, D. A. *The Novel and the Police.* Berkeley: U of California Press, 1988.

Mingay, G. E. *Land and Society in England, 1750–1980.* London: Longman, 1994.

Mitchel, John. *The Last Conquest of Ireland (Perhaps).* 1861. Edited by Patrick Maume. Dublin: U College Dublin Press, 2005.

"Modern Notions of Government: The Irish Question." *The Westminster Review,* Apr 1868, 163–80.

Moore, George. *A Drama in Muslin: A Realistic Novel.* 1886. Gerrards Cross, IRE: Colin Smythe, 1981.

————. "Literature at Nurse." *Literature at Nurse, or Circulating Morals.* London: Vizetelly, 1885.

————. "A New Censorship of Literature." *Pall Mall Gazette,* Dec 10, 1884, 1–2.

————. *Parnell and His Island.* 1887. Edited by Carla King. Dublin: University College Dublin Press, 2004.

Morash, Christopher. *Writing the Irish Famine.* Oxford: Clarendon, 1995.

Morris, Pam. *Imagining Inclusive Society: The Code of Sincerity in the Public Sphere.* Baltimore: Johns Hopkins UP, 2004.

Moynahan, Julian. *Anglo-Irish: The Literary Imagination in a Hyphenated Culture.* Princeton, NJ: Princeton UP, 1995.

Murphy, Sharon. *Maria Edgeworth and Romance.* Dublin: Four Courts, 2004.

Nardin, Jane. "*Castle Richmond,* the Famine and the Critics." *Cahiers Victoriens and Edouardians* 58 (2003): 81–90.

Norton, Caroline. *English Laws for Women in the Nineteenth Century.* 1854. Edited by Perry Willett. Library Electronic Text Resource Service (LETRS), Indiana University, Bloomington, IN, 1996. http://www.indiana.edu/~letrs/vwwp/norton/englaw.html.

Nunokawa, Jeff. *The Afterlife of Property: Domestic Security and the Victorian Novel.* Princeton, NJ: Princeton UP, 1994.

O'Day, Alan, and John Stevenson, eds. *Irish Historical Documents since 1800.* Dublin: Gill and Macmillan, 1992.

Owenson, Sydney. *Wild Irish Girl.* 1806. New York: Oxford UP, 1999.

Paine, Thomas. *The Life and Writings of Thomas Paine.* Edited by Thomas Clio Rickman. New York: Vincent Parke, 1908.

————. *Rights of Man.* 1791. In *Rights of Man, Common Sense, and Other Political Writings.* Edited by Mark Philp. Oxford: Oxford UP, 1998.

[Pelly, Lewis]. "The English in India." *Westminster Review* 69 (Jan 1858): 106.

Perkin, H. J. "Land Reform and Class Conflict in Victorian Britain." In *The Victorians and Social Protest: A Symposium,* ed J. K. Butt and I. F. Clarke, 177–217. Hamden, CT: Archon, 1973.

———. *The Rise of Professional Society in England Since 1880*. New York: Routledge, 1989.

Pettitt, Clare, *Patent Inventions: Intellectual Property and the Victorian Novel*. New York: Oxford UP, 2004.

Pinch, Adela. *Strange Fits of Passion: Epistemologies of Emotion, Hume to Austen*. Stanford, CA: Stanford UP, 1996.

Plotz, John. *Portable Property: Victorian Culture on the Move*. Princeton, NJ: Princeton UP, 2008.

Plummer, Alfred. "The Place of Bronterre O'Brien in the Working-Class Movement." *The Economic History Review* 2, no 1 (Jan 1929): 61–80.

Pocock, J.G.A. *Virtue, Commerce, and History*. Cambridge: Cambridge UP, 1985.

Poovey, Mary. *Uneven Developments: The Ideological Work of Gender in Mid-Victorian England*. Chicago: U of Chicago Press, 1988.

Pretto-Sakmann, Arianna. *Boundaries of Personal Property: Shares and Sub-shares*. Oxford: Hart, 2005.

The Provisional Government. "Proclamation of the Irish Republic, 1867." In O'Day and Stevenson, *Irish Historical Documents*, 76–77.

Quinn, James. "Dublin Castle and the Act of Union." In *The Irish Act of Union, 1800: Bicentennial Essays*, ed Michael Brown, Patrick Geoghegan, and James Kelly, 95–107. Dublin: Irish Academic Press, 2003.

Radin, Margaret Jane. *Reinterpreting Property*. Chicago: U of Chicago Press, 1993.

Ragussis, Michael. *Figures of Conversion: "The Jewish Question" and English National Identity*. Durham, NC: Duke UP, 1995.

Readman, Paul. *Land and Nation in England: Patriotism, National Identity, and the Politics of Land, 1880–1914*. Suffolk, UK: Boydell, 2008.

Rickman, Thomas Clio, ed. *The Life and Writings of Thomas Paine*. New York: Vincent Parke, 1908.

Robbins, Bruce. "How to Be a Benefactor without Any Money: The Chill of Welfare in *Great Expectations*." In *Knowing the Past: Victorian Literature and Culture*, ed Suzy Anger, 172–90. Ithaca, NY: Cornell UP, 2001.

———. *Upward Mobility and the Common Good: Toward a Literary History of the Welfare State*. Princeton, NJ: Princeton UP, 2007.

Rose, Mark. "The Author as Proprietor: Donaldson vs. Becket and the Genealogy of Modern Authorship." *Representations* 23 (Summer 1988): 51–85.

———. *Authors and Owners: The Invention of Copyright*. Cambridge, MA: Harvard UP, 1993.

Ross, Trevor. "Copyright and the Invention of Tradition." *Eighteenth-Century Studies* 26, no 1 (1992): 1–27.

Said, Edward. *Culture and Imperialism*. New York: Vintage, 1994.

Saint-Amour, Paul K. *The Copywrights: Intellectual Property and the Literary Imagination*. Ithaca, NY: Cornell UP, 2003.

Sanchez-Eppler, Karen. "Bodily Bonds: The Intersecting Rhetorics of Feminism and Abolition." *Representations* 24 (1988): 28–59.

Saville, John. *The Consolidation of the Capitalist State, 1800–1850*. London: Pluto, 1995.

Schmidgen, Wolfram. *Eighteenth-Century Fiction and the Law of Property*. Cambridge: Cambridge UP, 2002.

Scott, Walter. *Waverley*. London: Penguin, 1981.

Semmel, Bernard. *The Rise of Free Trade Imperialism: Classical Political Economy, the Empire of Free Trade, and Imperialism, 1750–1850.* Cambridge: Cambridge UP, 1970.

Shanley, Mary Lyndon. *Feminism, Marriage, and the Law in Victorian England, 1850–1895.* Princeton, NJ: Princeton UP, 1989.

Shaw, John, "Land, People, and Nation: Historicist Voices in the Highland Land Campaign, 1850–1883." In Biagini, *Citizenship and Community*, 305–24.

Shaw-Lefevre, J. George (Baron Eversley). *English and Irish Land Questions: Collected Essays.* 2nd ed. London: Cassell, Petter, Galpin, 1881.

Sherman, Brad, and Lionel Bently. *The Making of Modern Intellectual Property Law: The British Experience, 1760–1911.* Cambridge: Cambridge UP, 1999.

Simpson, A. W. B. *A History of the Land Law.* 2nd ed. Oxford: Clarendon, 1986.

Smiles, Samuel. *Self-Help.* 1859. Oxford: Oxford World's Classics, 2002.

Solow, Barbara Lewis. *The Land Question and the Irish Economy, 1870–1903.* Cambridge, MA: Harvard UP, 1971.

Sommer, Doris. *Foundational Fictions: The National Romances of Latin America.* Berkeley: U of California Press, 1991.

Spencer, Herbert. *Social Statics: The Conditions Essential to Human Happiness Specified, and the First of Them Developed.* New York: Robert Schalkenbach Foundation, 1970.

Steele, E. D. *Irish Land and British Politics: Tenant-Right and Nationality, 1865–1870.* Cambridge: Cambridge UP, 1974.

———. "J. S. Mill and the Irish Question: The Principles of Political Economy, 1848–1865." *The Historical Journal* 13, no 2 (1970): 216–36.

———. "J. S. Mill and the Irish Question: Reform and the Integrity of Empire." *The Historical Journal* 13, no 3 (1970): 419–50.

Stevenson, Lionel. *The Ordeal of George Meredith: A Biography.* New York: Charles Scribner's Sons, 1953.

Stewart, Robert. *The Speech of the Right Honourable Robert Stewart, 2nd Marquis of Londonderry upon Delivering to the House of Commons of Ireland His Excellency the Lord Lieutenant's Message on the Subject of an Incorporating Union with Gt. Britain.* Dublin: J. Rea, 1800.

Stone, J. S. *George Meredith's Politics: As Seen in His Life, Friendships, and Works.* Port Credit, ON: P. D. Meany, 1986.

Strathern, Marilyn. *Property, Substance, and Effect: Anthropological Essays on Persons and Things.* London: Athlone, 1999.

Sullivan, Samuel. "Land Commission in Ireland." *Dublin University Magazine,* 1845, 471–86.

Thompson, E. P. *Customs in Common.* London: Merlin, 1991.

Thompson, F. M. L. *English Landed Society in the Nineteenth Century.* London: Routledge and Kegan Paul, 1963.

———. "Land and Politics in England in the Nineteenth Century." *Transactions of the Royal Historical Society,* 5th ser, 15 (1965): 23–44.

Thompson, S. J. "Parliamentary Enclosure, Property, Population, and the Decline of Classical Republicanism in Eighteenth-Century Britain." *The Historical Journal* 51, no 3 (2008): 621–42.

Tierney, Michael. "Politics and Culture: Daniel O'Connell and the Gaelic Past." *Studies: An Irish Quarterly Review* 27, no 107 (1938): 353–80.

Tracy, Robert. "Maria Edgeworth and Lady Morgan: Legality versus Legitimacy." *Nineteenth Century Fiction* 40, no 1 (1985): 1–22.

———. *The Unappeasable Host: Studies in Irish Identities.* Dublin: University College Dublin Press, 1998.

Trollope, Anthony. *Can You Forgive Her?* 1864. Oxford: Oxford UP, 1982.

———. *Castle Richmond.* 1860. Oxford: Oxford UP, 1989.

———. *The Eustace Diamonds.* 1873. Oxford: Oxford UP, 1972.

———. *Phineas Finn, the Irish Member.* 1869. New York: Penguin, 1983.

———. *Phineas Redux.* 1874. Oxford: Oxford UP, 1973.

———. *The Prime Minister.* 1876. Oxford: Oxford UP, 1994.

———. *The Small House at Allington.* 1864. London: J. M. Dent and Son, 1965.

———. "Trollope's [Six] Letters to the Examiner." Edited by Helen Garlinghouse King. *The Princeton University Library Chronicle* 26 (1965): 76–101.

———. "What Does Ireland Want?" December 1869. In *Writings for St. Paul Magazine,* 286–301. New York: Arno, 1981.

Trumpener, Katie. *Bardic Nationalities: The Romantic Novel and the British Empire.* Princeton, NJ: Princeton UP, 1997.

Turnick, Mark. "Tolerant Imperialism: John Stuart Mill's Defense of British Rule in India." *The Review of Politics* 68 (2006): 586–611.

Underkuffler, Laura S. "On Property: An Essay." *Yale Law Journal* 100 (1990): 127–48.

Vanden Bossche, Chris R. "The Value of Literature: Representations of Print Culture in the Copyright Debate of 1837–1842." *Victorian Studies* 38, no 1 (Autumn 1994): 41–68.

Vandevelde, Kenneth J. "The New Property of the Nineteenth Century: The Development of the Modern Concept of Property." *Buffalo Law Review* 29, no 2 (1980): 325–67.

Vaughan, W. E. *Landlords and Tenants in Mid-Victorian Ireland.* Oxford: Oxford UP, 1994.

———, ed. *Ireland under the Union, I, 1801–1870.* Vol 5 of *New History of Ireland.* Oxford: Clarendon, 1989.

Veblen, Thorstein. *The Theory of the Leisure Class: An Economic Study of Institutions.* 1899. New York: Viking, 1931.

Wellman, Carl, ed. *Property Rights and Duties of Redistribution.* Vol 6 of *Rights and Duties.* New York: Routledge, 2002.

Whelan, Kevin. "The United Irishmen, the Enlightenment, and Popular Culture." In Dickson, Keough, and Whelan, *The United Irishmen,* 269–96.

Wiener, Martin J. *English Culture and the Decline of the Industrial Spririt, 1850–1980.* Cambridge: Cambridge UP, 1981.

Williams, Ioan. *Meredith, the Critical Heritage.* London: Routledge and Kegan Paul, 1971.

Williams, Raymond. *The Country and the City.* New York: Oxford UP, 1973.

Wilt, Judith. "Meredith's Diana: Freedom, Fiction, and the Female." *Texas Studies in Literature and Language* 18, no 1 (Spring 1976): 42–65.

Wolfreys, Julian. "Reading Trollope: Whose Englishness Is It Anyway?" *Dickens Studies Annual: Essays on Victorian Fiction* 22 (1993): 303–29.

Wollstonecraft, Mary. *A Vindication of the Rights of Woman.* 1792. Edited by Carol H. Poston. New York: W. W. Norton, 1988.

Woods, G. S. "Arnold, Sir (Robert) Arthur (1833–1902)." Revised by Jonathan Spain. In *Oxford Dictionary of National Biography*. Oxford: Oxford UP, 2004. http://www .oxforddnb.com/view/article/30454.

Wright, Julia. *Ireland, India, and Nationalism in Nineteenth-Century Literature*. Cambridge, Cambridge UP.

Young, Arthur. *General View of the Agriculture of the County of Suffolk Drawn Up for the Consideration of the Board of Agriculture and Internal Improvement*. London: B. Macmillan, 1807.

Zastoupil, Lynn. "Moral Government: John Stuart Mill on Ireland." *The Historical Journal* 26, no 3 (1983): 707–17.

Index

Akenson, Donald, 211n5
Allen, Grant, 173–74, 178
Anglo-Irish, 4, 8, 9, 11, 12, 13, 113, 118, 123, 126, 129, 212n8; and Edgeworth, 19, 22, 25–27, 30, 33, 37, 39, 45, 46, 51–52, 211n6, 213n16; and the Dublin Parliament ("Grattan's Parliament"), 30, 31
Armitage, W. H. G., 111
Arnold, Arthur, 169, 219n3
Arnold, Matthew, 124; on copyright, 171; on Irish land law, 2, 171–72, 207, 214n3; on property in land, 2, 207

Backus, Margot, 14, 212n8
Bagehot, Walter, *The English Constitution*, 140, 166
Bailkin, Jordanna, 16, 168, 169, 219n2
bard figures, 28–29
Bentham, Jeremy, 56–57, 103–5, 109, 117
Bentley, Lionel, 219n5
Berol, Laura, 135
Besant, Annie, 160, 219n9
Bessborough Commission of 1879, 127
Bew, Paul, 215n10
Bhabha, Homi, 45, 213–14n19
Biagini, Eugenio, 16
Bigelow, Gordon, 14, 211n4
"Black '47." *See* famine
Blackstone, William: on legal status of wives, 150–51; on property, 90, 98, 99, 215n3, 216n4
Bolton, G. G., 31
Boorstin, Daniel, 216n4
Boyce, D. George, 30, 115, 213n10
Brantlinger, Patrick, 141, 144
Brehon law, 124, 128, 215n10
Bright Clauses, 129

Brontë, Charlotte, 110; *Jane Eyre*, 102–3
Bull, Phillip, 127, 215n10
bundle of rights, paradigm of property. *See* property: bundle of rights, theory of
Burgess, Miranda, 212n3
Burke, Edmund: and Thomas Carlyle, 98; and Samuel T. Coleridge, 93, 97, 101; on custom, 21, 37, 45; and Maria Edgeworth, 21, 22, 24–26, 34–35, 37, 39, 42, 45, 53, 56; and free market, 42; on French Revolution, 21, 24, 50; nation as property, 21, 24, 25, 26, 32, 34–35, 39, 53, 56, 98, 105, 138; and Thomas Paine, 21, 105; on property as organic community, 93, 97, 98, 100
Butler, Marilyn: on Maria Edgeworth, 19, 23, 39, 212n1, 213n17, 214n23; on Robert Lovell Edgeworth, 19, 39, 212n1; on *Ennui*, 39, 213n17; on Walter Scott, 23
Butt, Isaac, 9, 124

Cahalan, James M., 213n13
Cain, P. J., 221n20
Campbell, George: and contract, 129; and current criticism, 130–31; and William Gladstone, 128; and India, 128, 128–31; and Land Acts, 128–29; and John Stuart Mill, 128, 130
Cardwell Act (1860), 218n21
Carlisle, Janice, 77, 214n3, 215n8
Carlyle, Thomas: "Chartism," 99; and feudalism, 98–99; and land as property, 106, 113; and Adam Smith, 98
Chartism: and Thomas Carlyle, 99; and constitutional rights, 217n17; and land reform, 109–13, 120; and John Stuart Mill, 79; and natural rights, 110–12, 217n17

Chartist Land Company, 111
Clark, Samuel, 218n21
Cleary, Joseph, 14
Coercion Acts, in Ireland, 1–2, 87, 181
Cohen, William A., 144
Coleridge, Samuel Taylor: and Blackstone, 90; and Burke, 93, 97, 101; and Maria Edgeworth, 89–90; and property as community, 89–90, 93, 97, 100, 101
Colley, Linda, 216n10
commodity fetishism, 105
commons land, 27, 29, 99, 112, 208; and public domain, 170; restoration of, 168, 169, 170
Commons Preservation Society, 169. *See also* Shaw-Lefevre, John George
Connolly, Claire, 212n2
Connolly, S. J., 214n21
conscription, 28
copyright: as absolute, individual property, 99–100, 173, 219n6; as estate, 110; international, 170, 177, 178; and land law, 99–100, 167, 168–77, 179; and public good, 167, 171, 173, 174, 176, 197; and railway law, 173, 175; 1774 debates, 95, 99, 215n3; and spatial models of property, 95–96, 215n3
Corbett, Mary Jean, 14, 213n14, 219n7; on Mill, 214n3; on the national tale, 24; on Trollope, 161, 218n1
Corn Laws, repeal of, 192, 195–96, 201, 220n13, 221n18, 221n21
Crofters Act of 1886, 168, 219n1
Crossman, Virginia, 211n5

Davis, Thomas Osborne: on Irish autarky, 118, 119, 122, 123; on Irish language, 121; on property in land, 118
Davitt, Michael, 129, 215n10
Deane, Seamus, 14, 35
Deasey's Act (1860), 218n21
Defenders, 212n7
Dewey, Clive, 215n6, 219n1
Dicey, Edward, 175, 219n6, 221n16
Dickens, Charles: *Dombey and Son*, 138; *Great Expectations*, 106–10
Dickson, David, 212n4
Divorce Act, 219n6

Dolin, Tim, 189, 220n10
Dougherty, Jane Elizabeth, 219n7
Dublin Castle, 75, 165, 182, 185–86
Dublin Parliament, 8, 9, 25, 30–33; and Edgeworth, 34, 47, 52
Dunne, Tom, 20

Eagleton, Terry: on Edgeworth, 20, 36, 213n12, 214n22; on Irish Land Acts, 130, 131
Easby, Rebecca Jeffrey, 216n8
Edgeworth, Maria: *The Absentee*, 11, 22, 40, 214n20; and British state, 4, 11, 22, 42, 46–50, 52, 53, 56; and Edmund Burke, 21, 22, 24–26, 34–35, 37, 39, 42, 45, 53, 56; Marilyn Butler on, 23, 39, 212n1, 213n17, 214n23; *Castle Rackrent*, 11, 23, 25–27, 30–38, 46; Mary Jean Corbett on, 213n14; Tom Dunne on, 20; Terry Eagleton on, 20, 36, 213n12; and Robert Lovell Edgeworth, 19, 26, 39–40, 46, 50, 212n1, 213n18, 214n20; *Ennui*, 11, 38–46; *Essay on Irish Bulls*, 11, 36; *Essays on Professional Education*, 19, 214n20; Thomas Flanagan on, 213n13; Daniel Hack on, 33–34, 212n9; and John Stuart Mill, 55–56, 89–90; *Memoirs of Richard Lovell Edgeworth*, 213n18; Sharon Murphy on, 20; and national identity, 13, 19, 20, 211n6, 213n12, 214n22, 214n23; *Ormond*, 11, 46–53; and Walter Scott, 19, 22, 23, 27, 212n2; "Simple Susan," 22, 27–30; and the national tale, 11, 22–25, 27–28, 144, 212n3; Robert Tracy on, 25–26, 30
Edgeworth, Richard Lovell, 19, 26, 39–40, 46, 50, 212n1, 213n18, 214n20
Egenolf, Susan, 212n9
Egeria, 194, 221n19
Elam, Diane, 189, 192, 220n11
Eliot, George: *Middlemarch*, 106; *Mill on the Floss*, 138; *Silas Marner*, 138
Elliott, Marianne, 212n7
emigration, Irish, 10, 209
Engels, Friedrich, 116, 118, 124
English Land Restoration League, 168
entail, 39, 137; and Edmund Burke, 21, 24, 98; as debt, 33, 39, 58; and the free market, 97, 101, 169, 173, 175, 216n12; Irish, 218n21

Epping Forest, 169
Epstein, James A., 110, 217n17

famine: Ireland 1817, 46; Ireland 1847, 10; and John Stuart Mill, 65, 83, 133; and Anthony Trollope, 133–35, 218n1; and Young Ireland, 119, 120, 133
Farrer, T. H., 174
Fenians, 6, 10, 83, 129
Ferguson, Moira, 218n3
Ferris, Ina, 14, 24, 212n2, 212n3, 212n5
Finn, Margot, 217n17, 219n5
Flanagan, Thomas, 40, 41, 49, 213n13, 214n22
Foster, John, 32
Foucault, Michel, 15, 109, 212n13
franchise, reform, 94, 101, 109–10, 112, 140, 160, 220n11; women's, 156, 161, 219n6, 220n11
Frank, Catherine O., 219n7
Fraser, Murray, 211n4
Frazier, Adrian, 179, 211n7, 220n7
Freedgood, Elaine, 208, 211n3
Free Land League, 168–69. *See also* Arnold, Arthur
free market property, 41–42, 169, 175
free trade, 99, 101, 112, 147, 170, 201, 218n24
Frey, Anne, 15, 212n12
Froude, J. A.: on copyright, 173, 175; on Irish property, 87, 215n7
Fulford, Tim, 215n2

Gallagher, Catherine, 26, 36, 216n6
Gavan Duffy, Charles, 118, 126, 215n10
Geoghegan, Patrick, 213n11
Gladstone, William Ewart: and Home Rule, 191–92; and Irish Land Acts, 87, 114, 124, 126–29, 131, 218n22
Goodlad, Lauren: and governmentality, 15, 212n12; and John Stuart Mill, 61, 62; and Trollope, 136–37
Gordon, Robert W., 215n3
governmentality, 15–16, 63, 109, 212n12, 212n13
"Grattan's Parliament." *See* Dublin Parliament
Gray, Kevin, 217n13

Grey, Thomas C., 217n13
Griffin, Ben, 219n5

Habeas Corpus, 1; suspension of, in Ireland, 182
Hack, Daniel, 33–34, 212n9
Hadley, Elaine: on George Meredith, 189; on Mill, 60–61; on self-possessed individualism, 214n2
Heller, Michael A., 217n13
Helsinger, Elizabeth, 208, 216n9
Hilton, Boyd, 221n18
Home Rule, 209; and Corn Law repeal, 192, 202; and George Meredith, 12, 168, 177, 192, 202; and George Moore, 12, 168, 177, 187; and Charles Parnell, 129, 191; and public domain, 168, 177, 187; and Anthony Trollope, 162
Honore, A. M., 216n13
Hopkins, A. G., 221n20
House of Commons, English: and copyright, 173; in Trollope's novels, 148, 159, 161, 163, 166
House of Commons, Irish, 32
Howe, Anthony, 221n20
Howitt, William, 70–71, 73, 139
Howkins, Alun, 111

improving agriculture, 97
intellectual property. *See* copyright
Irish Land Act (1870), 12, 91, 125, 217n21; Bright Clauses of, 129; and British land reform, 167, 169, 176; and George Campbell, 128–31; and William Gladstone, 87, 126–28, 131, 218n22; and Henry Sumner Maine, 128–30; and John Stuart Mill, 87, 128, 131; and tenant right, 126–27, 129, 130–31; and Anthony Trollope, 132, 165, 206
Irish Land Act (1881), 12, 91, 125, 217n21; and British land reform, 167, 169, 176; and William Gladstone, 87, 126–28, 131; and Henry Sumner Maine, 128–30; and John Stuart Mill, 87, 128, 131; and tenant right, 126–27, 129, 130–31; and Anthony Trollope, 132, 165
Irish Revolutionary Brotherhood. *See* Fenians

Jones, Mervyn, 211n8
Jones, Richard, 64

Kennedy, Duncan, 215n3
Kiberd, Declan, 27, 45
Kinzer, Bruce L., 84, 211n9
Kirkpatrick, Kathryn J., 211n6
Klein, Lawrence E., 215n2
Kostal, R. W., 172–73
Kowaleski-Wallace, Elizabeth, 212n1
Kumar, Krishan, 207

Laing, Samuel, 70, 73
laissez-faire economics. *See* free trade
Lalor, James Fintan, 119–23, 135
Land Courts, 129–30
Land Law Reform League, 168
Land League (Irish): and Irish Land Acts,
    126, 129; and Land War, 129, 179, 183,
    185, 202, 220n9; and John Stuart Mill,
    215n10; and Kitty O'Shea, 191
landlord, state as, 62, 66, 84, 86, 174, 176
landlords, Anglo-Irish, 30, 46, 52, 87, 115,
    209, 218n21, 218n24; and Matthew
    Arnold, 172; and George Campbell, 130,
    132; and Maria Edgeworth, 20, 22, 26, 33,
    35, 39–41, 46, 47, 52–53, 56, 89, 214n20,
    214n23; and George Meredith, 202; and
    John Stuart Mill, 64, 66, 72, 75; and
    George Moore, 179–80, 182, 183–85; and
    Anthony Trollope, 132, 134–36; and
    Young Ireland, 118, 120, 122–23
landlords, English, 139, 168, 206–7
Land Nationalization Society, 168
Land Tenure Reform Association, 58
Land War, 10, 129, 202; in *Drama in Muslin*,
    179–85
Langbauer, Laurie, 144–45
Leslie, T. E. Cliffe, 172
liberal individual: and C. B. MacPherson,
    91–92, 146–47; and John Stuart Mill,
    59–62, 66–69; and the impossibility of
    self-possession, 146–49, 214n2; and the
    state, 95–96
Liberty and Property Defence League,
    168
Lloyd, David, 14, 213n15

Locke, John: and Jeremy Bentham, 103;
    and Irish property, 119, 120; and C. B.
    MacPherson, 92; and Henry Sumner Maine,
    84–85; John Stuart Mill's revision of, 59–61,
    63, 215n5; and postcolonial critics, 5; and
    property in one's own person, 56, 84, 91; and
    the state, 7, 10, 57, 63, 74, 91, 95
Lockhart, J. G., 22–23

Macaulay, Thomas, 1–2
MacDonagh, Oliver, 130–31
MacPherson, C. B., 16, 61, 92, 146–47
Maine, Henry Sumner, 12; *Ancient Law*,
    84–85, 128; and Matthew Arnold, 171;
    Lectures on the Early History of Institutions,
    218n23; and John Stuart Mill, 85, 128–29;
    modern usage of, 130–31; and the Irish
    Land Acts, 128–31, 215n10, 218n24; *Village
    Communities*, 85
Mandler, Peter, 139, 216n8
Marcus, Jane, 220n10
married women. *See* wives
Married Women's Property Act (1870), 159–60
Married Women's Property Act (1882),
    159–60, 169
Married Women's Property Act, Amend-
    ment (1874), 219n6
Matrimonial Causes Act (1857), 219n6
Matthews-Kane, Bridget, 218n1
McCaw, Neil, 211n10
McCulloch, J. R., 215n5
McDowell, R. B., 212n4
McGraw, Sean, 217n19
McKenna, Theobald, 31, 33
McLoughlin, T. O., 212n9
McMaster, Juliet, 141
Mehta, Uday Singh, 5–6, 8
Meredith, George, 4, 12, 15; Gillian Beer on,
    220n12; and blended space, 199–205;
    Elizabeth Bradburn on, 199–200; Celtic
    identity of, 13, 205, 211n8, 221n22, 221n23;
    and Corn Law repeal, 192, 195, 201–2,
    220n3; *Diana of the Crossways*, 167,
    187–205; Timothy Dolin on, 189, 220n10;
    Diane Elam on, 189, 192, 220n11; feminist
    readings of, 189–92, 220n10, 220n12,
    220n14; Elaine Hadley on, 189; and Home

Rule, 13, 15, 167–68, 177, 192, 220n17; and
Irish land on British soil, 188, 192, 202,
204–5; and married women's property,
190–91, 220n12, 220n15; and Caroline
Norton, 187, 191–92, 220n13; and Kitty
O'Shea, 191–92, 220n16; and public domain,
190, 192–98; Judith Wilt on, 199; and
women's involvement in politics, 191,
193–97, 220n11; Virginia Woolf on, 199
Merrill, Thomas W., 217n13
Metropolitan Public Gardens Association,
168
Michelet, Jules, 72
Mill, Harriet Taylor, 55, 64
Mill, John Stuart, 4, 13; *Autobiography*, 55,
64; Janice Carlisle on, 77, 214n3, 215n8;
Considerations on Representative Government,
57, 59, 64, 72, 83; Mary Jean Corbett on,
214n3; and Maria Edgeworth, 53, 55–56,
89; "England and Ireland," 83–87, 215n10;
Lauren Goodlad on, 61; Elaine Hadley on,
60–61; as imperialist, 56, 214n1, 215n6,
215n7, 215n8, 215n10; and Ireland, 58, 62,
65, 71–72, 74, 76–77, 83, 85–87, 90,
128–29, 131, 133–35; Irish essays in the
Morning Chronicle, 65, 67–77, 79, 84–86, 172,
214n3; Bruce Kinzer on, 84, 214n3, 215n6;
and Henry Sumner Maine, 84–86, 128–29,
131, 171; *On Liberty*, 56–57, 59–60, 62–64,
68–69, 71, 73, 77, 80; *On the Subjection of
Women*, 151; and peasant proprietors, 15,
53, 58, 62, 64, 66–74, 77–81, 108, 133, 207,
209, 215n7; *Principles of Political Economy*,
60, 63–65, 69, 71, 73, 78, 79–80, 85, 87;
revision of Locke, 59–61, 63–64, 74, 215n5;
"The Right of Property in Land," 58; E. D.
Steele on, 84, 214n3; and the British state,
4, 11, 53–54, 59, 62–63, 66, 73–76, 82, 84,
86–87, 133–35, 172, 207; and the liberal
individual, 57–61, 65–70, 73; and utilitarian
theory, 56–57; and women's suffrage,
219n6; and workers' cooperatives, 77–82
Miller, Andrew H., 2, 141
Miller, D. A., 157
Mitchel, John, 119
Moore, George, 4; and Anglo-Irish identity,
15, 179, 184, 211n7; and copyright, 178–79;

Drama in Muslin, 177–87, 188, 192; and
Home Rule, 13, 168, 177, 187; and Land
War, 182–83, 185, 188; "Literature at
Nurse," 220n9; *A Modern Lover*, 178, 220n8;
and Mudie's Circulating Library, 178–79; *A
Mummer's Wife*, 178; and nursemaids, 179,
220n9; *Parnell and His Island*, 220n9; and
public domain, 15, 167, 168, 177, 179,
181–82, 188, 192; and the British state, 12,
15, 179, 185–86; and Zola, 178, 220n7
Morash, Christopher, 218n1
Morgan, Lady. *See* Owenson, Sydney
Morris, Pam, 15, 212n12
Mudie's Circulating Library, 178–79, 220n8,
220n9
Municipal Corporations Act (1869), 219n6,
220n11
Murphy, Sharon, 20

Naipaul, V. S., 213n19
Nardin, Jane, 218n1
Nash, Joseph, 99, 139
national tale, 11, 14, 22–28, 144, 198, 212n3,
212n8
Norton, Caroline, 151, 187, 191–92, 220n13,
220n14
Nunokawa, Jeff, 2, 151

O'Brien, Bronterre, 111–12
O'Connell, Daniel, 117, 184, 217n19
O'Connor, Feargus, 110–12
O'Hagan, John Lord, 124
O'Shea, Katherine "Kitty," 191, 220n16
Owen, Robert, 81, 112
Owenson, Sydney, 9, 25–26

Paine, Thomas, 104–5, 109; influence on
Ireland, 212n4; and precedent, 21–22
Parliament (British), 1, 8, 13, 112, 140;
consolidation with Dublin parliament
("Grattan's Parliament"), 31, 32, 52, 213n11;
and copyright, 170, 173, 174; in *Diana of
the Crossways*, 188, 193, 194; and Irish Land
Acts, 128, 217n21, 217n22; Irish participation in, 129, 135, 163, 185, 209, 217n22; the
landed class's domination of, 101, 221n20;
reform of, 105, 110, 117; in Anthony

Parliament (British) (*continued*)
  Trollope's novels, 132, 135, 137, 140–41,
    147–48, 153, 155–59, 161, 163, 164, 166,
    219n8; and women, 140–41, 153, 155–59,
    160–61, 194, 219n6, 219n8
Parnell, Charles, 129, 191, 215n10
patents, 211n3, 215n1, 219n5
peasant proprietor: German, 70, 73; as
    liberal individual, 57–62, 68–69, 73; and
    John Stuart Mill, 15, 53–54, 58–59, 62–77,
    78–82, 108, 122, 133, 207, 209, 215n7;
    Norwegian, 122
Pelly, Lewis, 17
Perkin, H. J., 217n18
Pettitt, Clare, 211, 215n1
Pinch, Adela, 216n6
Plotz, John, 208, 211, 217n15
Plummer, Alfred, 111
Pocock, J. G. A., 96, 215n2
police force in Ireland, 8, 46, 211n5
Poovey, Mary, 100, 151–52, 216n11, 220n14
Pretto-Sakmann, Arianna, 217n13
primogeniture, 101, 168–69
property: bundle of rights, theory of, 11, 103,
    104, 112, 113, 127, 216n13; fetishism, 105–9,
    136; Irish, 91, 113–16, 125–32, 216n12; and
    liberalism, 16–17, 61, 63, 67, 91–93, 95–96,
    146–47; literary, 99–100; in one's labor, 3,
    5, 39–40, 74, 91–93, 102–3, 104–5, 110,
    128, 170–74; property in land, exceptional
    status, 62, 112–13, 136, 168–76; from
    status to contract, 127–32; as symbol of
    community, 89, 90, 93, 97–99, 100, 139; in
    the free market, 42–43; as thing (reification
    of), 101–9, 215n3; as zone of autonomy, 90,
    92, 93–97, 100
public domain, 16; and copyright debates,
    167–68, 170–71, 175–77, 197; and Home
    Rule, 12, 168, 177; and land, 170, 176, 188,
    197; and George Meredith, 187–88, 190–97;
    and George Moore, 179, 184–87; and the
    British state, 168, 177, 185, 195

Quinn, James, 213n11

Radin, Margaret Jane, 92, 96
Ragussis, Michael, 164

railways and property, 75, 172–73, 176,
    190, 207
Rau, Karl, 70
Reade, Charles, 219n6
Readman, Paul, 16, 217n18
Rebellion of 1798, 30–31, 46, 212n4
Reform Act, Third (1884), 189, 220n11
Reform Acts, 112
Ribbon Men, 10, 124
Ricardo, David, 215n5
Robbins, Bruce, 109, 217n16
Rockites, 10, 76, 77, 124
Romilly, John, 1–2
Rose, Mark, 96, 100, 215n3
Ross, Trevor, 100, 176

Said, Edward, 5
Saint-Amour, Paul K., 170, 219n5
Sanchez-Eppler, Karen, 150
Saville, John, 211n5
Schmidgen, Wolfram, 216n7
Scotland, 216n10, 217n20
Scott, Walter, 19, 22, 23, 27, 212n2, 218n2
Scrope, George Poulet, 76
self-possessed individual, 16, 61, 92
Settled Land Act of 1882, 169
Shanley, Mary Lyndon, 160, 220n11
Shaw, John, 219n1
Shaw-Lefevre, John George, 169, 219n4
Sherman, Brad, 219n5
Simpson, A. W. B., 215n3
Sismondi, Simonde de, 70
slavery, 64, 150–51, 155
smallholder. *See* peasant proprietor
Smiles, Samuel, 61
Smith, Adam, 85, 99; *Philosophy of Moral
    Sentiments*, 96, 98; *Wealth of Nations*, 41,
    215n5
Smith, Henry E., 217n13
Solow, Barbara Lewis, 87
Sommer, Doris, 24, 212n8
Spence, Thomas, 112
Spencer, Herbert, 113
Steele, E. D., 84, 86, 126, 129, 211n1, 214n3,
    215n9, 215n10
Stevenson, Lionel, 221n23
Stewart, Robert, 32

Stone, J. S., 221n17, 221n21
Strathern, Marilyn, 123
Sullivan, Samuel, 115–16, 118

tenant right, 125–27, 129–30, 217n20, 218n21
"thing theory," 211n3
Thompson, E. P., 216
Thompson, William, 150
Thornton, William, 64
Tierney, Michael, 217n19
Tithe War, 10, 50, 124
Tracy, Robert, 25, 26, 30
Trollope, Anthony, 4, 13; Patrick Brantlinger
    on, 144; and British Parliament, 132, 135,
    137, 140–41, 147–48, 153, 155–59, 161, 163,
    164, 166, 219n8; *Can You Forgive Her?*, 138,
    152, 153, 154, 156, 160, 164, 166, 218n4;
    Castle Richmond, 134, 218n1; William A.
    Cohen on, 144; Mary Jean Corbett on,
    161, 219n7; Paul Delaney on, 141; *The
    Eustace Diamonds*, 141–45, 149, 157;
    Examiner letters, 133–35; Phineas Finn,
    135, 145, 154, 155, 156, 162, 163, 164; and
    Ireland, 125, 133–37, 141, 161–64; and Irish
    Land Acts, 165, 206; and Jews, 137, 163–64;
    The Kellys and the O'Kellys, 135; Laurie
    Langbauer on, 144–45; *The MacDermots of
    Ballyclaron*, 135; Juliet McMaster on, 141;
    Andrew H. Miller on, 141; D. A. Miller
    on, 157; *North America*, 209; *Phineas Redux*,
    142, 145, 147, 148, 149, 157, 162, 219n8;
    The Prime Minister, 143, 144, 145, 154, 155,
    158, 159, 161, 162, 164, 165, 206–7; and
    self-possession, 146–49; *The Small House
    at Allington*, 145; and the British state,
    133–34; on the famine, 133–35, 218n1; and
    vicarious enjoyment of property, 12, 15,
    132, 136, 138, 153–57, 165–66; "What Does
    Ireland Want?," 125; and wives, 12, 136,
    138, 140, 150–56, 159–61, 207, 209, 219n8
Trumpener, Katie, 14, 23

Ulster Custom. *See* tenant right
Underkuffler, Laura S., 95, 216n5, 217n14
Unencumbered Estates Act (1849), 218n21
Union of Great Britain and Ireland, 4, 17, 31;
    British attempts to preserve, 86, 87, 129;

and dissolution of Dublin Parliament
    ("Grattan's Parliament"), 30–33, 52, 213n11;
    and Maria Edgeworth, 20, 22–23, 25, 30,
    33–34, 45, 47, 50, 52, 212n8, 212n9, 214n20;
    Irish rebellion against, 6, 10, 83, 117, 120,
    129, 202, 209; and George Meredith, 177,
    202–4; and John Stuart Mill, 83, 86; and
    George Moore, 177; and the marriage plot,
    23–24, 25–26, 161–62, 198, 219n7; and
    Anthony Trollope, 12, 136–37, 161, 162
Union between Great Britain and Ireland
    Act (1801), 4, 8, 20, 23–25, 212n9; and
    bribery, 213n11; debate on the passage of,
    30–34
United Irishmen, 30, 31, 212n4, 212n7
United Irishmen Uprising. *See* Rebellion of
    1798
Uprising of 1798. *See* Rebellion of 1798

Vanden Bossche, Chris R., 100, 219n5
Vandevelde, Kenneth J., 217n13
Veblen, Thorstein, 152

welfare state, 109
Whelan, Kevin, 212n7, 217n19
White Boys, 10, 76, 77, 124
W. H. Smith Lending Library, 220n8
Williams, Raymond, 96
Wilt, Judith, 199
wives: and politics, 137, 141, 155–59, 220n11;
    and property, 12, 36–38, 137, 141, 150–55,
    159–61, 189–91, 220n11, 220n12
Wolfreys, Julian, 164
Wollstonecraft, Mary, 150
Women's Suffrage Bill (1866), 219n6
Woods, G. S., 219n3
Wyndham Acts, 129

Young, Arthur: and improving agriculture,
    97; and the "magic of property," 67, 70–71,
    215n7
Young, Edward, 100
Young England, 99
Young Ireland, 4, 12, 13, 89, 91, 117–25, 127,
    133

Zastoupil, Lynn, 214n3, 215n9